The New Users Guide to the iPad, iPad 2 & the New iPad.

by

Mack N. Tosh

Copyright 2012
ISBN: 978-1-105-66338-3

COPYRIGHT NOTICE
All material in this book is
copyrighted by The original author.
COPYRIGHT©2012

THE NEW USERS GUIDE TO THE IPAD

Special Thanks to:

Sierra Jones
Shyanne Jones
Angélica Alves de Moraes
Ryan Hutsell
Frosty Wise
Laura Feingold
Connie Shidler
Jim Zakoura
Lee Smithyman
Glen Paulson
Skylar, Keith, Aiden, & Claire
and
Everyone who contributed to this book.

Table of Contents

History of the iPad   4
Specifications   8
Settings   14
Contacts, Calendar and Email   94
App Store   136
Calendar   146
Contacts   160
Notes   166
Maps   176
Video   188
YouTube   194
Game Center   204
iTunes   212
Safari   238
Reminders   256
Photos   264
iPod / Music Player   282
Messaging   292
Notifications   302
IBooks   304
Newsstand 322
AirPlay   332
AirPrint   336
Files and Folders   338
Keyboard   342
Tips, Tricks and Secrets   360
Find My iPhone   406
FaceTime   412
Home Sharing   416
Apple TV   419
iCloud   422
Misc.   428

HISTORY OF THE IPAD

The iPad is a line of tablet computers designed, developed and marketed by Apple Inc. primarily as a platform for audio-visual media including books, periodicals, movies, music, games, and web content. Its size and weight fall between those of contemporary smartphones and laptop computers. The iPad runs the same operating system as the iPod Touch and iPhone—and can run its own applications as well as iPhone applications. Without modification, and with the exception of websites, it will only run programs approved by Apple and distributed via its online store. Like iPhone and iPod Touch, the iPad is controlled by a multitouch display—a departure from most previous tablet computers which used a pressure-triggered stylus—as well as a virtual onscreen keyboard in lieu of a physical keyboard. The iPad uses a Wi-Fi data connection to browse the Internet, load and stream media, and install software. Some models also have a 3G wireless data connection which can connect to HSPA or EV-DO data networks. The device is managed and synced by iTunes on a personal computer via USB cable.

April 3, 2010, was the release date of the original iPad. Steve Jobs, founder of the Apple, personally talked about the new revolution known as the iPad in a release broadcast worldwide. On the official release date, the demand was so great that lines in some places wrapped around the block. Less than 80 days after its release, the iPad had sold more than 80 million units. During the remaining months of 2010, Apple sold over 14.1 million iPads. These sales figures represented 75% of the total Tablet PC sales for 2010.

HISTORY

The original iPad was only available initially online at Apple.com and through the retail Apple stores. The iPad was eventually release for sales through retails such as Wal-Mart and Best Buy.

Apple's CEO, Steve Jobs unveiled the iPad 2, the second generation of the device, at a March 2, 2011, press conference, despite being on medical leave at the time. Steve Jobs was actually suffering from cancer at the time, but the information was not known until he passed away on October 11, 2011.

The pricing on the new generation of iPad's was the same as the pricing on the first generation. The same models and configurations were kept. The primary differences were:

33% lighter in weight
Forward and rear facing cameras
Weight dropped from 1.35 pounds to 1.33 pounds
Depending on the model, the weight difference can be 15%
Option of white case or black (Original was only black)
Processing power of iPad 2 is 512 MB RAM vs 256 MB on iPad
Processor on iPad2 is dual-core A5 chip vs dual-core A4 on iPad
A three-axis gyro sensor that is used by GPS, Games, etc...
Additional software is also on the iPad 2, such as FaceTime for video conferencing. Movie software for using the onboard video capability. Photo software for working with picture from the cameras.

To some, upgrading from a first generation iPad to the iPad 2 did not make sense. If you were a business person relying on the communication aspects of the product, the second generation's features make sense. Ultimately, it will come down to individual preference and what is right for each of us.

THE NEW USERS GUIDE TO THE IPAD

On March 7, 2012, Apple President, Tim Cook had a press conference in San Francisco to officially release the third generation of the iPad. This new generation was called "The New iPad".

Preorder on March 7, 2012 and available on March 16, 2012.

The features of "The New iPad" are as follows:

Support for LTE wireless cellular network with speeds up to 73 MB, depending on the network.

Forward and rear facing 5 megapixel camera.

Built-in Hotspot capability. This capability will allow multiple devices (computers, iPods, phones, anything that works with Wi-Fi) to connect to the iPad and use the iPad as a means of getting to the internet.

HD 1080p video. The iPad can create 1080p high definition videos that can be used on the device or shared.

Retina Display. This new display has a resolution of 2047 x 1533 which is almost double the resolution of the iPad 2 at 1024 x 768.

Available in either black or white.

Still thin and light. The New iPad is a bit heavier and thicker than the iPad2.

A5x Intel Processor. This faster processor will allow applications to run much better and faster.

Same pricing structure as the iPad 2.

New key on the keyboard that will accept voice recognition for dictation.

The New iPad will have higher resolution and more memory than the popular gaming system—Xbox 360.

Increased battery capacity with up to 10 hours of usage.

HISTORY

Screen

- The display is the same size as previous iPad iterations, at 9.7 inches diagonal
- Doubles the number of pixels packed into the 9.7-inch screen
- 2048 x 1536 resolution, 264 pixels per inch, total of over 3.1 million pixels

Processor and RAM

- New A5x chip, an upgrade from the A5 found in the iPhone 4S and iPad 2
- Sports a quad-core graphics processor
- It has not yet been made known what the new iPad's RAM is, though the iPad 2 doubled the original's iPad RAM, bumping it up to 512 MB

Cameras

- 5-megapixel iSight camera with 5-element lens, IR filter, and in-plane switching
- Has autofocus, automatic exposure and lock, automatic face detection and lock, and image stabilization
- Records HD video at 1080p

4G LTE

- The new iPad will come in either Wi-Fi only or mobile broadband models
- First iPad to offer LTE network support, with Verizon, AT&T, Bell, Telus, and Rogers
- All iPads will still offer 3G

Other Features

- 10 hour battery life, 9 hours on LTE
- 9.4 mm thin, weighs 1.4 pounds
- Will follow the usual model sizing and pricing: 16 GB for $499, 32 GB for $599, and 64 GB for $699
- Models with LTE support will cost $130 more

SPECIFICATIONS

Model		iPad (original)	iPad 2
Announcement date		January 27, 2010	March 2, 2011
US release date		April 3, 2010	March 11, 2011
Discontinuation date		March 2, 2011	March 2012
Display		9.7 inches (250 mm) multitouch display at a resolution of 1024 × 768 pixels with LED backlighting and a fingerprint and scratch-resistant coating	
Processor		1 GHz Apple A4 system-on-a-chip	1 GHz (dynamically clocked) dual-core Apple A5 system-on-a-chip
Memory		256 MB DDR RAM built into Apple A4 package	512 MB DDR2 (1066 Mbit/s data rate) RAM built into Apple A5 package
Storage		16, 32, or 64 GB	
Wireless	Wi-Fi	Wi-Fi (802.11a/b/g/n), Bluetooth 2.1+EDR	
	Wi-Fi+3G	3G cellular HSDPA, 2G cellular EDGE on 3G models	
Geolocation	Wi-Fi	Wi-Fi, Apple location databases	
	Wi-Fi+3G	Assisted GPS, Apple databases, Cellular network	
Environmental sensors		Accelerometer, ambient light sensor, magnetometer	Additionally: gyroscope

SPECIFICATIONS

	Model	iPad (original)	iPad 2
Operating system			iOS 5.0.1
Battery		Built-in lithium-ion polymer battery; (10 hours video, 140 hours audio, 1 month standby)	
	Weight	Wi-Fi model: 1.5 lb (680 g) 3G model: 1.6 lb (730 g)	Wi-Fi model: 1.325 lb (601 g) GSM 3G (AT&T) model: 1.351 lb (613 g) CDMA 3G (Verizon) model: 1.338 lb (607 g)
	Dimensions	9.56×7.47×0.528 in (243×190×13.4 mm)	9.5×7.31×0.346 in (240×186×8.8 mm)
	Mechanical keys	Home, sleep, volume rocker, variable function switch (originally screen rotation lock, mute in iOS 4.2, either in 4.3)	
Camera	Back	N/A	720p HD still and video camera 0.7 MP, 30fps and 5x digital zoom
	Front	N/A	VGA-quality still and videocamera, 0.3 MP
	Greenhouse gas emissions	130 kg CO2e	105 kg CO2e

Apple IOS 5

On October 12, 2011, just days after the passing of Apple CEO Steve Jobs, Apple released their version 5.0 of their Operating System. This new version had over 200 new features.

iOS updates are delivered free to users through their iTunes application or wirelessly to their device from the internet.

iOS (formerly iPhone OS) is Apple Inc.'s mobile operating system. Originally developed for the iPhone, it has since been extended to support other Apple devices such as the iPod Touch, iPad, and Apple TV. Unlike Windows CE (Mobile and Phone) and Android, Apple does not license iOS for installation on non-Apple hardware. As of March 6, 2012, Apple's App Store contained more than 550,000 iOS applications, which have collectively been downloaded more than 25 billion times. It had a 16% share of the smartphone operating system units sold in the last quarter of 2010, behind both Google's Android and Nokia's Symbian. In May 2010 in the United States, it accounted for 59% of mobile web data consumption (including iPod Touch and the iPad).

The user interface of iOS is based on the concept of direct manipulation, using multi-touch gestures. Interface control elements consist of sliders, switches, and buttons. The response to user input is immediate and provides a fluid interface. Interaction with the OS includes gestures such as swipe, tap, pinch, and reverse pinch, all of which have specific definitions within the context of the iOS operating system and its multi-touch interface. Internal accelerometers are used by some applications to respond to shaking the device (one common result is the undo command) or rotating it in three dimensions (one common result is switching from portrait to landscape mode).

iOS is derived from Mac OS X, with which it shares the Darwin foundation, and is therefore a Unix operating system.

SPECIFICATIONS

Home Button

On / Off
Sleep / Wake

Screen Rotation
and
Volume Control

Volume up/down   Screen rotation lock

THE NEW USERS GUIDE TO THE IPAD

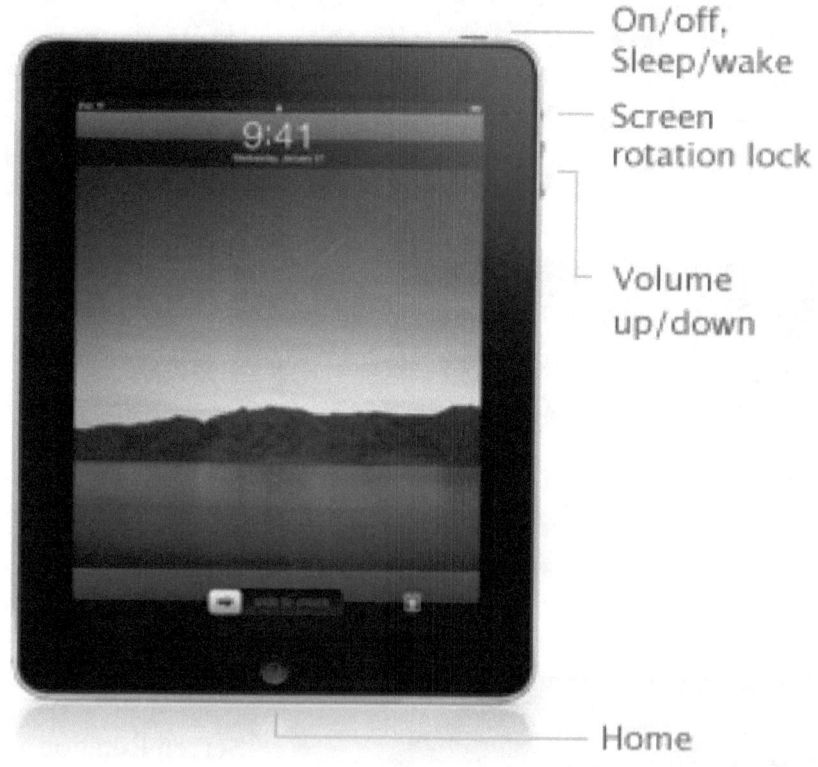

SPECIFICATIONS

SETTINGS

On the main screen, there is an icon to open the settings for the iPad.

Select the Settings Icon for iPad Settings

SETTINGS

Within the settings area, there are a few key things to look for.

To select an option, simply touch the option with your finger.

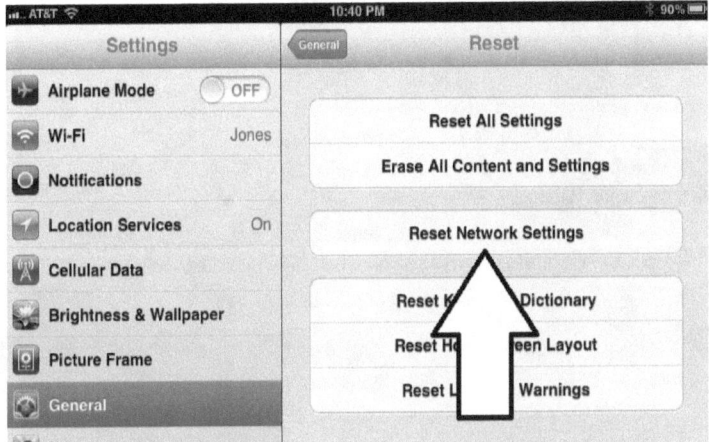

Once you have selected an option, there will be a grey arrow box at the top pointed to the left. This is your Back-Up button. Selecting this will take you back one step from where you were. If you are several layers down into the options, simply keep selecting the left arrow until the grey arrow disappears, which means you are at the main menu and there are no more options to back-up from.

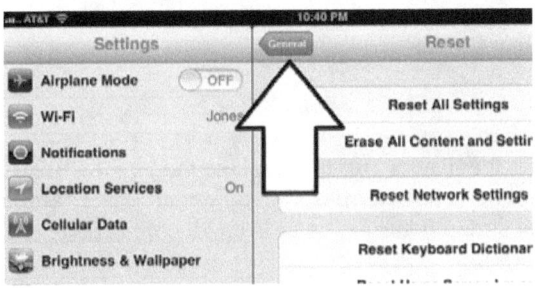

Page 15

THE NEW USERS GUIDE TO THE IPAD

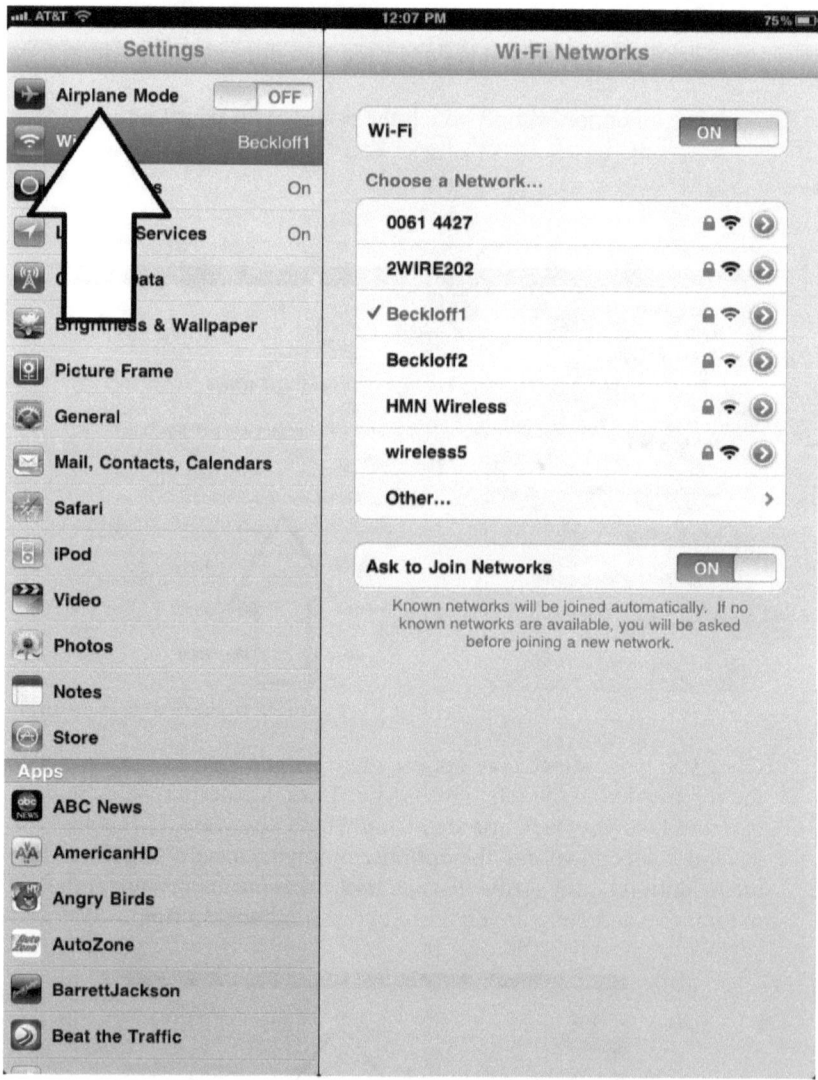

When the iPad is put into airplane mode, all wireless and cellular reception is turned off at the same time. Select airplane mode and make sure it is turned on to keep all connections in the off state.

SETTINGS

Some of the iPad models have technology known as 3G. If the device has 3G capability, the iPad can access internet resources anywhere there is cellular coverage. The 3G option is similar to a cell phone that uses a cellular signal for communications.

All iPads have 802 wireless connectivity options. This wireless signal, which is also known as Wi-Fi is only available at certain locations. If you have wireless in your house, this will be the signal type that is being used with an internet connection at home. This is also the signal type that is available at cafes, gas stations, hotels, and more.

Which connection is better or faster?

3G is slower than wireless but it is available everywhere cellular technology is available. 3G signals typically have monthly limits on the amount of data that can be used. If a device goes over the limits, the user will either be billed for another segment of data or possibly on a per megabyte basis.

Wi-Fi is much faster, depending on the supplying internet access. If Wi-Fi is used, the 3G monthly data limits are not impacted since that technology is not used.

The Wi-Fi only models are typically less expensive than the 3G and Wi-Fi models. The Wi-Fi only models do not have monthly data plans. Once the device is purchased, there are no additional costs to use the device on Wi-Fi networks.

THE NEW USERS GUIDE TO THE IPAD

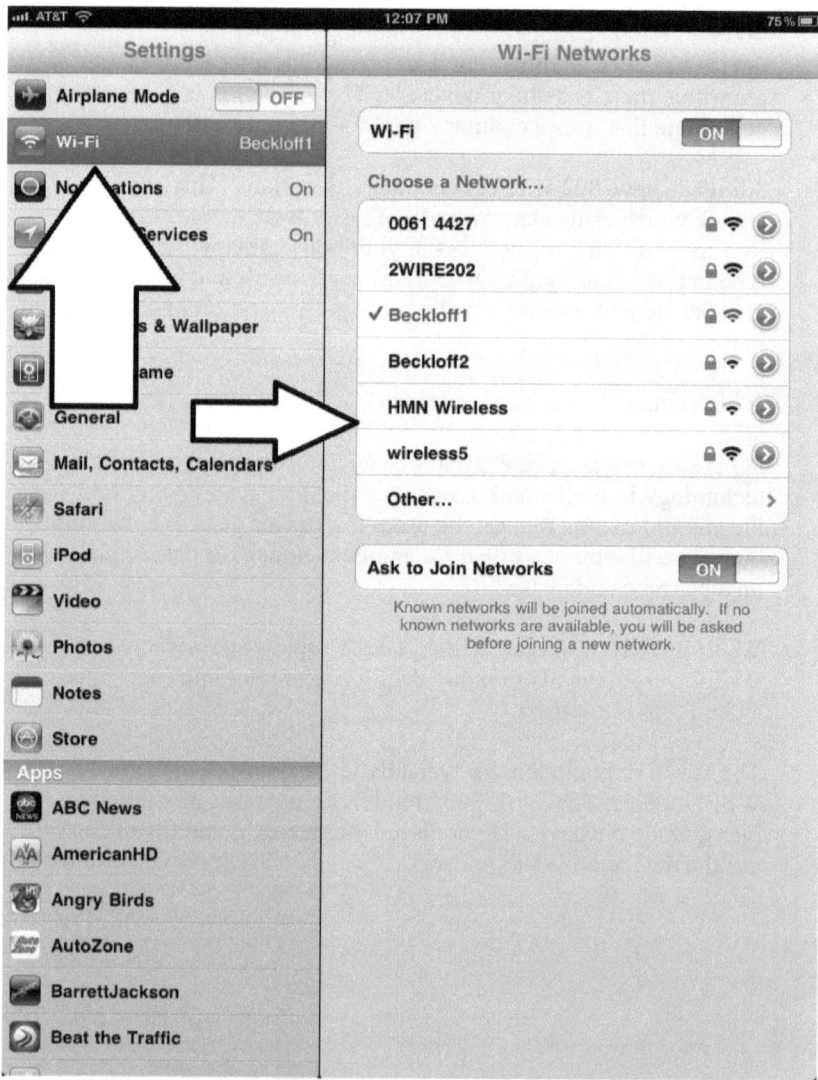

Select Wi-Fi, the networks that are available will show up on the right. Touch the network you would like to join. A checkmark will appear next to the network that is attached.

SETTINGS

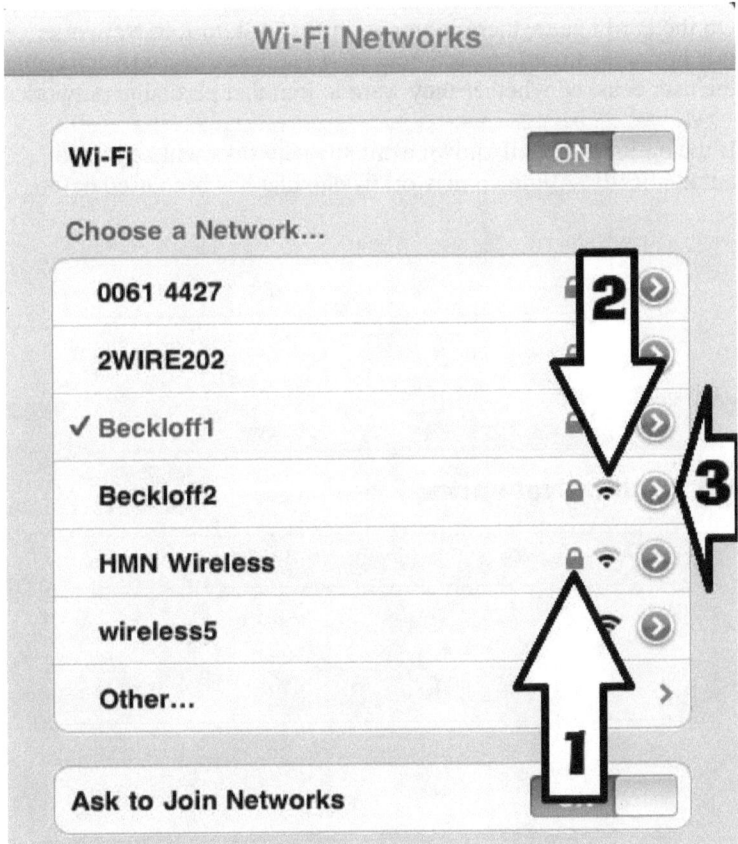

In the Wi-Fi networks that are listed there are some additional icons to help describe the network.

Arrow one, the lock indicates that the wireless network is secure and will need a password.

Arrow two, this shape indicates the signal strength of the wireless network.

Arrow three, this button shows more information about the individual network.

THE NEW USERS GUIDE TO THE IPAD

On the Wi-Fi page, there is an option for "Ask to Join Networks". If this option is turned on, as a new Wi-Fi network becomes available, the user is asked whether they want to join that particular network.

If the option is on, all known available networks will be joined automatically. A known network is one that has been used before.

Ask to Join Networks　　　　　　　　ON

Known networks will be joined automatically. If no known networks are available, you will be asked before joining a new network.

SETTINGS

The button with the greater than sign, will give you more information about that network. The photo at the bottom on the left will show you the detail page on a network. A check mark will show up next to the network you are connected to. The lock means that it is a secure network.

An IP Address is a unique number given to you to access the internet. DHCP (Dynamic Host Control Protocol) means that there is a device giving you numbers. The Renew Lease button will get a new IP address. The other settings will come from your Internet Provider. Forget this Network button will remove it from previously joined networks.

When the Renew Lease button is clicked, you will see a message asking you if you would really like to do this.

If you are attached to a Wi-Fi network but are unable to get to any websites, this is the first diagnostic thing to try.

SETTINGS

When the renewal is complete, you should see the new IP listed on the screen show below.

Sometimes we will connect to a network that is either slow or too much of a problem to keep attaching to automatically. So if a network gets saved that you no longer want to connect to automatically, we will need to forget this network. When the Forget this Network button is clicked, the system will no longer automatically connect to that network.

Wi-Fi Networks	Jones	
	Forget this Network	
IP Address		
DHCP	BootP	Static
IP Address		192.168.1.101
Subnet Mask		255.255.255.0
Router		192.168.1.1
DNS		192.168.1.1
Search Domains		
Client ID		
	Renew Lease	
HTTP Proxy		
Off	Manual	Auto
Server		
Port		
Authentication		OFF

SETTINGS

Notifications are sounds or alerts that will display information on your iPad main screen. A good example of an alert would be a local news app that is installed on your iPad. If you enable alerts on the news app and some ground-breaking news happens, there will be an alert displayed on the main screen along with a sound. A weather app might pop up with local bad weather alerts. A Traffic app might show news on major accidents in your area. Notifications are set up on a per-app basis. If you find after enabling an alert on an app, that you do not want alerts from that app, you will find the app under the alerts option on the left, locate the specific app, select it, then turn the notification off for the app.

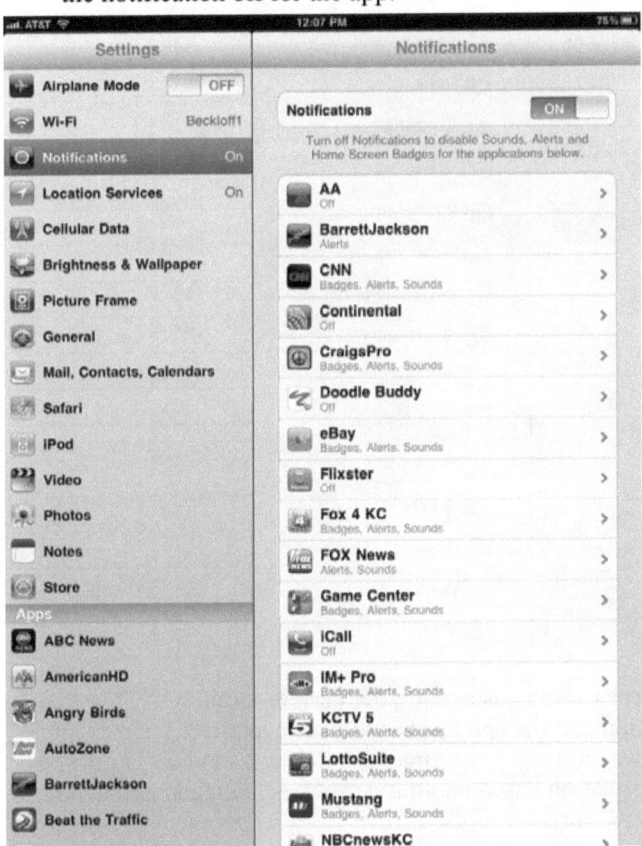

Page 25

THE NEW USERS GUIDE TO THE IPAD

Location services try to ascertain your current location and use that for information that the app can use to your benefit. A good example would be a weather app which may use location services to get you weather information based on your current location geographically.

SETTINGS

If the iPad has 3G on it, this option will allow you to toggle the Cellular service on or off. The View Account option will allow a user to see how much data they have consumed. Since many cellular companies bill based on data usage, this is a great place to regularly check your data usage. You will need to use your user id and password to access this information. These will be the credentials that were set up with your cellular provider.

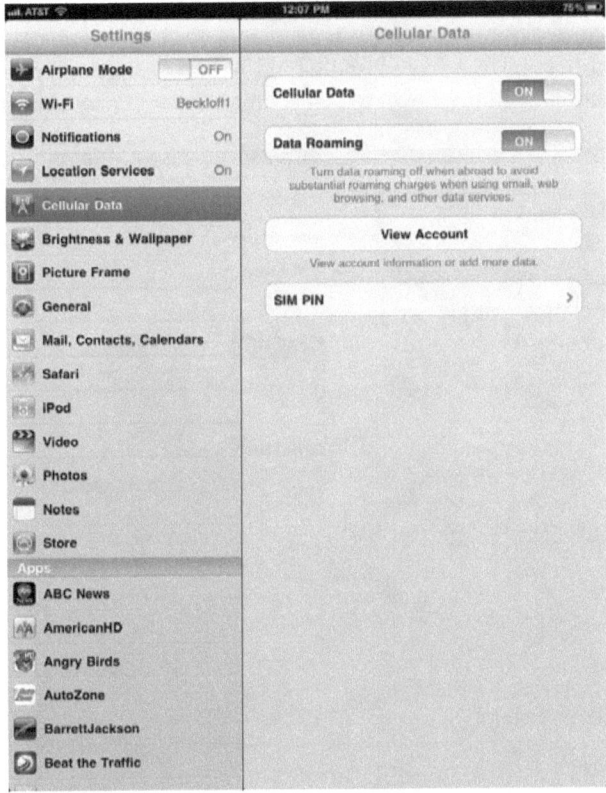

Page 27

THE NEW USERS GUIDE TO THE IPAD

The brightness and wallpaper option is where you can adjust the brightness of the iPad, so setting the Auto Brightness option will dim the brightness after a predetermined amount of time.

The wallpaper option will allow a user to change the photo or design used for their lock screen and their main desktop wallpaper. The photo below shows a flag photo for the lock screen and a landscape photo for the main wallpaper. The lock screen is the initial screen that is shown when the iPad is in the lock position. The main wallpaper is the photo that will show on the main screen with all of the icons and apps that are used regularly. To change either one, simply touch the screen you would like to change and photo locations will be shown to select an alternate photo or design.

SETTINGS

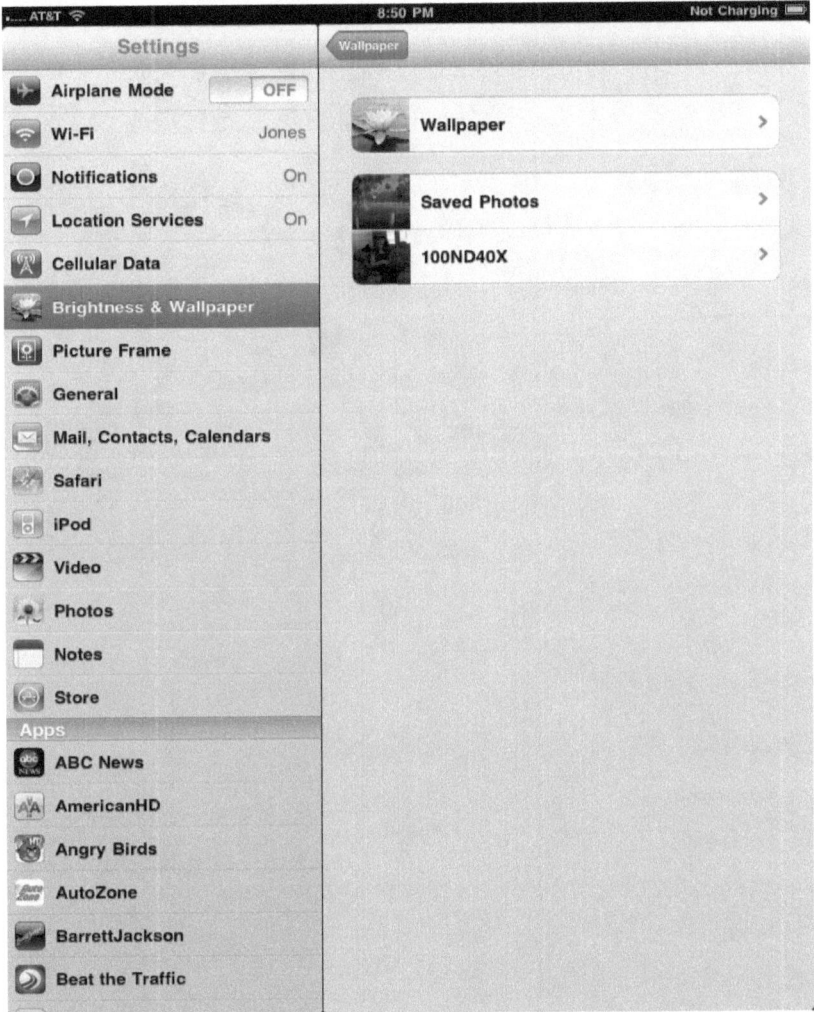

On this screen we have selected to change our wallpaper to a different design. This screen shows us where our photos are stored. Select one of the folders with pictures or designs in it.

Here are the pictures that are available in this folder. Select the one to use for your background. Select it by simply touching it.

SETTINGS

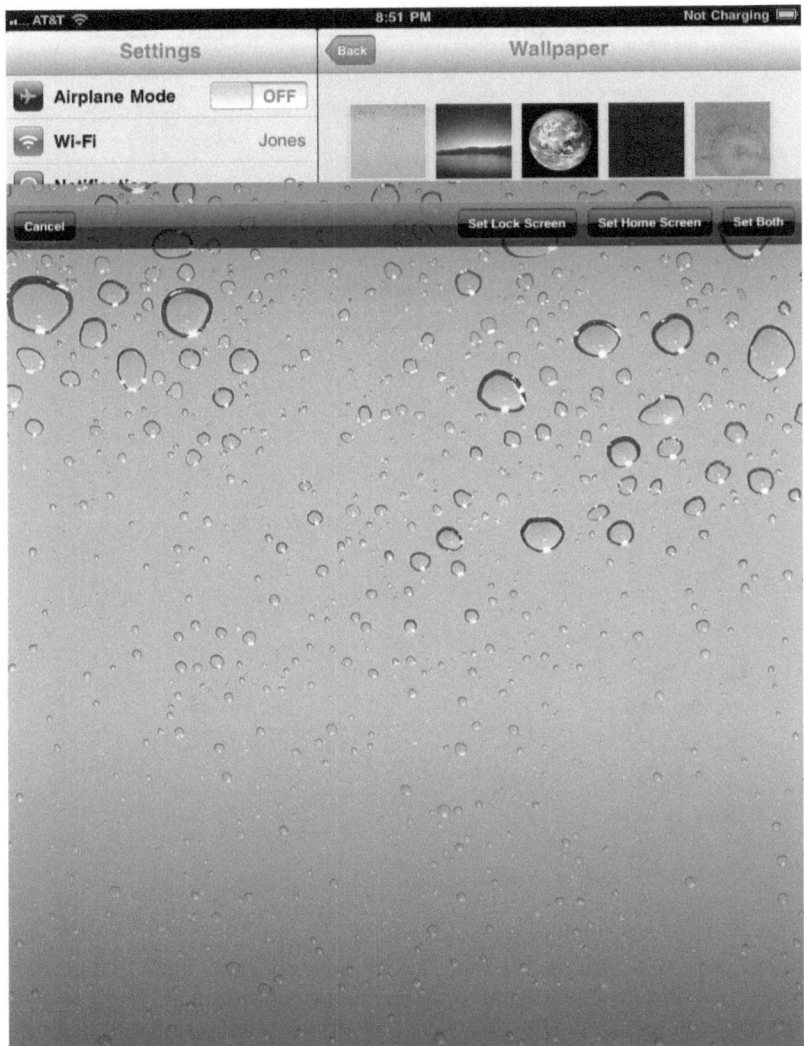

The picture we selected will open up to give a better view. There are two buttons available at the top right of the photo. "Set Lock Screen" and "Set Home Screen" are your options to set with this picture.

THE NEW USERS GUIDE TO THE IPAD

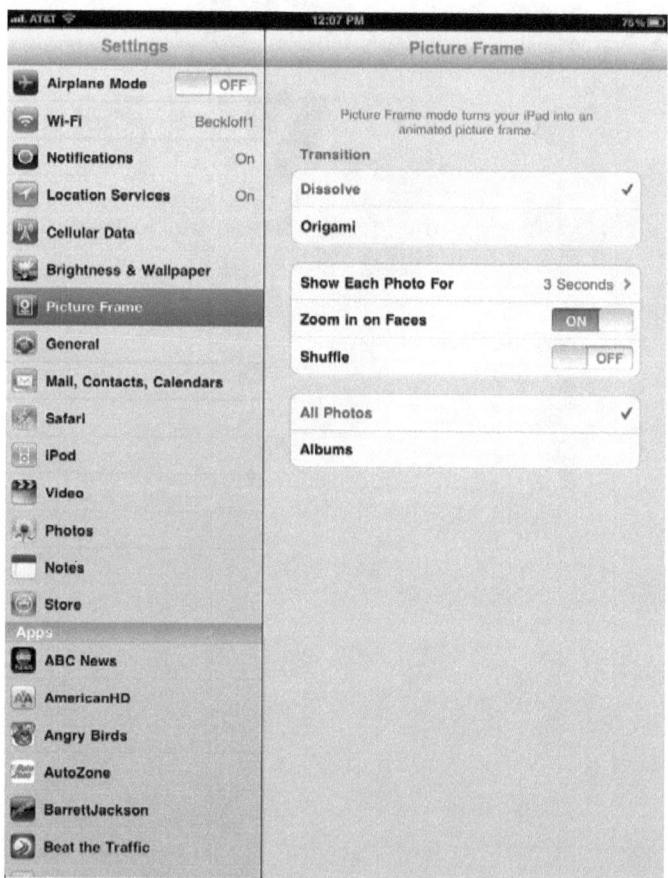

Photo Frame will turn the iPad into a digital photo frame that will cycle photos. The dissolve or origami options are the transitions that will be used between pictures. The "show each photo for X seconds" will be how long the photo is displayed. "Zoom in on faces" will simply zoom in on photos of people. "Shuffle" will randomize the photos. The last option is what photos to use. All photos or specific albums can be selected.

SETTINGS

The About option has several options about the iPad itself.

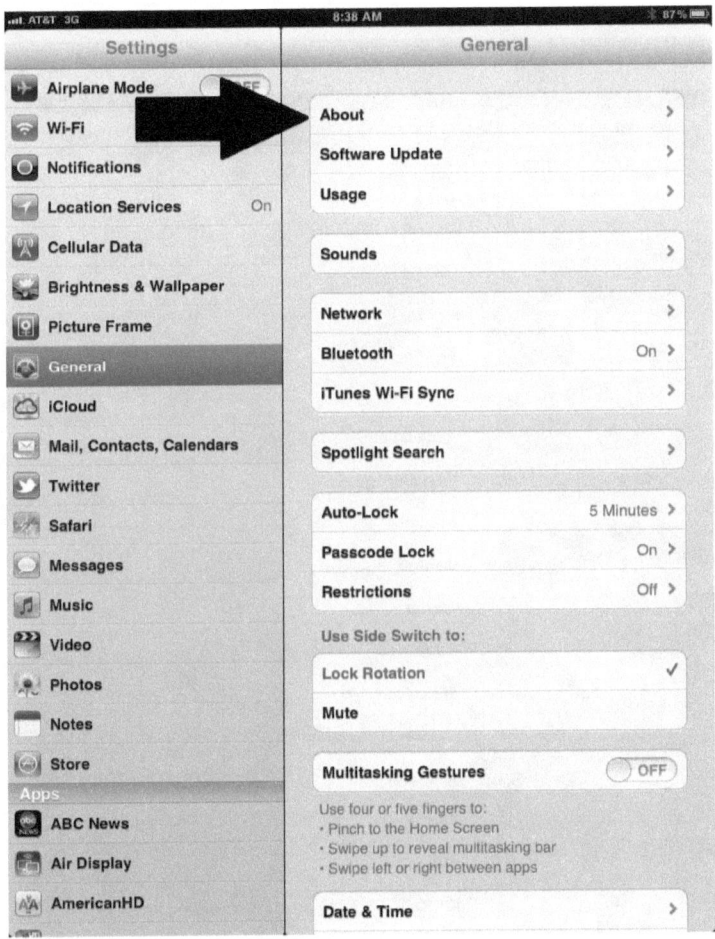

THE NEW USERS GUIDE TO THE IPAD

The options in the About screen are listed below. We have the name of our iPad. We see the Cellular Network as ATT. The volume of music, videos, and photos is listed here. The total capacity of storage on the iPad is listed here. The amount of free space on the iPad is listed here. Many of the Cellular Carrier data options are listed here.

SETTINGS

On this screen, we have selected to rename our iPad. You can type a new name in this box for the iPad.

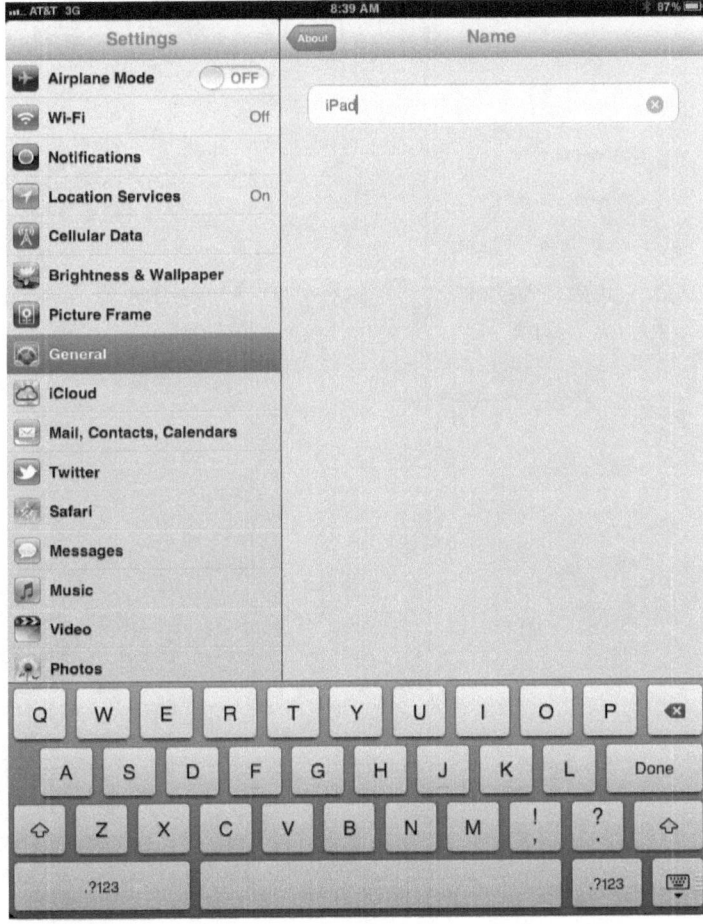

THE NEW USERS GUIDE TO THE IPAD

The diagnostic and usage information is data that can be sent back to Apple regarding problems that happen with the software on the iPad. Sending the information to Apple will help them correct problems that are recurring. This step sends usage information about the iPad. This option is completely up to each individual user.

SETTINGS

The software update option is where you will find updates to the Operating System on the iPad. If the iPad is up to date, you will see a screen similar to the one below. If there are updates available, you will see them listed on this screen.

THE NEW USERS GUIDE TO THE IPAD

In this example, there are no software updates available for this iPad. This page will display the Operating System version as well, this is also known as the IOS version number.

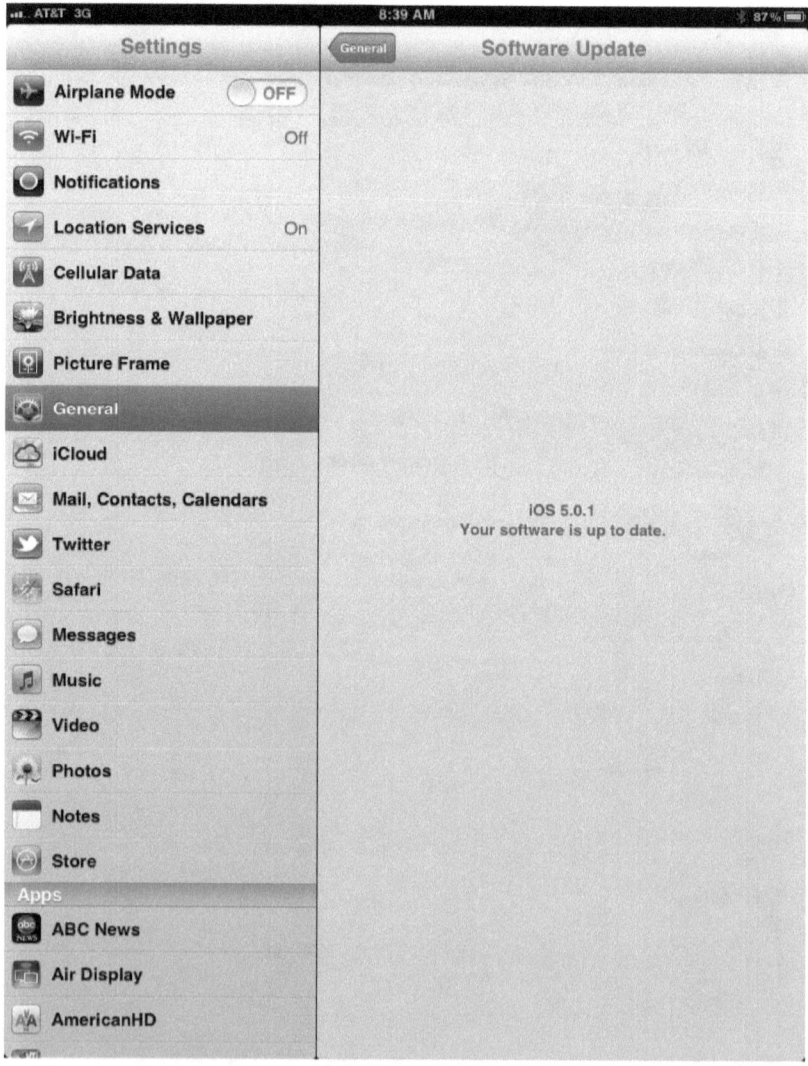

SETTINGS

The Usage option will show us more information in regard to how the iPad is being used.

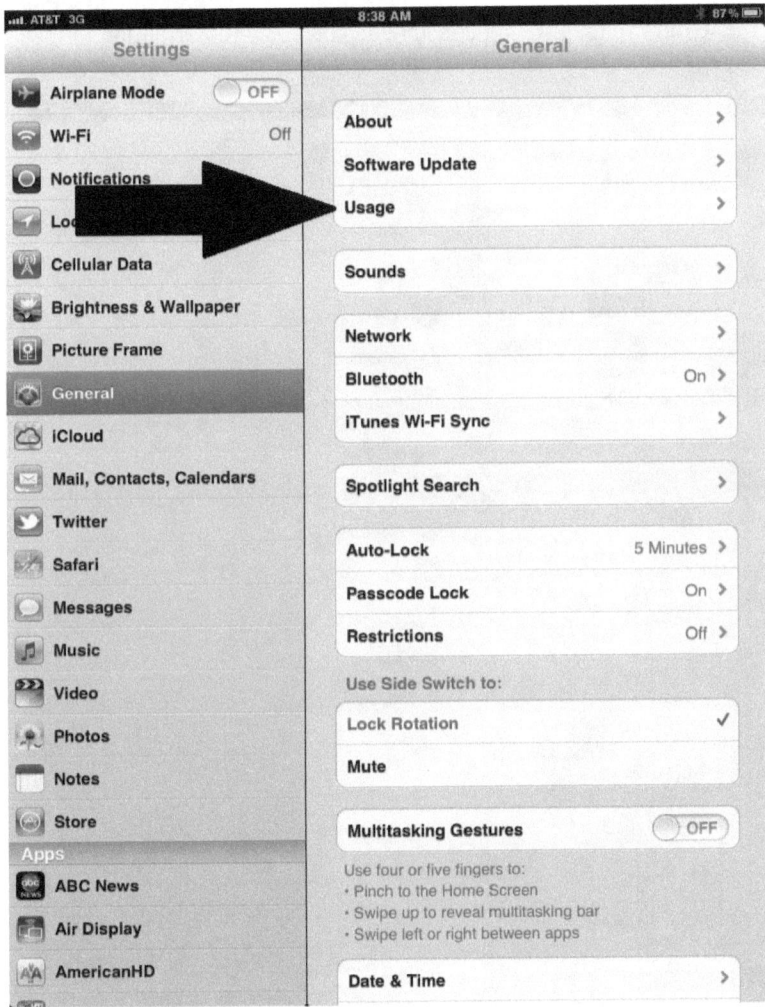

The Usage screen will show us how much space is being consumed by the larger applications. On this iPad, we can see a large number of video files are being stored. We also see the iCloud information and how much of the iCloud space is being consumed. There is another option to manage the storage of the iCloud information.

SETTINGS

Manage Storage is the option to show the breakdown of information on our iCloud account. It will also show other devices that are using on the same iCloud account. There is a button to purchase more storage space for the iCloud account.

THE NEW USERS GUIDE TO THE IPAD

This option will show the cellular usage for a given period. There is a Reset Statistics button that will allow users to erase the current statistics to start tracking for a new period of time. This is one of two places where a user can see what the cellular data statistics are for a time period. The other screen is located in the options, under cellular data. Inside the cellular data options is a button to view your account. Click this button and log in to your cellular account to see statistics for the current billing period.

SETTINGS

The sounds option is where individual sounds can be set for the different functions that happen on the iPad, such as new email arriving.

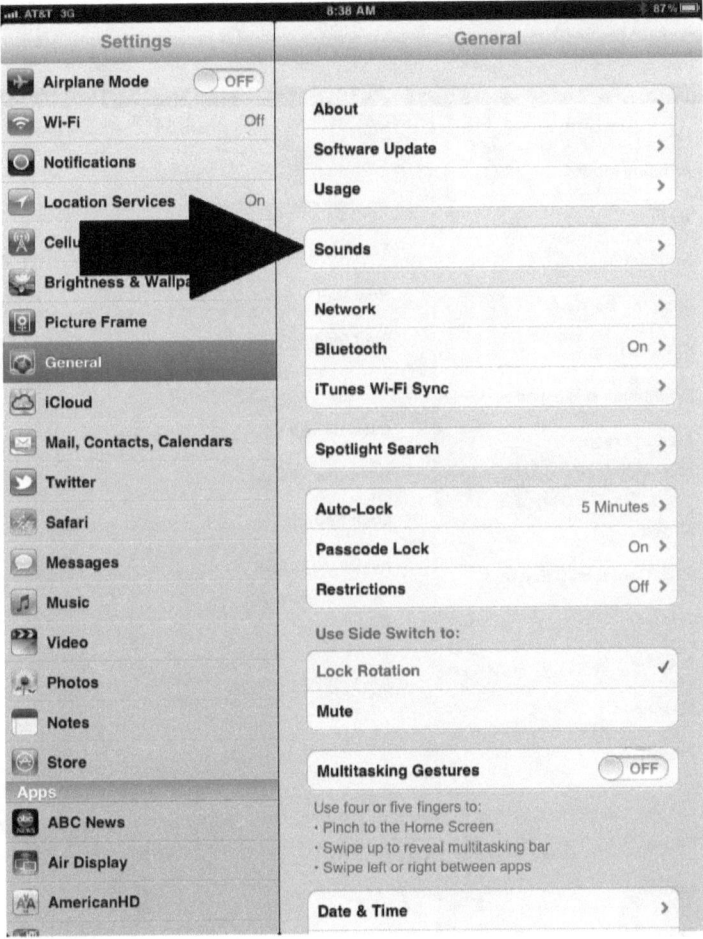

Page 43

THE NEW USERS GUIDE TO THE IPAD

This screen shows the many options where you can select alternate sounds for your iPad if you do not like the original sounds. There is also a volume control for the sounds on this same page.

SETTINGS

The Network option will allow us to use a VPN or Wi-Fi network.

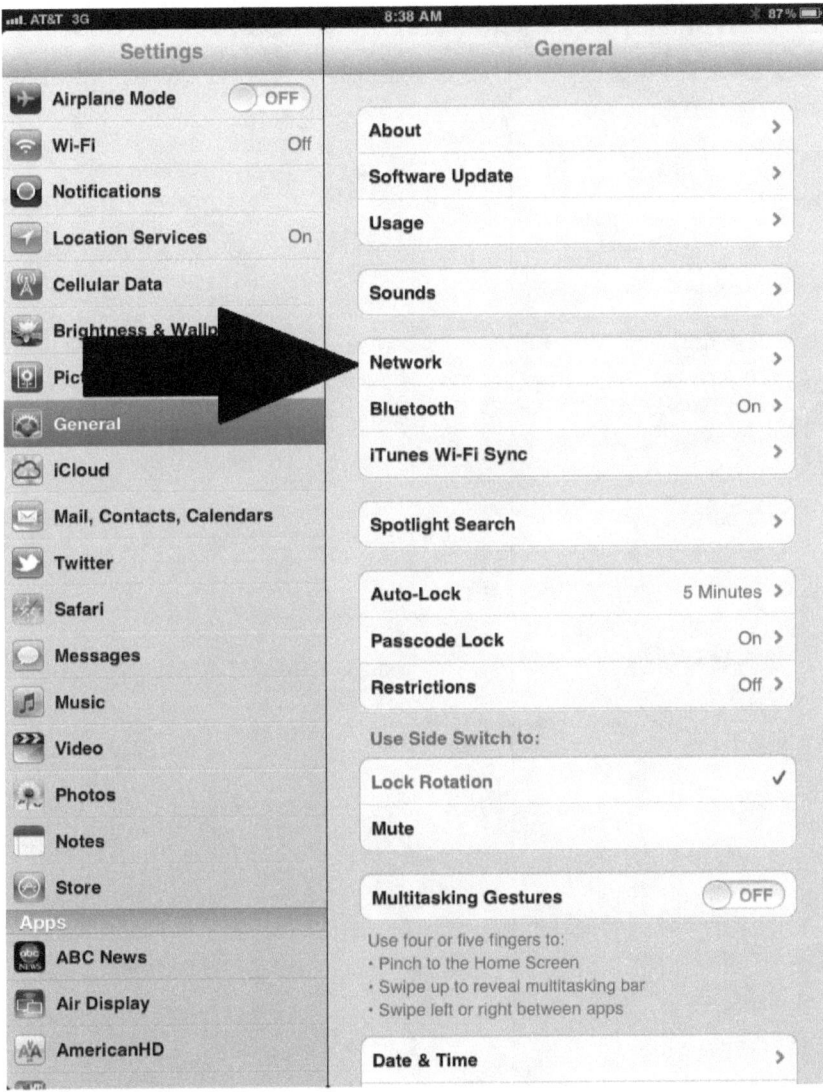

THE NEW USERS GUIDE TO THE IPAD

Here are the options that are listed in the Network options list. You can turn on or off a VPN or Wi-Fi connection here.

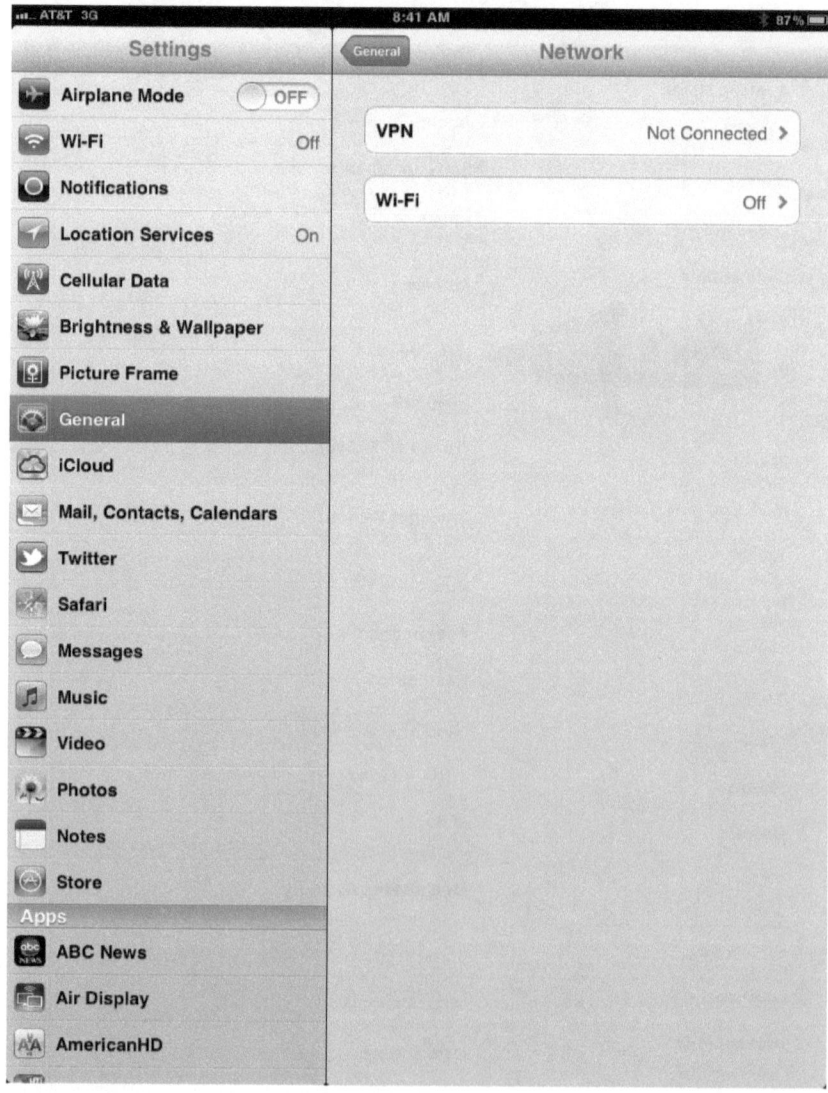

SETTINGS

The iPad has a Bluetooth connection built into it for connecting to other Bluetooth devices. This is the option to go into the Bluetooth settings.

Page 47

THE NEW USERS GUIDE TO THE IPAD

Inside the Bluetooth options we will see the toggle to turn the option on or off. Under the Devices tab, we see the devices that we have paired with or connected to in the past. We also can see if the iPad is discoverable by other Bluetooth devices. If the iPad is discoverable, the name you specified in the About option is what others will see.

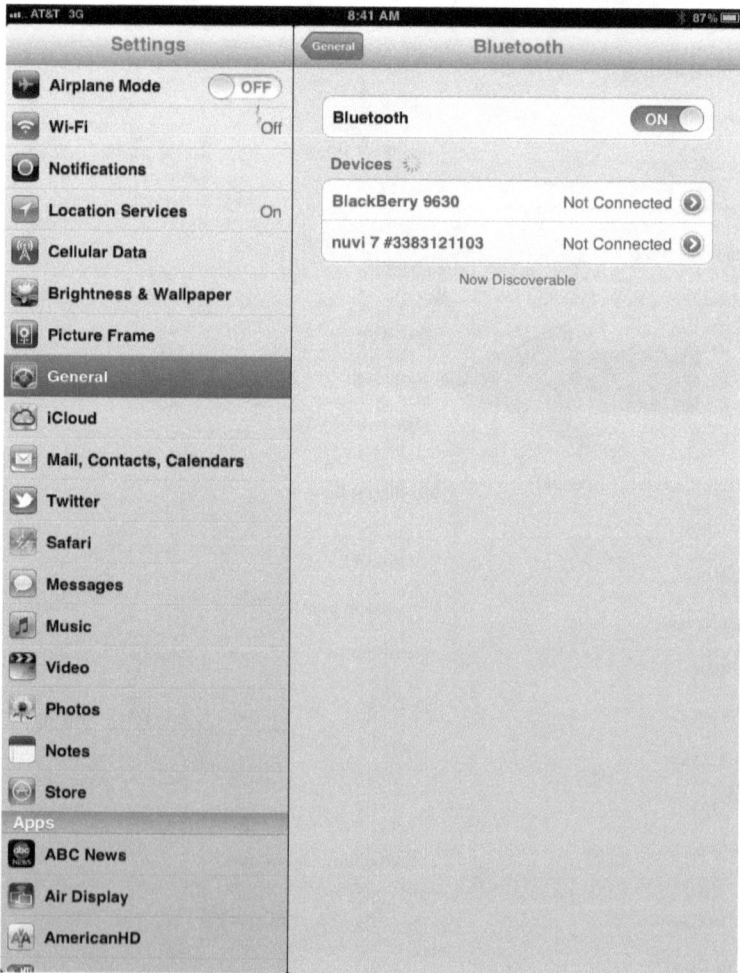

Page 48

SETTINGS

The iPad can Sync its content to a computer running iTunes. This process has always worked with the USB cable; however, starting with Version 5 of the IOS, we can now sync wirelessly on our wireless network. This is the option screen for the wireless sync setup.

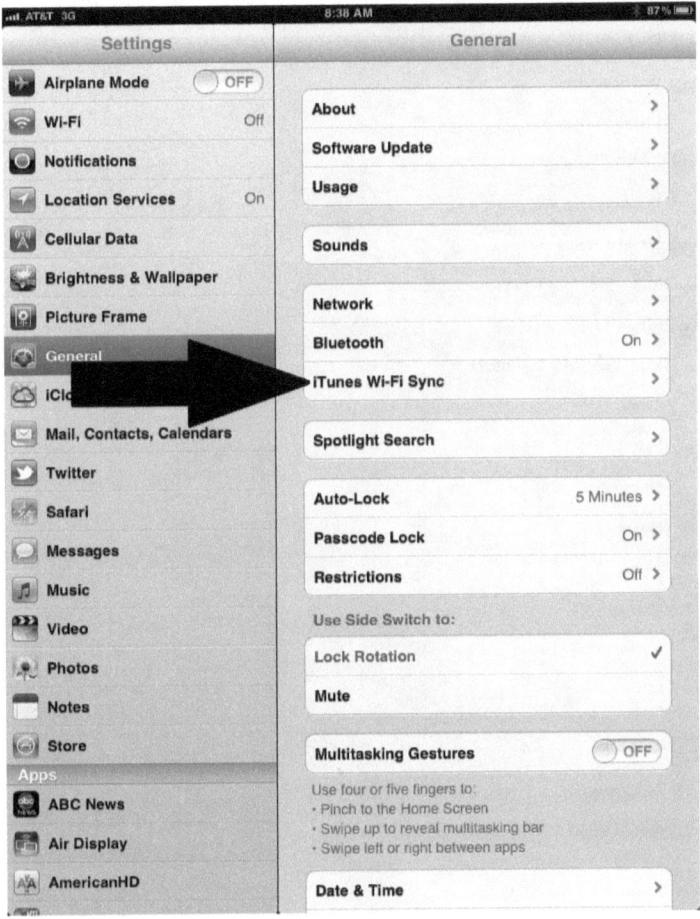

THE NEW USERS GUIDE TO THE IPAD

The wireless sync option will show the computer that is configured to sync with this iPad. It will show the last successful sync with that computer. If you are on the same wireless network as this computer, there is a button initiating a sync from the iPad.

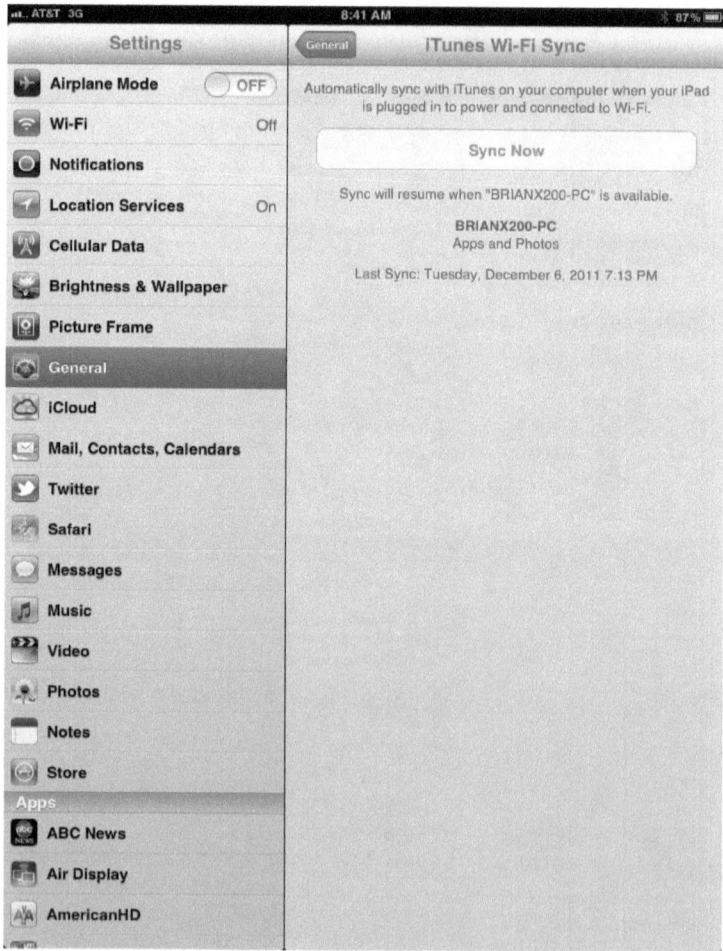

SETTINGS

Spotlight search is our search tool that allows us to look in many locations at one time. We can type a name and it will look at contacts, emails, notes, and much more. Simply search for a given thing, and this is where you will find it fast.

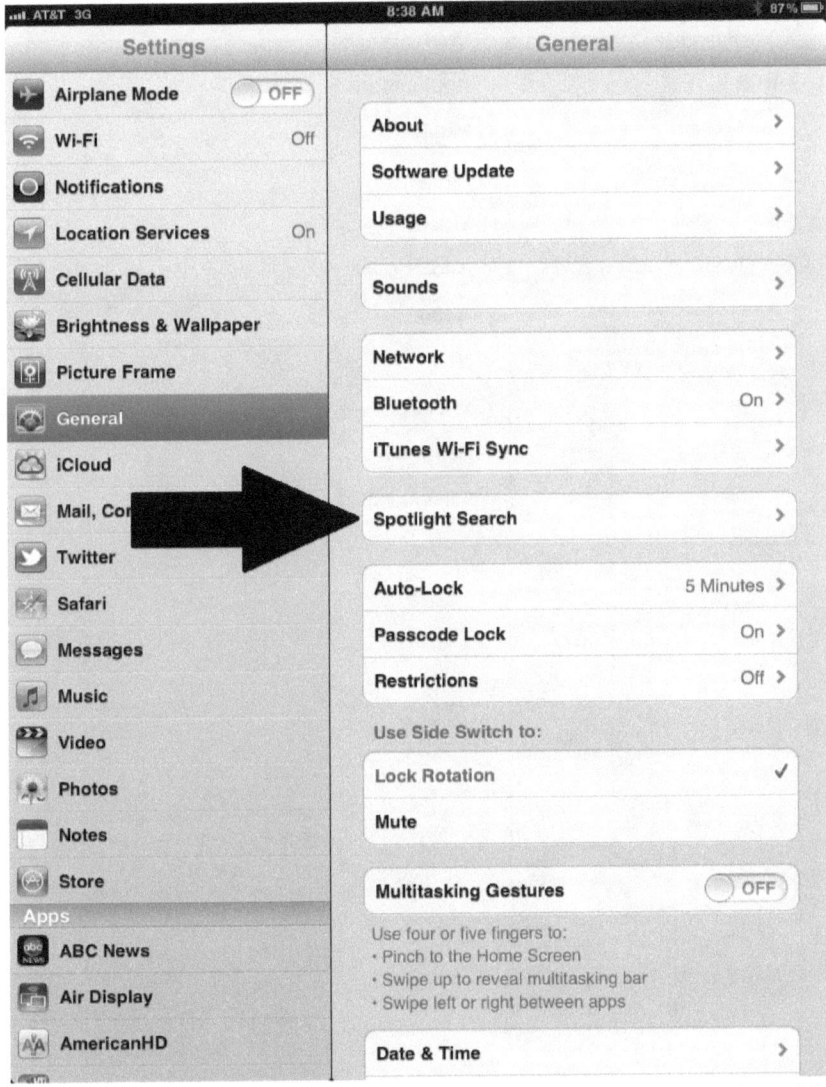

THE NEW USERS GUIDE TO THE IPAD

These are the areas that can be searched using the Spotlight Search tool. You can select or deselect places to look for the search terms.

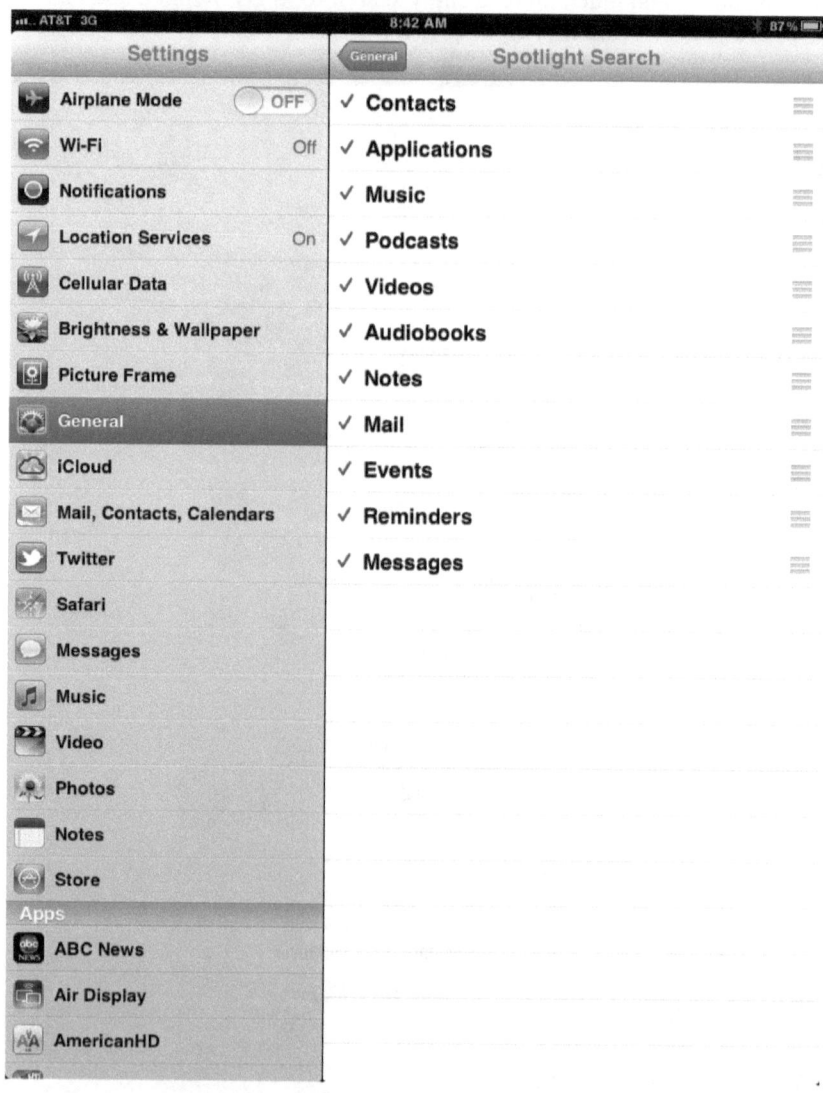

SETTINGS

Auto-Lock is the function that will start at the predefined amount of time as specified in the option below and lock the iPad. In this example, after two minutes of inactivity, the iPad will lock and require a password to access it.

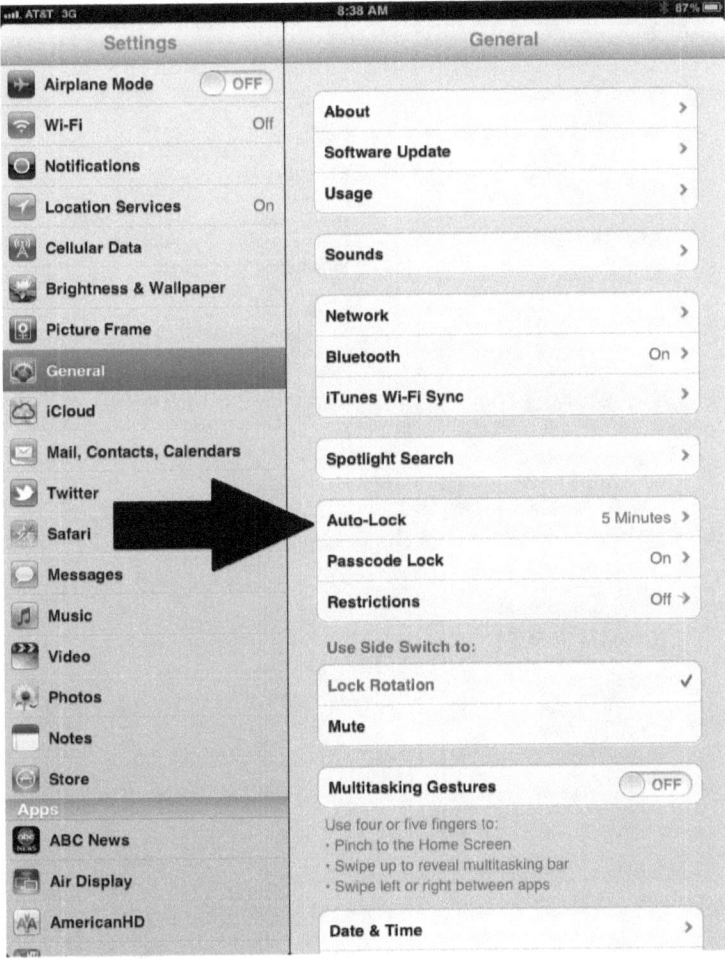

THE NEW USERS GUIDE TO THE IPAD

This photo shows the options that are available to use with the Auto-Lock function. If the "Never" option is selected, the Auto-Lock function will be disabled.

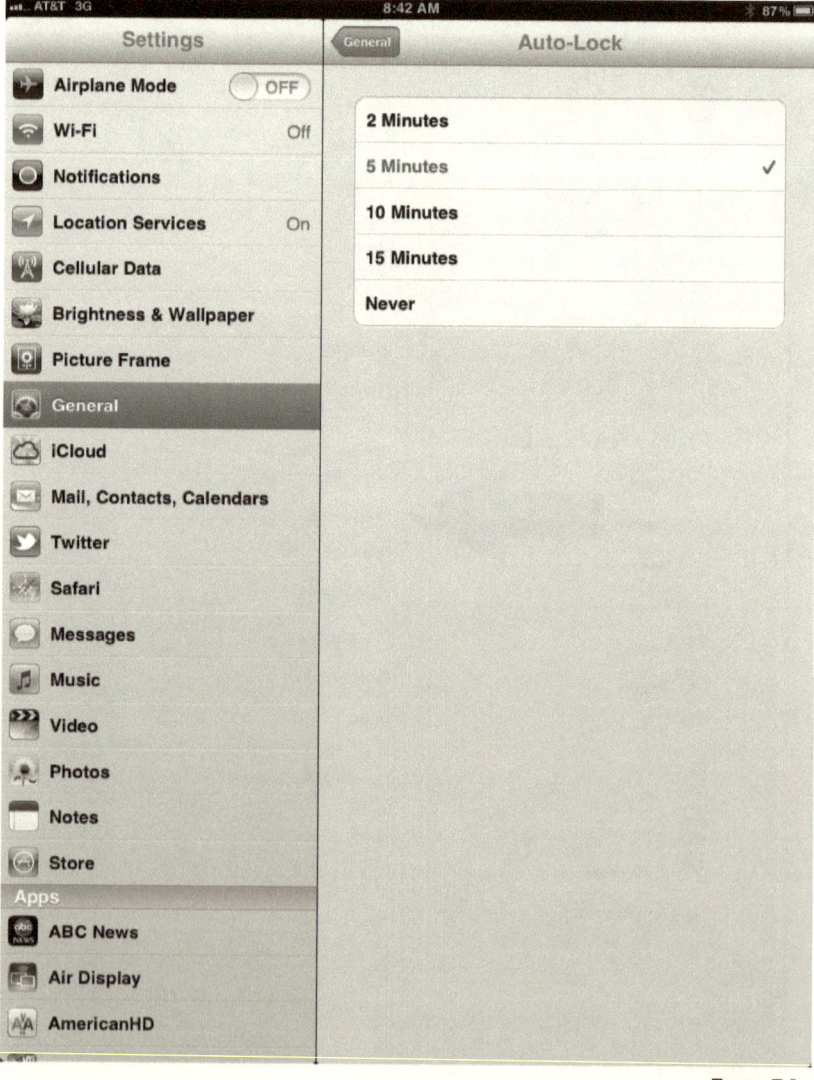

Page 54

SETTINGS

The Passcode Lock option will allow the iPad to be securely locked with a password either after a set amount of time or if manually locked. The default passcode is a four digit numeric code. The passcode type can be changed to be more complex if desired.

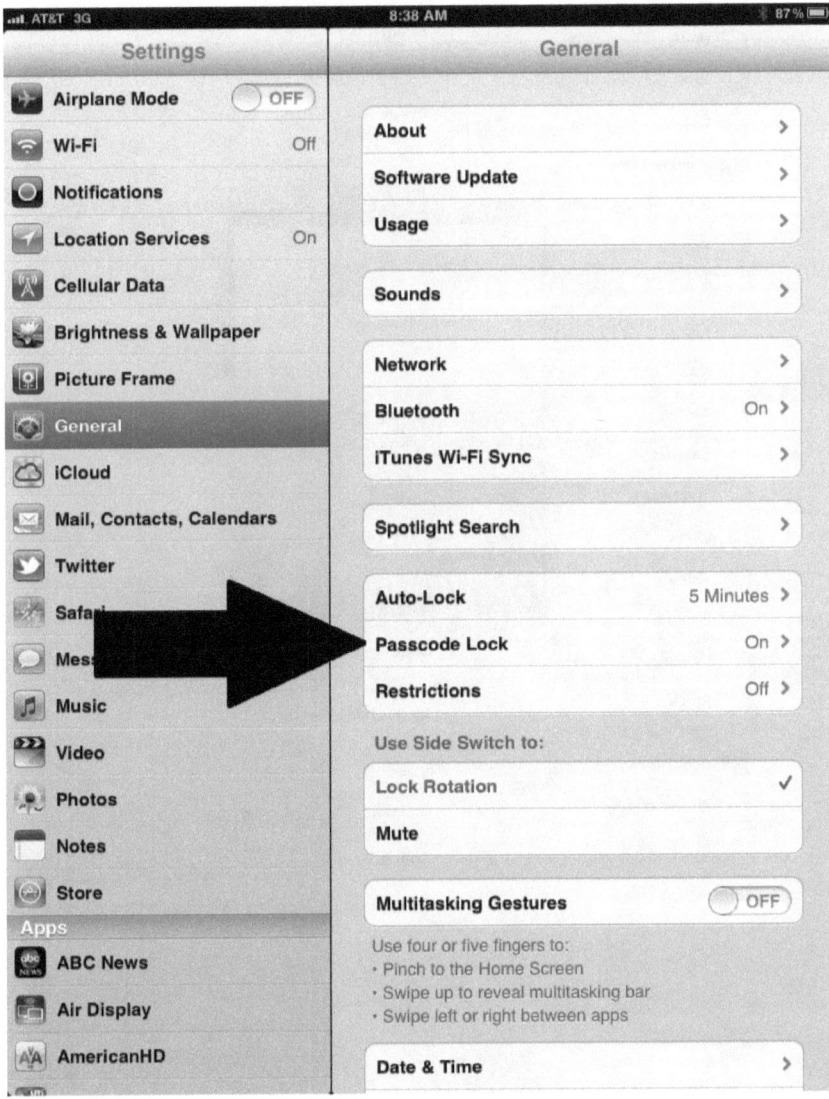

THE NEW USERS GUIDE TO THE IPAD

To make changes to the Passcode Lock options, the current passcode will need to be entered before getting to the passcode options.

SETTINGS

The Passcode Lock options screen has several options.

There is an option to turn the passcode lock completely off.

There is an option to change the existing passcode. If the passcode is changed, it will be changed to match the passcode type currently selected, simple or complex.

The required passcode will indicate when the passcode will be initiated.

The Simple passcode option will allow the passcode lock to be changed to something more complex than four numeric numbers. If Simple is set to off, the iPad passcode can be more complex.

The picture frame option will allow photos to be shown as a display of photos when the iPad is locked.

The erase data option is a security setting that will allow the iPad will be completely erased if a passcode is attempted more than 10 consecutive times. If confidential data is kept on the device that could be compromised if the iPad is lost or misplaced, this option is a great idea. I have also seen children pick up a locked iPad to play with the device and when the parents return, they realize that the iPad is completely erased as a result of the children typing letters.

THE NEW USERS GUIDE TO THE IPAD

The Restrictions option allows an iPad to lock out certain applications or functions. A great example of this might be to lock out the Safari browser so that internet usage quota (if carrier has a monthly quota) cannot be exceeded.

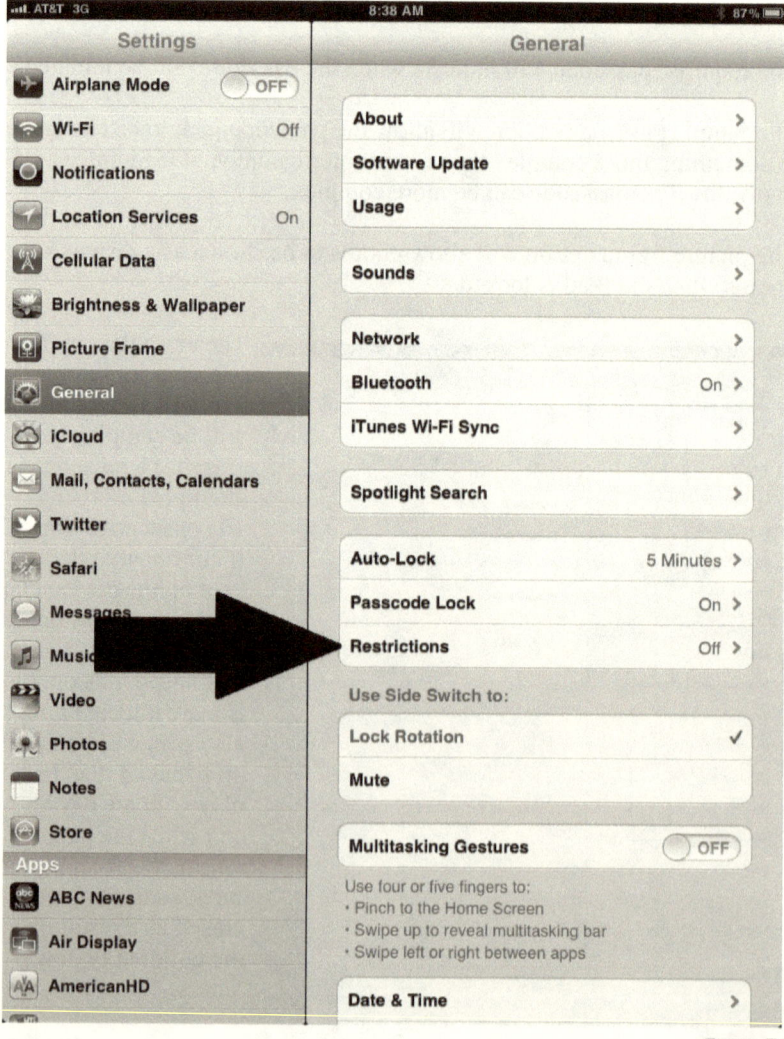

SETTINGS

Here are the apps and functions that can be restricted, if restrictions are enabled.

THE NEW USERS GUIDE TO THE IPAD

On the right side of the iPad is a slide switch. When the original iPad was released, this switch locked the screen from being automatically rotated. A later version of the IOS converted the functionality of the switch so that it became a mute button. The latest version of the software allows a user to select the function that the slide switch will perform.

SETTINGS

In the photo below, we can see that the option for the side slide switch is set the mute function.

THE NEW USERS GUIDE TO THE IPAD

When the iPad was released, developers realized that the iPad had much more screen area for finger and gestures to be used. As a result of the larger screen, Multitasking Gestures was introduced. If this function is enabled, there are several functions that will work with the device.

The Pinch to Close option will close the app if the user pinches their fingers together in the middle of an app.

Take four or five fingers to swipe up to see the window that shows all the apps that are currently running.

Take four or five fingers and swipe left or right to change to other apps that are currently running.

SETTINGS

The Date & Time option will allow the iPad to have the time zone changed and several other options.

Page 63

THE NEW USERS GUIDE TO THE IPAD

The Time & Date options are shown below. The iPad has the option to display time in 24 hour format. The iPad has a "Set Automatically" option for the iPad to sense Daylight Savings Time as well as location services to match time and time zone settings based on the geographic location of the iPad.

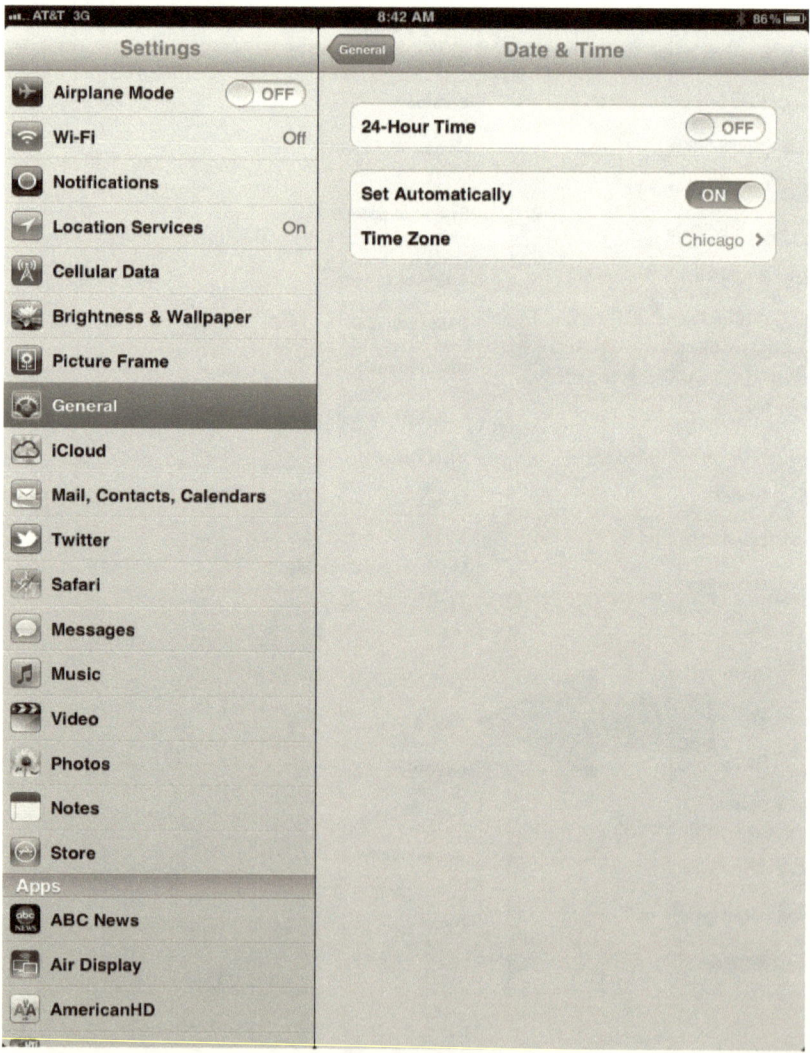

SETTINGS

Page 65

THE NEW USERS GUIDE TO THE IPAD

Keyboard options allow for the iPad to have functions such as "Auto Capitalization", "Auto Spellcheck", and more. These options can be turned on or off.

Shortcuts can be set up. A shortcut is a series of letters that when entered will be substituted for the shortcut words. In the example below, the letters "OMW" when typed would automatically be changed to the words "On my way." Create additional shortcuts that make sense to your iPad usage.

SETTINGS

The International option allows the iPad to be configured for other languages.

The Accessibility option will allow the iPad to be used by users with such disabilities as low vision, hearing impairment, or motor challenges.

SETTINGS

Some of the Accessibility functions are great for everyone. Some of the Vision accessibility options make the iPad more visible in bright sunlight. The Voice Over option, if enabled, will turn your eBooks into audio books. Take a look at the different options and see if any of them would be beneficial to you.

THE NEW USERS GUIDE TO THE IPAD

The Reset option will allow the iPad to be completely reset. This option will also reset other things as well.

SETTINGS

Below are the Reset options. These options allow the iPad to be set back to default. All files and settings can be erased here. Take a look below at the other options that can be reset.

Reset All Settings-This will default all settings to factory settings but will leave all data (photos, notes, music, etc...) on the iPad.

Erase All Content and Settings-Removes everything and then defaults iPad back to factory settings like new. Use this before giving iPad away.

Reset Network Settings-Resets all network settings (for network problems).

Reset Keyboard Dictionary-Erases all words that were learned by usage.

Reset Home Screen Layout-Resets the layout of the icons on the main page.

Reset Location Warnings-Clears all warnings that have occurred.

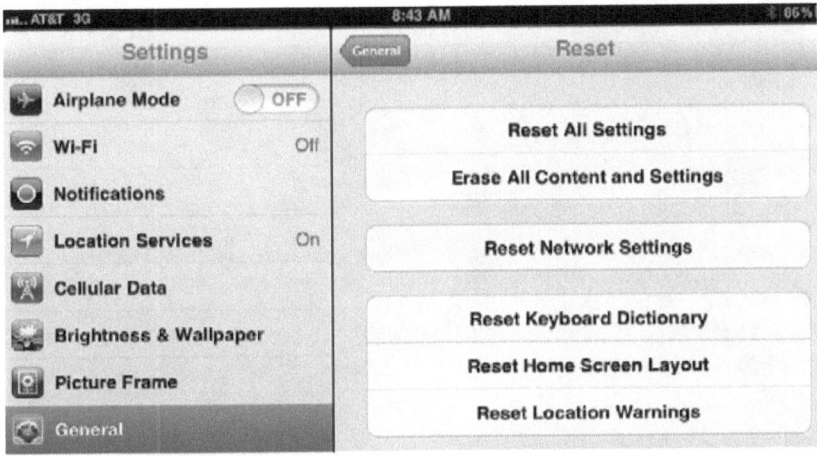

Starting with IOS Version 5, the iCloud became standard on all iPads. By default, Apple will give you five gig of storage space free. Additional space may be purchased, if needed. There is a list of items that can be backed up to the iCloud. "Storage & Backup" will allow the user to manage their iCloud account. The big red button will allow all content on the iCloud to be deleted.

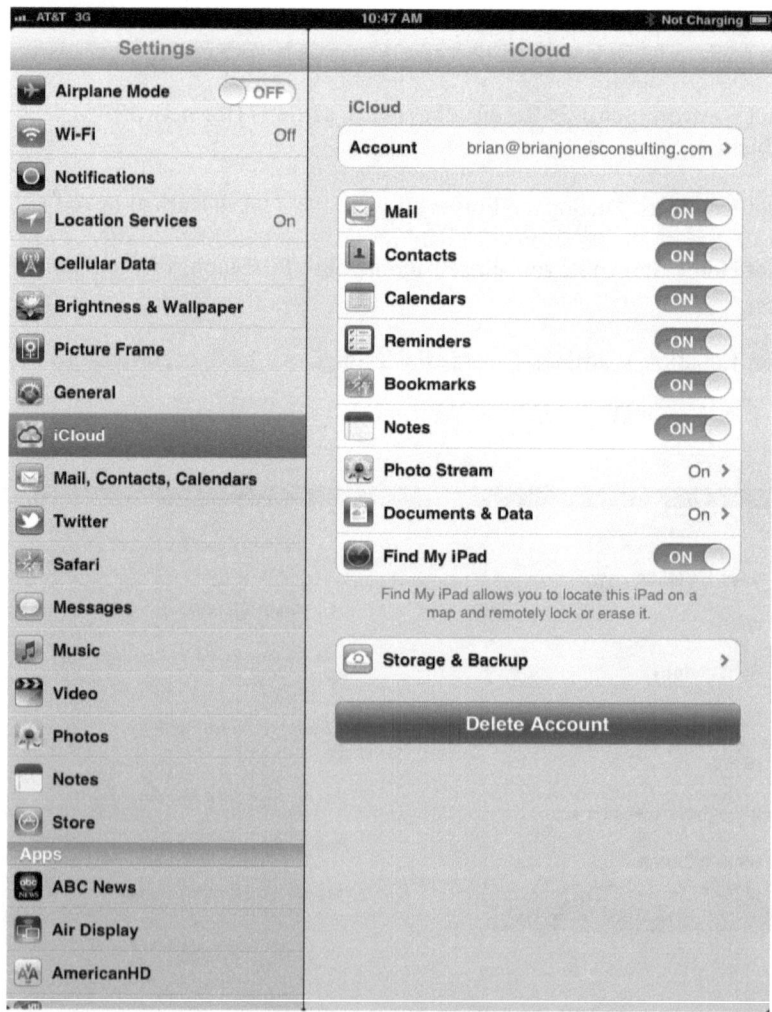

SETTINGS

The "Storage & Backup" option is where you can view your iCloud storage limits. There is a "Manage Storage" option with additional capabilities. If you find you need more storage space, there is a button on this page to purchase additional storage.

THE NEW USERS GUIDE TO THE IPAD

"Mail, Contacts, Calendars" is where the email accounts are set up and configured.

The screen on the left demonstrates four different email accounts set up on this iPad.

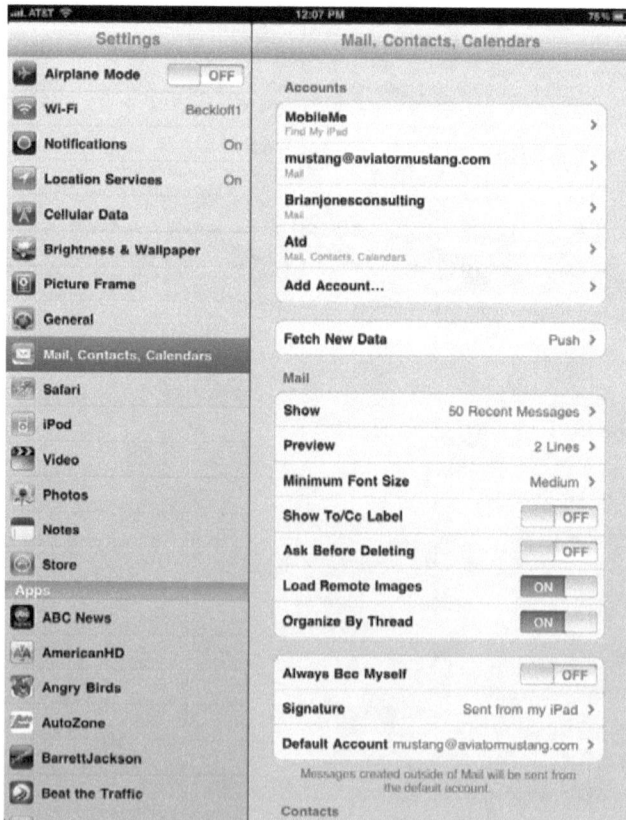

SETTINGS

Here we see the options for this configured email account. We can turn on or off the many options for the email accounts. These settings are global and are applied to all different account setups.

Here we see the options for this email account. Here is where we can turn on or off the many options for the email accounts. These settings are global and are applied to the different account setups.

SETTINGS

Here we see the options for this particular email account. Some accounts may have more or less options.

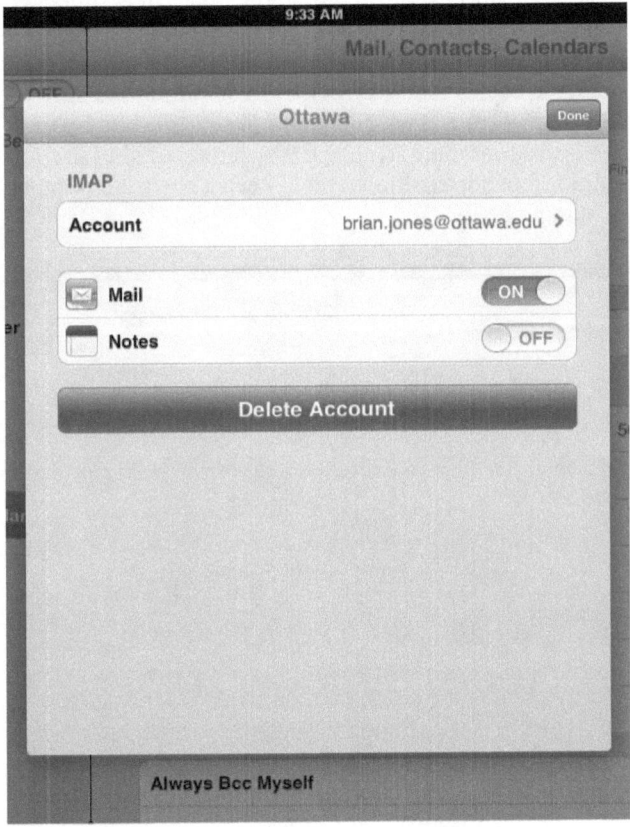

THE NEW USERS GUIDE TO THE IPAD

The Safari options are set for your Internet browser. This is the application that allows a user to get to web pages.

The "Search Engine" box allows a change to a different search provider such as Yahoo or Bing. Autofill will allow user names and passwords to prepopulate if Safari has saved them from a previous setting. "Private Browsing" will allow you to go to web pages and there are no traces of where you have been. "Accept Cookies" will allow web sites to write certain information to a small file on the iPad for future reference. JavaScript is programming language that some websites use for functionality. The pop-up blocker will keep a site from popping up other windows automatically.

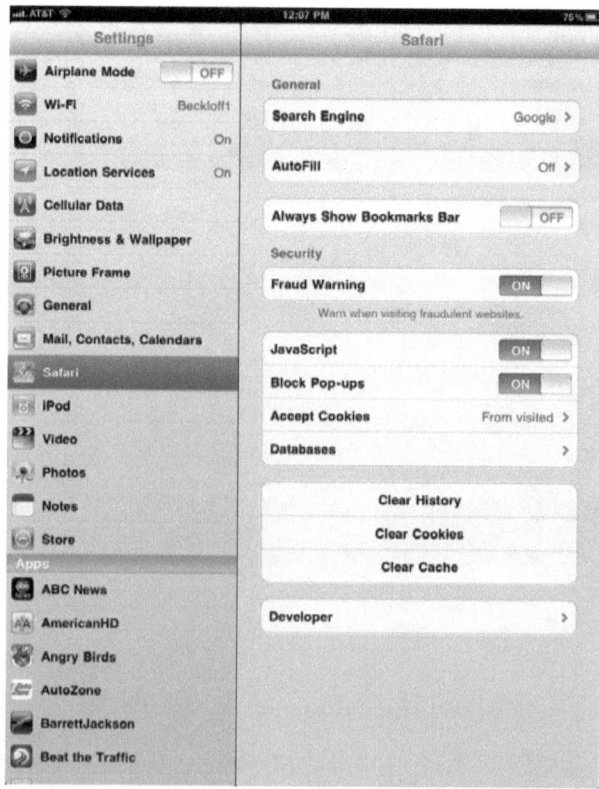

Page 78

SETTINGS

The Music options are used for the music player on the iPad. The look and feel is similar to the Apple iPods that have been used for years.

Sound Check can be turned on. Equalizer (EQ) can be turned on.

iTunes Match is a service that allows you store your entire collection, iTunes purchases as well as music you've imported from CDs or purchased somewhere other than iTunes, in the Cloud. The service is sold with a yearly subscription.

The Home Sharing box is where you will put your iTunes Apple ID and Password. This will be used for the Home Sharing option. Home Sharing a way that music and media files on other computers in your network can be shared and played on different devices inside your wireless network. Home Sharing is also what is used by the Apple TV products that are discussed later in this book.

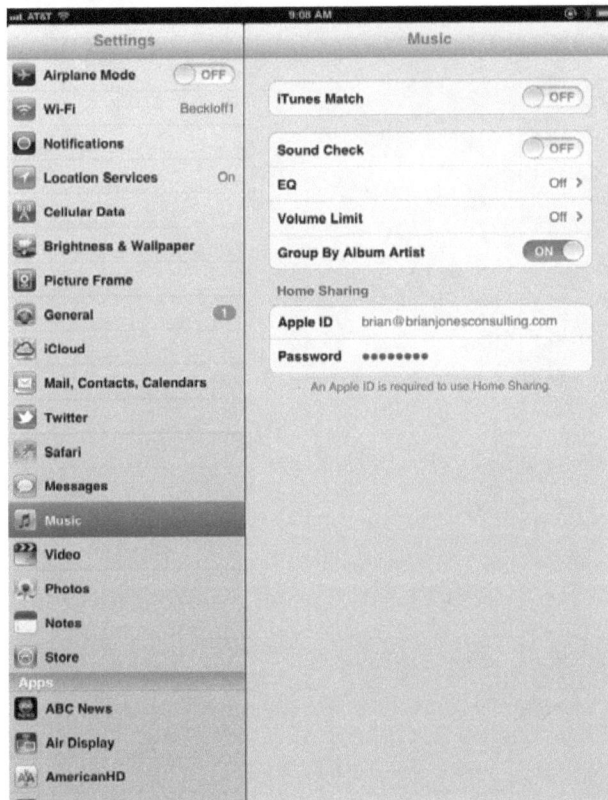

The video options are used for the video media player. If you have movies or videos stored on your iPad, these will be the settings that will be utilized. The "Start Playing" option will let a user stop watching a movie then continue where they left off once the movie is restarted. Closed captioning can be toggled on or off.

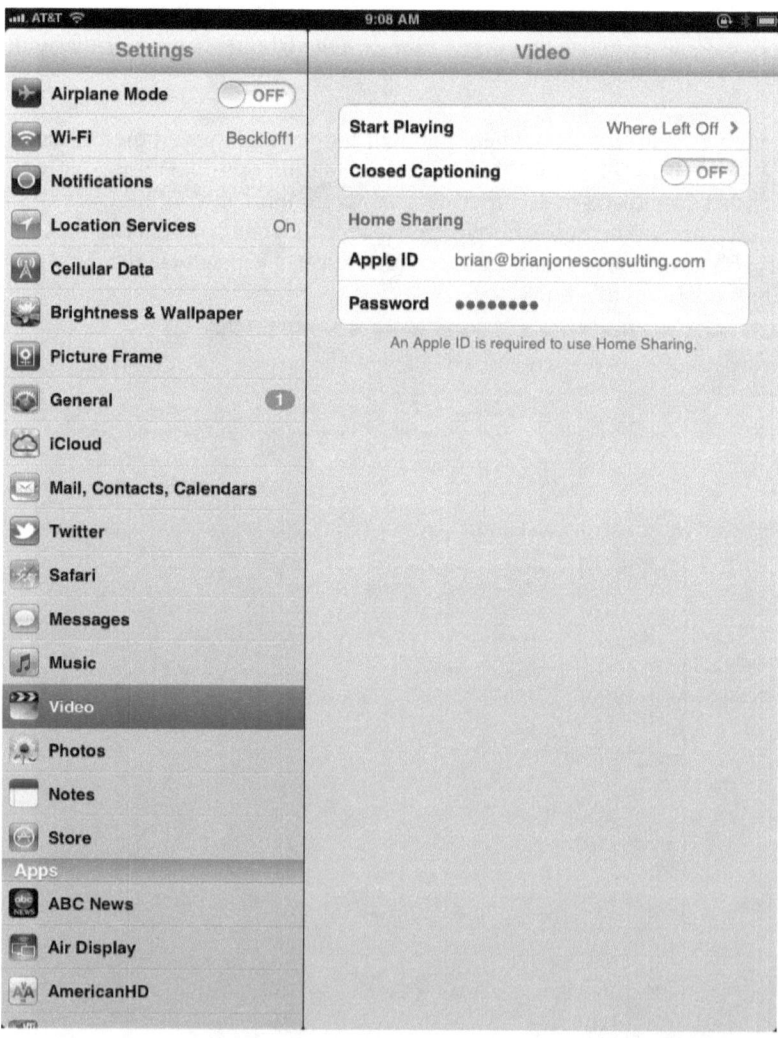

SETTINGS

The Photos options will be what are used when you are displaying photos on your iPad.

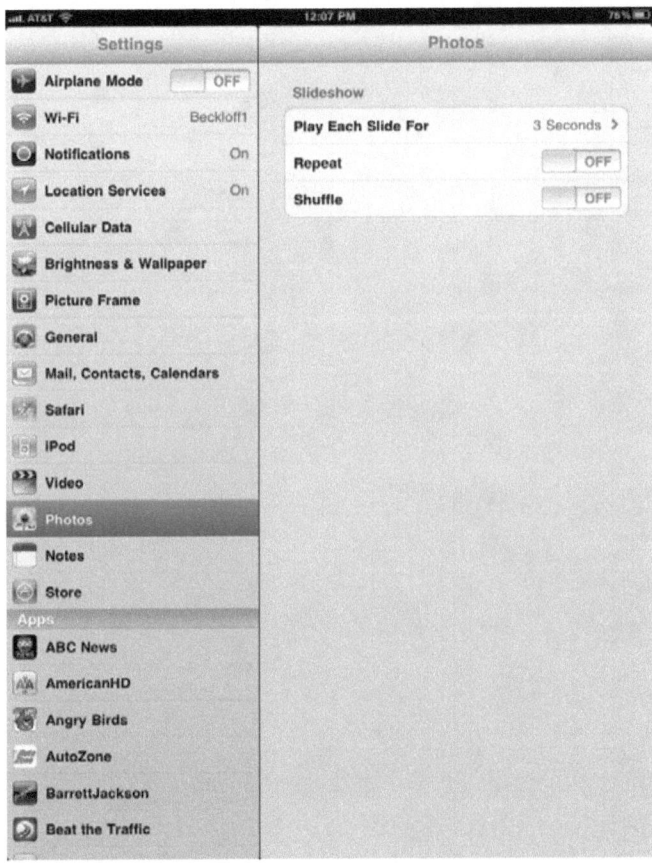

THE NEW USERS GUIDE TO THE IPAD

The Notes options will allow the change of fonts and the look of the lettering when a note is created or used.

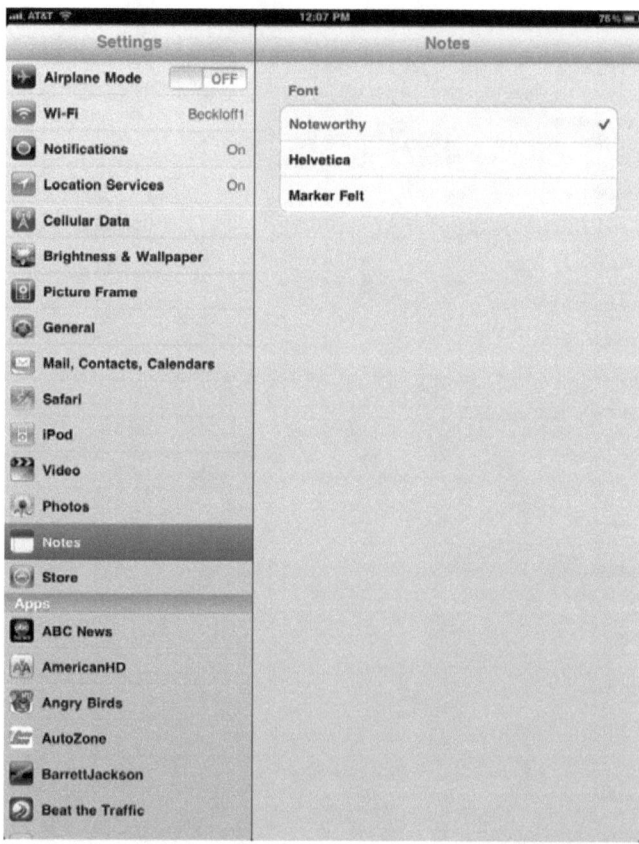

SETTINGS

The Store option will be the information that is used at the online iTunes store for music, books, videos, TV shows, and more.

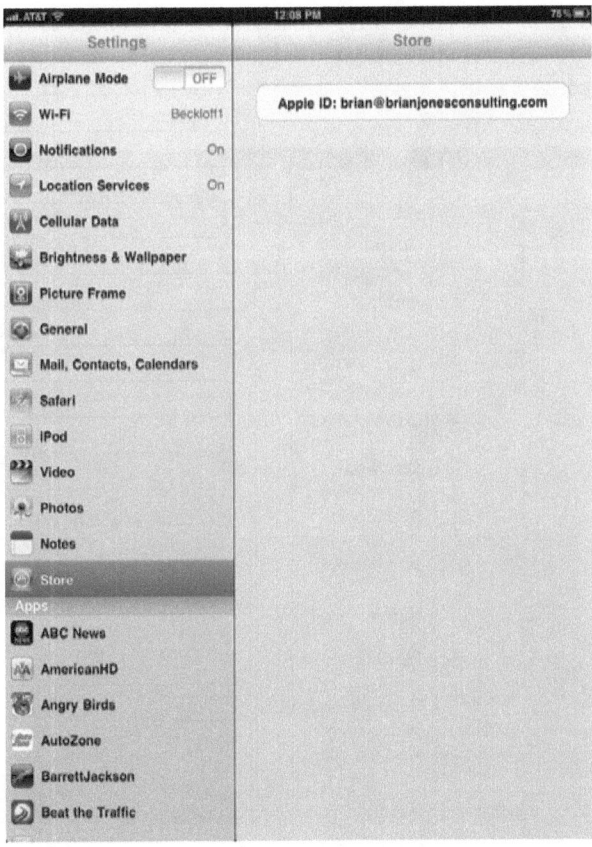

The iCloud option became available with Version 5 of the software. The iCloud option will let a user create an account where data and information about the iPad can be stored on a cloud server. A cloud server is simply a server that is hosted on the internet where data can be kept securely. On this screen, you will see the information that can be stored on the iCloud. An iCloud account can be created for no charge. The free account will only allow you a limited amount of storage. This amount will usually be enough for most users with no problem. If you need more storage available on your iCloud account, additional space can be purchased on a yearly basis.

SETTINGS

Below the standard options, you will see the applications that are installed on the iPad. Each application may have individual settings for their app. This example shows the ABC News app and the options that are available for it.

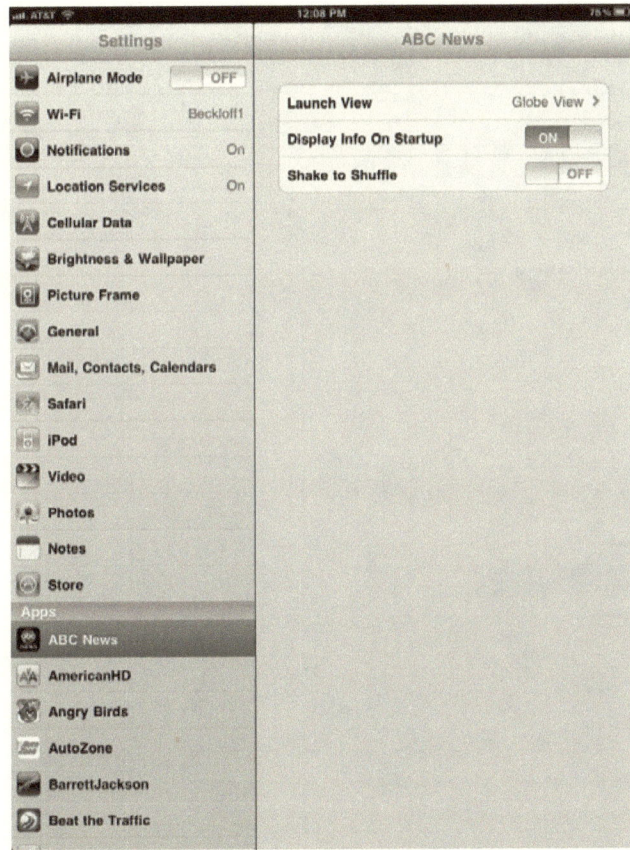

The American Airlines app has a few settings that can be changed.

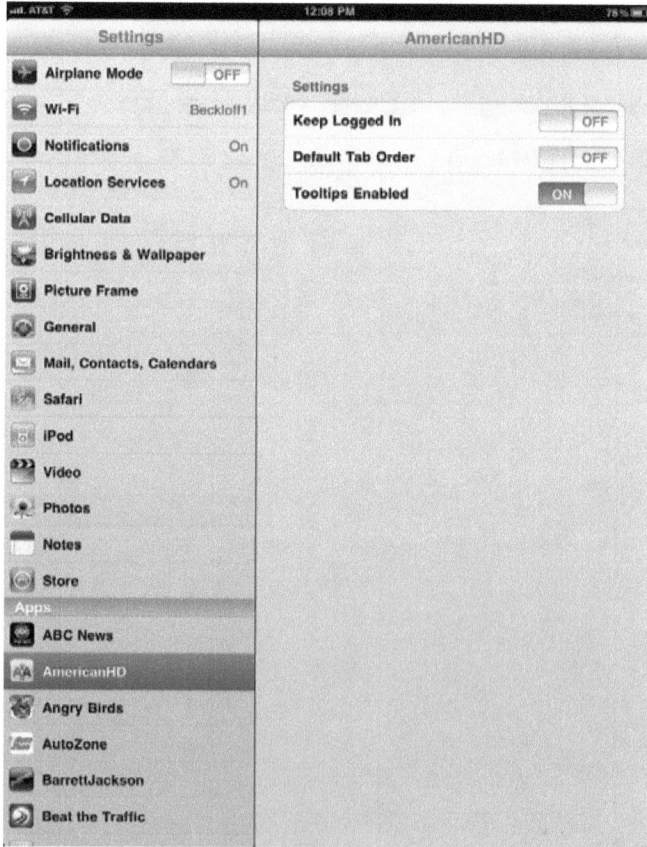

SETTINGS

The game Angry Birds has a few settings that can be changed.

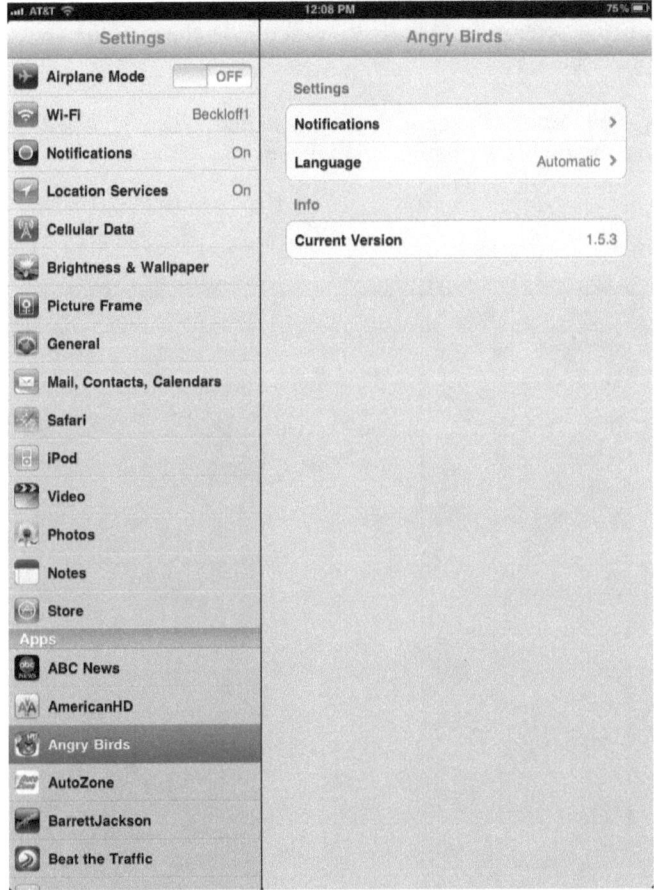

THE NEW USERS GUIDE TO THE IPAD

Some apps will only have the version number of the app listed in the options. In this example, the Barrett Jackson Antique Auto Auctions will only show the version and toggle to reset the database of the cars that are being sold or have sold.

On your iPad, look at the apps that are installed to see what settings and options are available for the individual apps.

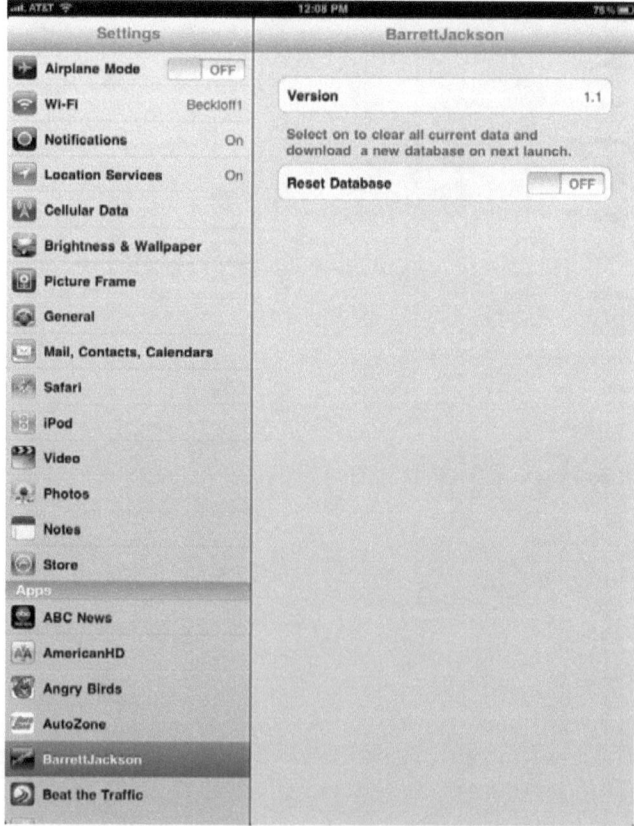

SETTINGS

 Initial Setup of iPad

So you have purchased this new and wonderful device known as an iPad and you are all ready to get it out and start using it right? Not quite yet. There is a series of steps that have to be completed before you can start using this new and magical device known as an iPad.

Once the iPad has been unboxed, you will need the device and the USB connector cable.

iTunes will need to be loaded on a computer for the initial set up steps. It is a good idea to make sure that your iTunes is updated to the latest version before starting. If you do not have iTunes loaded on a computer, it is a free download from www.apple.com.

To update your iTunes to the latest version, we will start by opening the iTunes application. If a new version is available, you may see a window indicating there is a new version and asking to download the latest version.

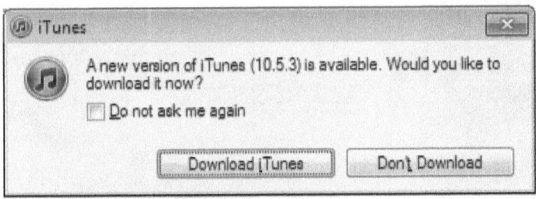

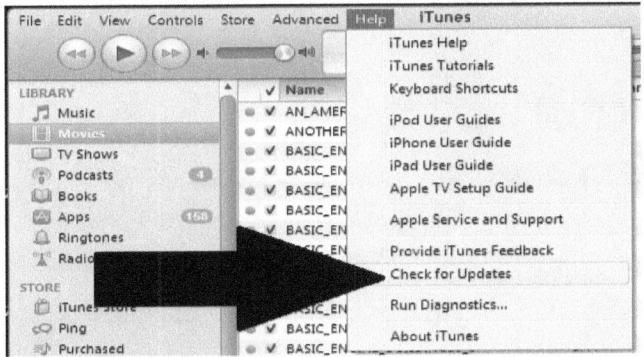 When iTunes opens, click on Help and look for the "Check for Updates" option and select it.

Page 89

THE NEW USERS GUIDE TO THE IPAD

With iTunes open on the Computer, we can connect the USB cable to the iPad and to the computer. iTunes should show the iPad as connected and as a new device; however, allow a few minutes for it to show up for the first time. Once the device is recognized, the iPad wizard will start.

While registration is not required to use your iPad or to take advantage of your warranty if broken, it does offer you some additional protections in the event your iPad is lost or stolen and later recovered. It also helps Apple keep you up to date with the latest software updates and product releases in the iPad line.

In our example, we are going to just click the continue button.

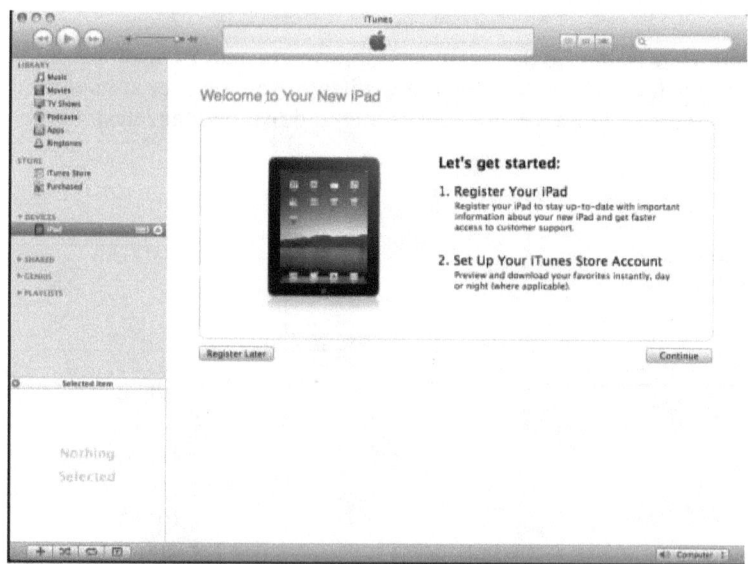

SETTINGS

The License Agreement will display on the screen, and you can agree to the terms and then click the continue button.

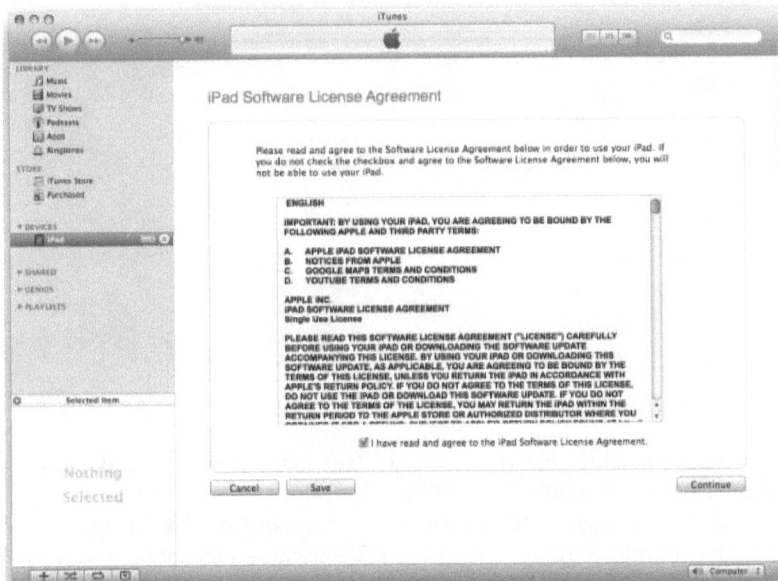

If you currently have an Apple ID, you can enter it on this screen and continue. If you do not have an ID, select the "I do not have an Apple ID" and create one. Click the "Continue" button to advance to the next step in the process.

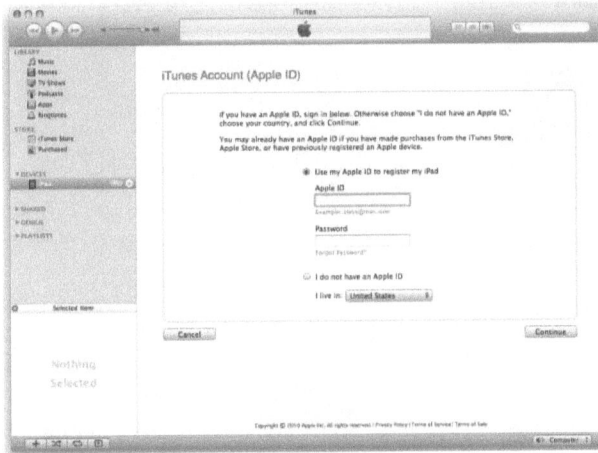

Since this is a new iPad and initially being set up, select the option for "Set up as a new iPad".

You will have to give your iPad a name. This is the name that will show up in the iTunes application as well as what others will see if the Bluetooth option is set to "Discoverable". This name can be changed later in the settings options. This is the screen where you set up how your iTunes will sync music, photos and applications. These settings can be changed later in the iTunes settings.

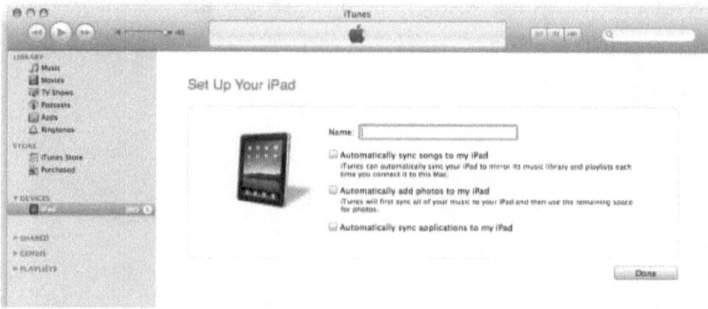

SETTINGS

At this point, the iPad is set up and ready to start using.

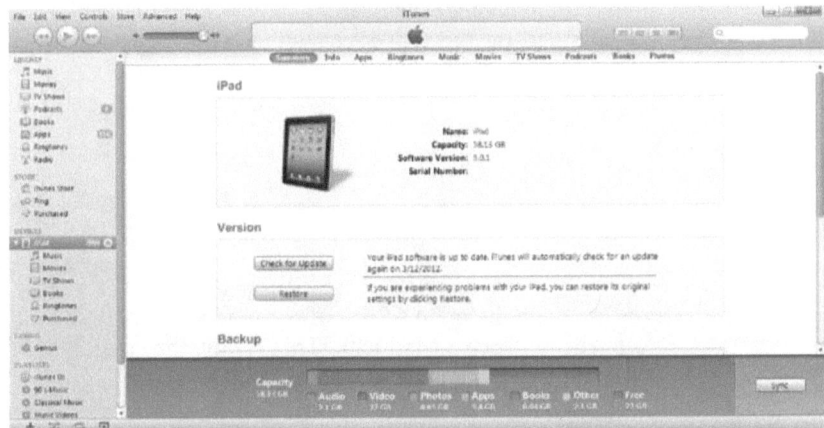

The iPad can be disconnected from the USB cable. A great habit to start would be to "Eject" the iPad before unplugging the USB cable.

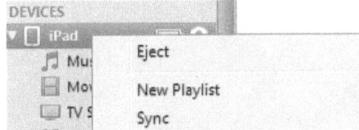 Right click on the iPad and select "Eject".

At the top of the iPad options when connected to iTunes, there are settings for how each item will sync with iTunes.

At the bottom of the iPad options, when connected to iTunes, is a graphical display of the quantity of data stored on the iPad.

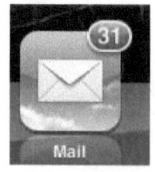 

Mail, Contacts, Calendars is where you will check your email, your contact and your calendars from the different email accounts that will be configured on the iPad. Multiple accounts can be created and accessed from the same screen, making organization and tracking of email a complete breeze. Emails as the arrive are announced with a sound and an icon change.

On the main screen of the iPad at the bottom you will see a Mail icon. This is how the email will be accessed once it is configured and working.

This is a shot of the same icon but the number in the red circle indicates that there is one new email in all the accounts configured to receive email.

CONTACTS, CALENDAR, AND EMAIL

Configure Your Email

On the main screen look for the Settings icon and select it.

When Settings open; select Mail, Contacts, Calendars on the left, then look for the Add Account option and select it.

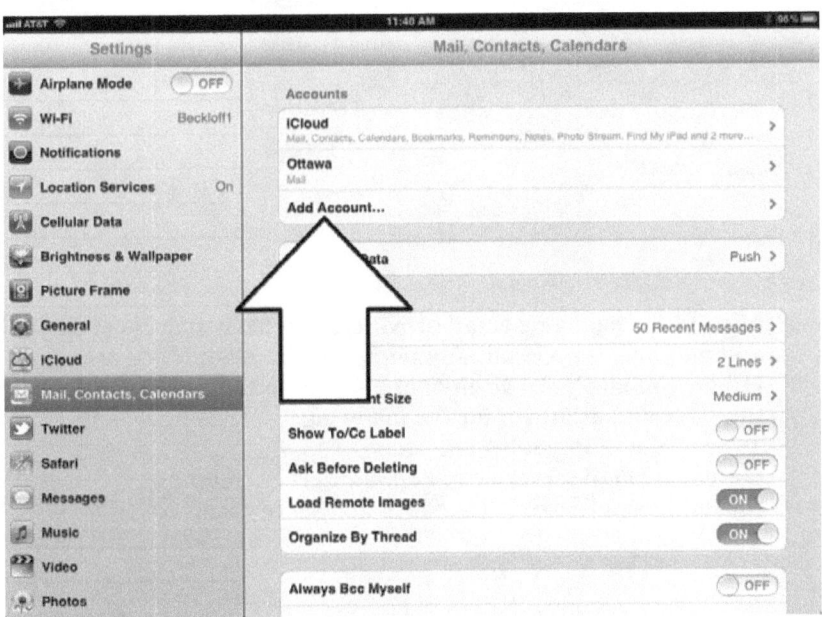

THE NEW USERS GUIDE TO THE IPAD

Select the type of email account that you would like to set up. On some account set ups, you may need to know the incoming and outgoing mail server names. If the email wizard asks for that information, you will need to contact your email provider for those settings.

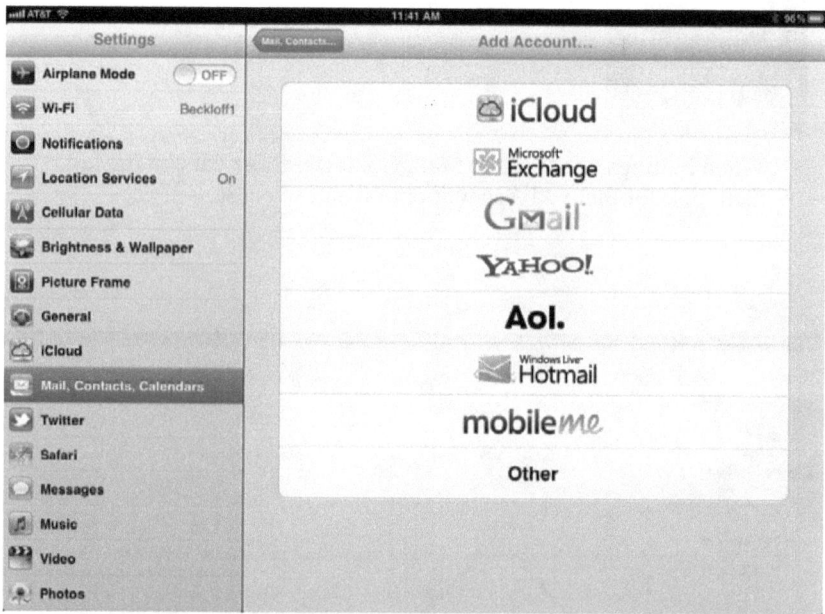

Most of the big name email providers will have their incoming and outgoing servers already set up for the iPad. If you select, Other, you may need additional information. Contact your email provider and ask them for the following:
Type of Email Pop3, IMAP, etc.
Outgoing email server : e.g. Pop.mailserver.com
Incoming email server: e.g. Smtp.mailserver.com

CONTACTS, CALENDAR, AND EMAIL

In our example, we are setting up a Gmail address. So we selected Gmail as our email type, and then the wizard lists the required information. Once complete, select the Next button in the upper right hand corner.

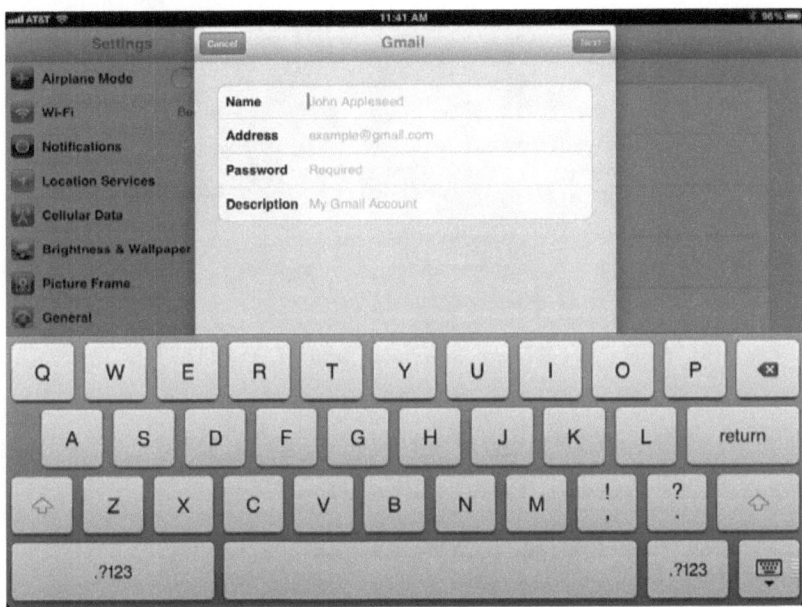

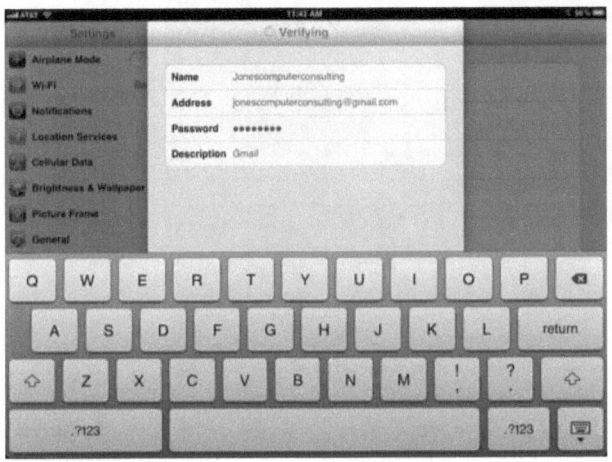
After clicking Next, there should be a window that indicates the system is verifying your information.

THE NEW USERS GUIDE TO THE IPAD

Error messages shown below indicate that there is a problem with the information you listed in the wizard for user name and password. Check your information and make sure it is correct.

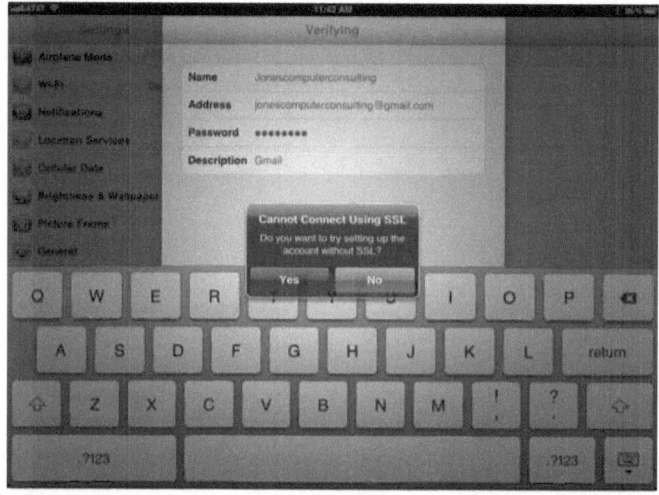

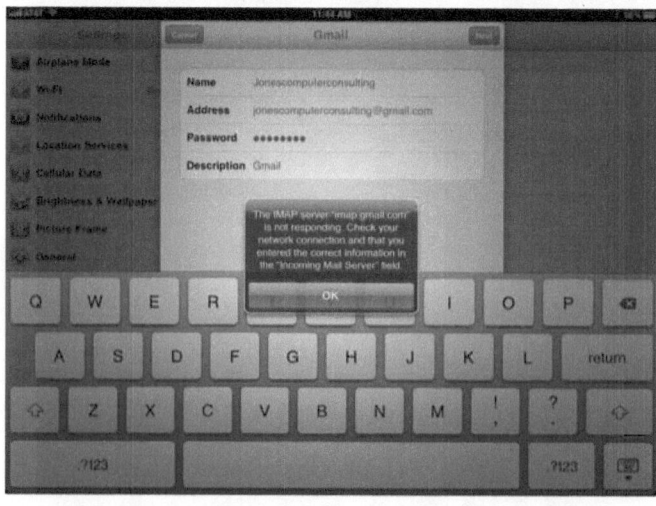

CONTACTS, CALENDAR, AND EMAIL

When the email address has finished configuring, a screen similar to the one below will be displayed. This screen will show the options that can by Sync'd with the Gmail servers. If the value is set to On, the items will remain in Sync. In Sync, means that the information in the items that are turned on will also be kept up to date on the Gmail servers. This will allow the user to also use a computer to check email, calendar, contacts and notes and always have up-to-date information.

The new Gmail account will now show up and be ready to use.

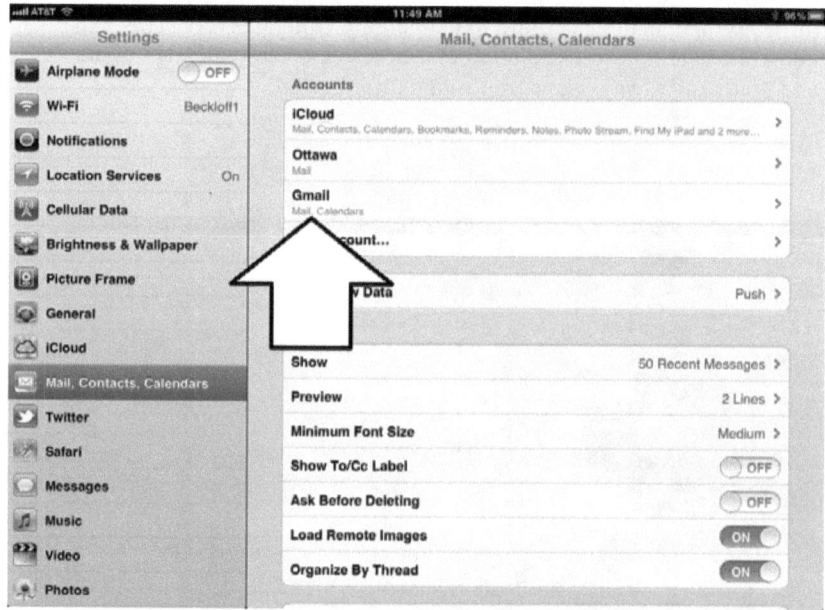

In the next few pages, we will talk about some of the global options that will apply to all email accounts.

CONTACTS, CALENDAR, AND EMAIL

The Fetch New data option is used to set a time frame to push email to the iPad. The more often it fetches, the more it will look at the servers for the email information. Setting this time to a higher number can sometimes help with battery life.
Here are the options for the fetch of email.

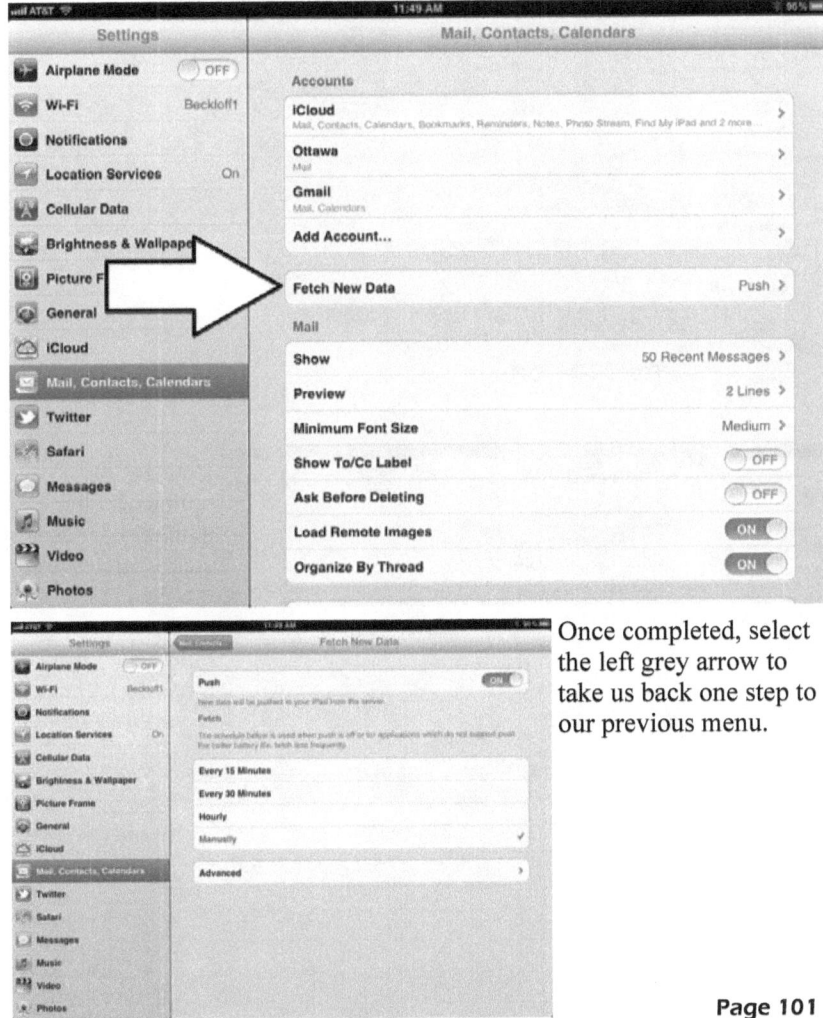

Once completed, select the left grey arrow to take us back one step to our previous menu.

Page 101

THE NEW USERS GUIDE TO THE IPAD

The Show option will let you specify how many of the most recent messages you would like to keep on the iPad.

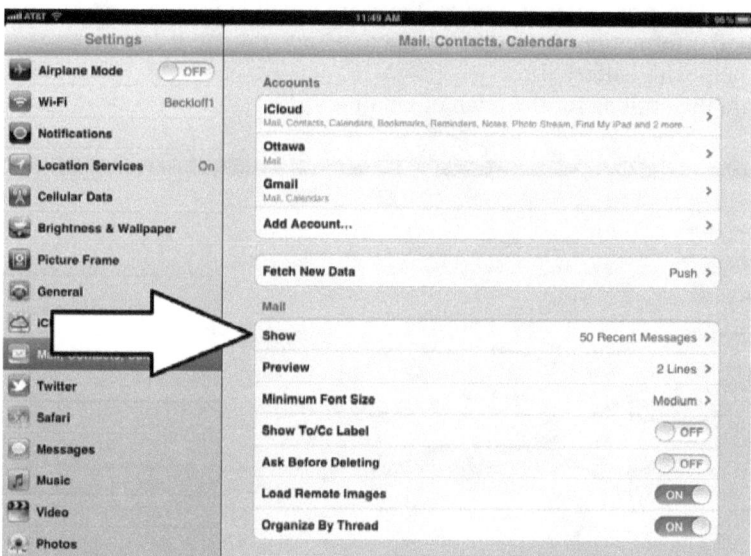

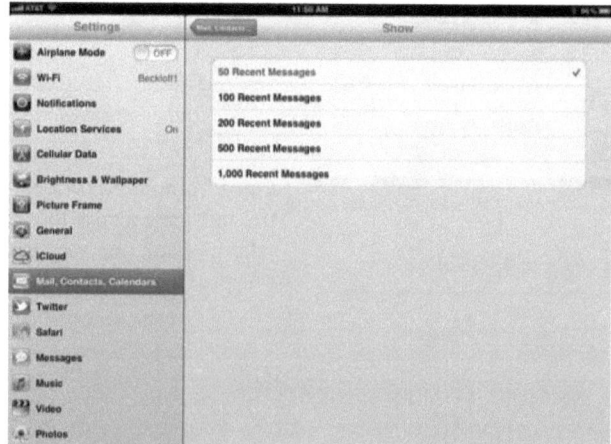

Here are the options for the number of recent emails to keep on the iPad.

Select the grey arrow to go back to previous menu.

Page 102

CONTACTS, CALENDAR, AND EMAIL

The Preview option will indicate how many lives of a new message are shown in the Inbox without opening the email. This is a user preference on what you would like.

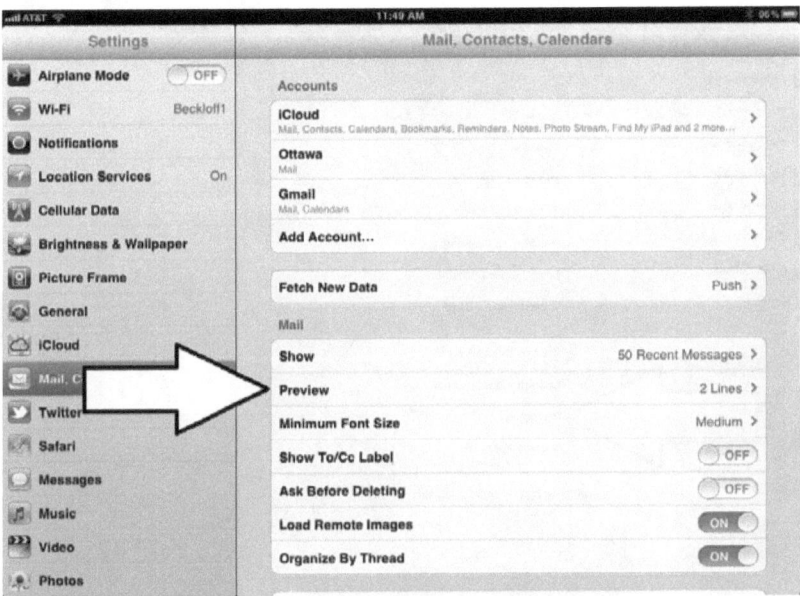

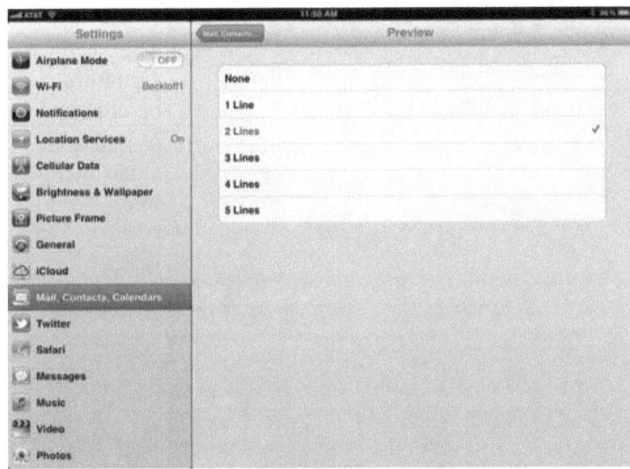

Here are the options in regard to the number of lines to preview in the Inbox.

THE NEW USERS GUIDE TO THE IPAD

The Signature option is what will appear at the bottom of every new email. By default, the signature block indicates Sent from my iPad.

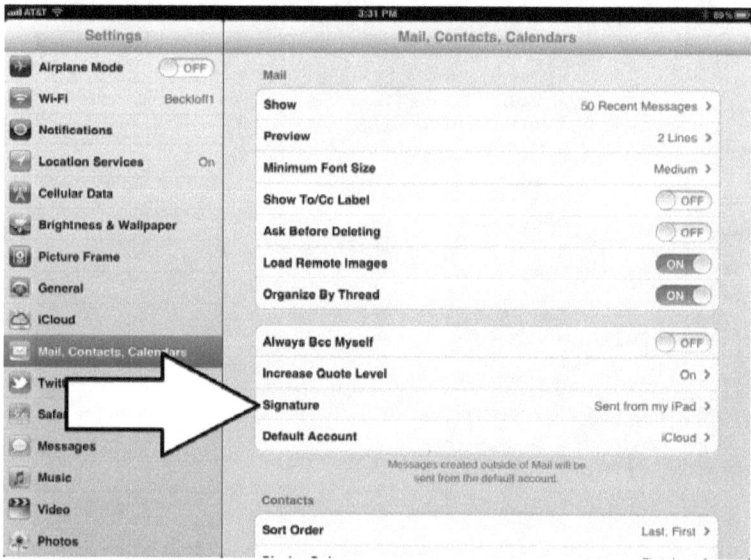

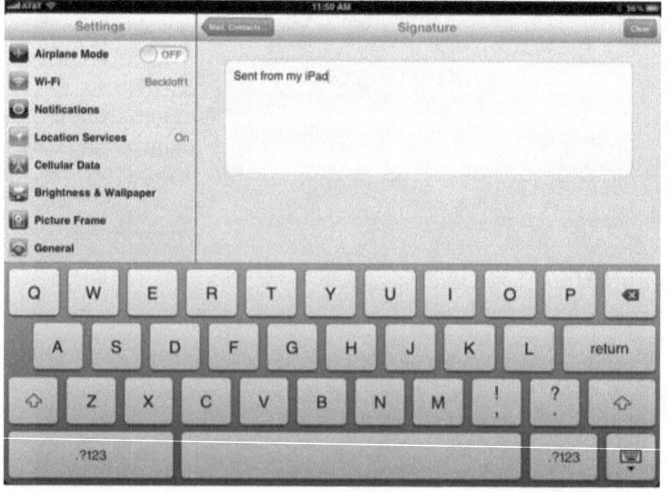

The signature can be changed to whatever a user would like.

CONTACTS, CALENDAR, AND EMAIL

The Default Account will be the preferred account that is used to send email if the user does not explicitly select an account. This is where the default email account is selected.

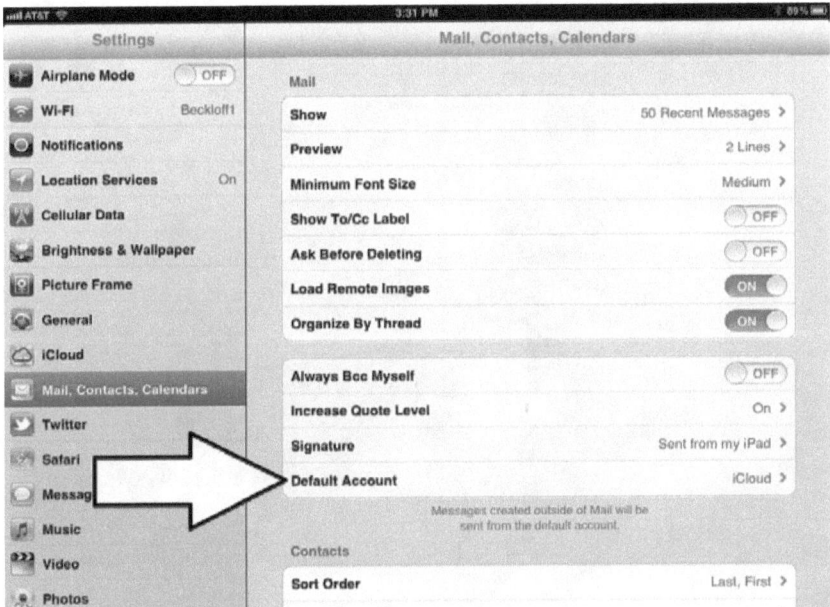

Let us start using our email. Look for the mail icon at the bottom of the main page.

CONTACTS, CALENDAR, AND EMAIL

When our email client opens, we see all of our accounts, our mailboxes and the most recent email.

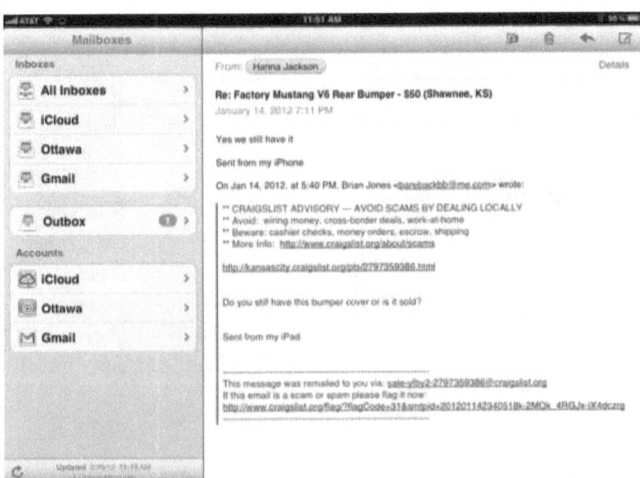

These are the different email accounts that are configured for the iPad. The top option will open all mailboxes at one time. If you prefer, you can select any of the accounts to check only that one account.

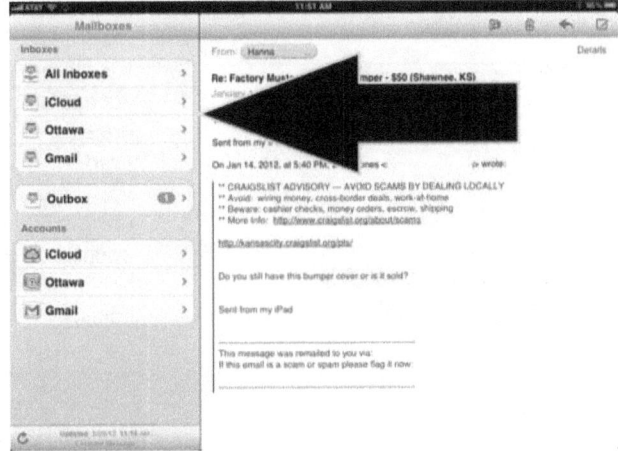

THE NEW USERS GUIDE TO THE IPAD

In the top diagram, the arrow is pointing to a number one in a colored circle. This number one indicates that there is one email in that box. So in this case, we see that there is one email in an outbox trying to be sent.

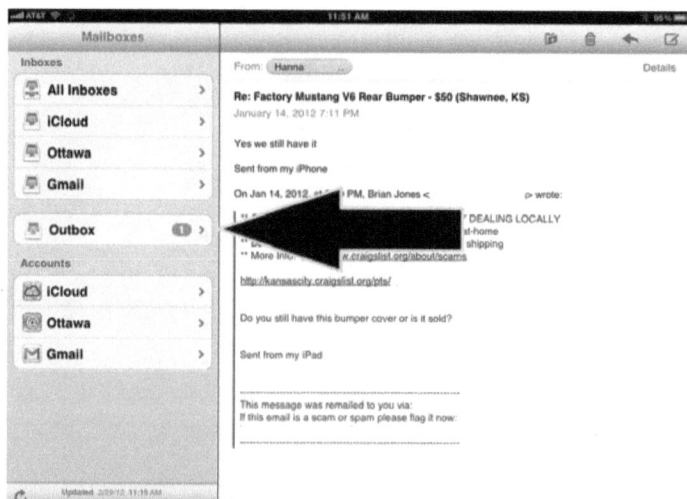

In the photo below, the arrow is pointed to the individual accounts. Select the email account that you would like to look closer at. Each of these options, when opened, will show all the different folders for that particular account such as Inbox, Outbox, Archive, Sent, and more. There is not a way to open all the folders for all the accounts at once. Folder views have to be opened on a per-account basis.

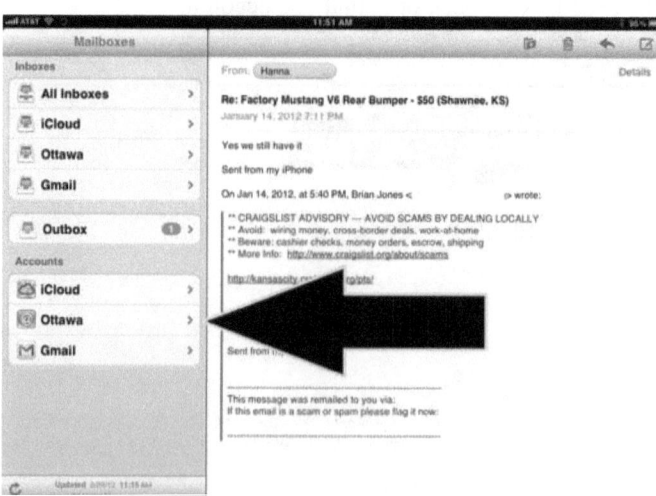

CONTACTS, CALENDAR, AND EMAIL

Any time there is a number in a circle, it indicates how many new emails are in that folder. By looking at the numbers, you will be able to tell which account the new emails are in.

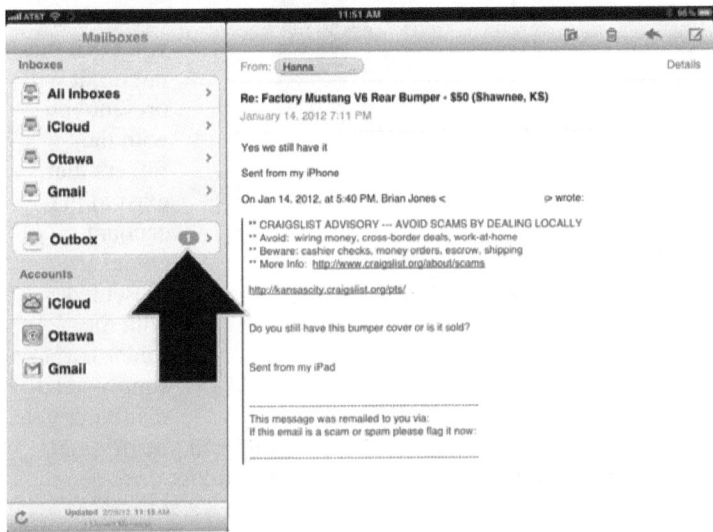

At the bottom of the window is a date and a time. This will be the last time that the email was updated. To the left of the date and time, is a Circle symbol with an arrow head. Click on this symbol to have the system go out right now and update all of your email accounts. Clicking on this button will force a send and receive action to happen in all folders.

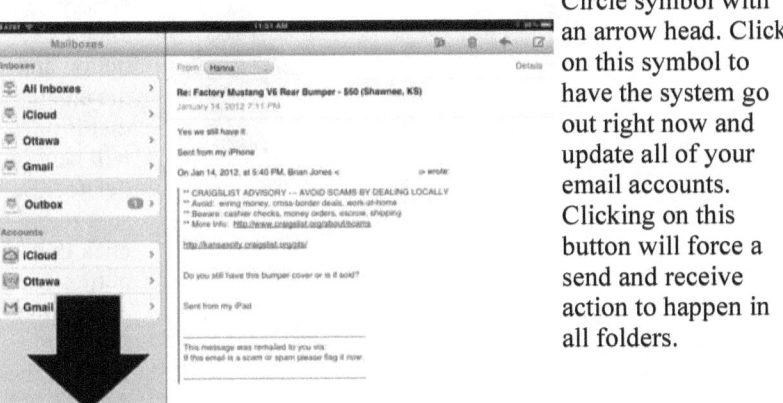

Page 109

THE NEW USERS GUIDE TO THE IPAD

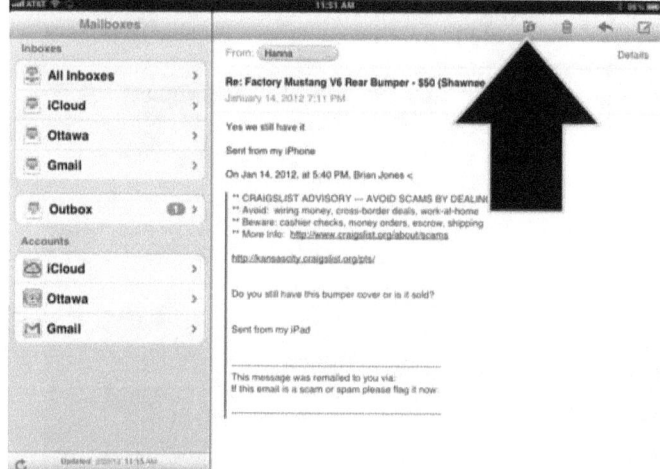

This arrow is pointing to the Move action. When you click this button, it will present you with the folders that exist in that account. Once presented with the folder list, simply touch the folder you would like to have the email moved into. Once completed, the original email will be moved and not copied into that specific folder.

The button the arrow below is pointing to, is the Delete function. While an email is open, simply click that button and the email that is open will be deleted. Be sure to only click that button once or the email that follows will also be deleted.

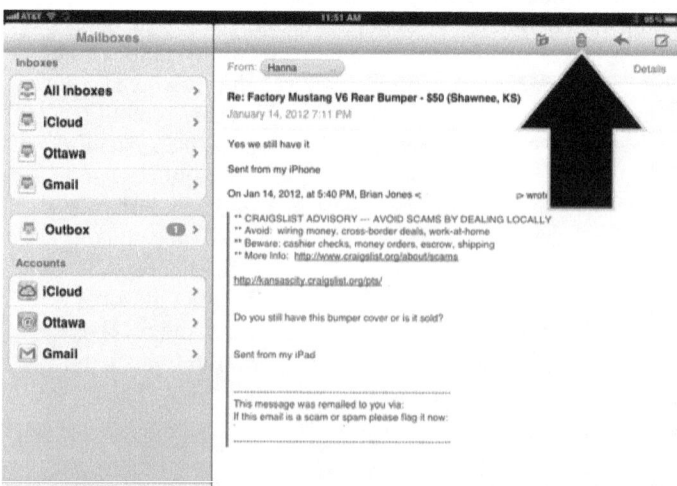

CONTACTS, CALENDAR, AND EMAIL

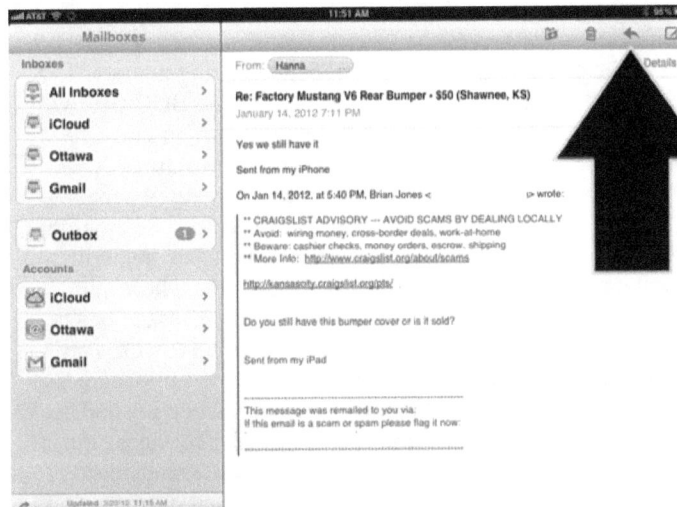

This button is to forward or reply to the email that is open. Once selected, you can then reply to the original sender or forward it on.

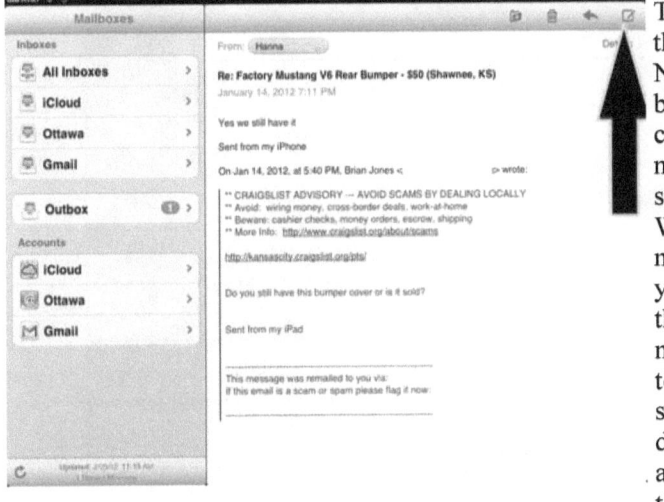

This button is the Compose New Message button. It will create a new message to send out. When the new message opens you can use the default mail account to send out or select a different account to use to send with.

THE NEW USERS GUIDE TO THE IPAD

In the photo below, we see the Compose New Message windows. At the top of the window we can type an email address or use the plus sign in the circle to the right to select an existing contact. The CC field is used to copy someone on the email. The BCC field will allow you to send that user a copy of the email with no one else involved in the email, the ability to see it was sent to the BCC person. The From box will allow you to see which email account is sending this email out. The subject of the message can be anything; however, if left blank, there will be a warning window that will pop up before the email is sent. The body of the email is where you would type the actual message. In the body of the message below, you should see the words "Sent from my iPad". Those words are the signature block that is attached to every outgoing message. You have the capability to change each one on the message itself. The signature block can be deleted from the message. The signature block can be changed in the Settings option for different words or no words at all. This signature setting is a global setting that will apply to all emails from all email accounts. Once the email is ready to go, simply select the Send button in the upper right-hand corner of the window. The message will disappear and then be on its way to its intended recipients.

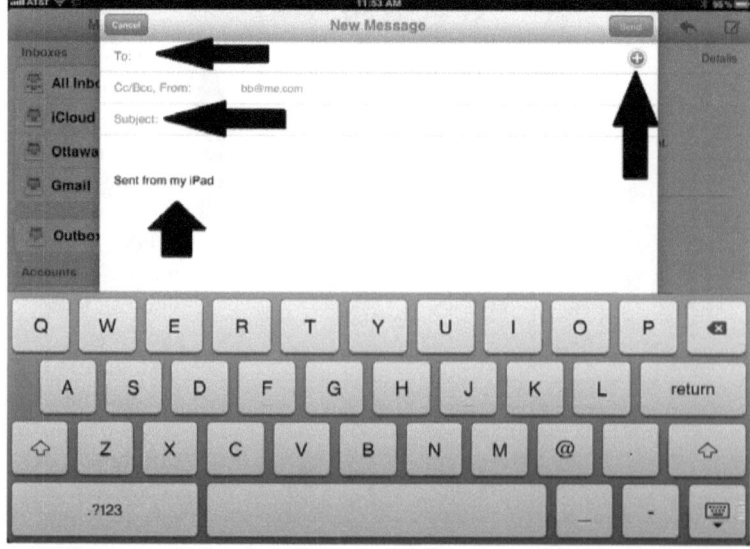

CONTACTS, CALENDAR, AND EMAIL

In this photo, we are showing you the add existing contact to an email option. Select the plus sign and a window will open with all your contacts for that account. Each email account can have its own separate list of contacts associated with it. Find the contact you are looking for by scrolling with your finger through the list of names. When the name appears in the list, simply select it.

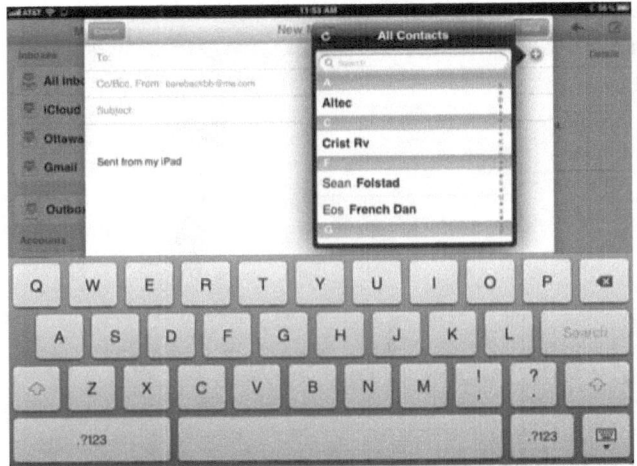

In the photo below we are showing another way to select an existing contact record. Start typing a name in the To: field, and the iPad will start to compare that information against your contact records. If you see the one you want, simply select it.

Page 113

THE NEW USERS GUIDE TO THE IPAD

In the photo below, we have typed the word "electronics". The iPad does a spell check as you type. If the suggested word is the correct one, select it by touching it or tap the space bar. There is an X next to the suggested word, if the word is not correct. The iPad will start

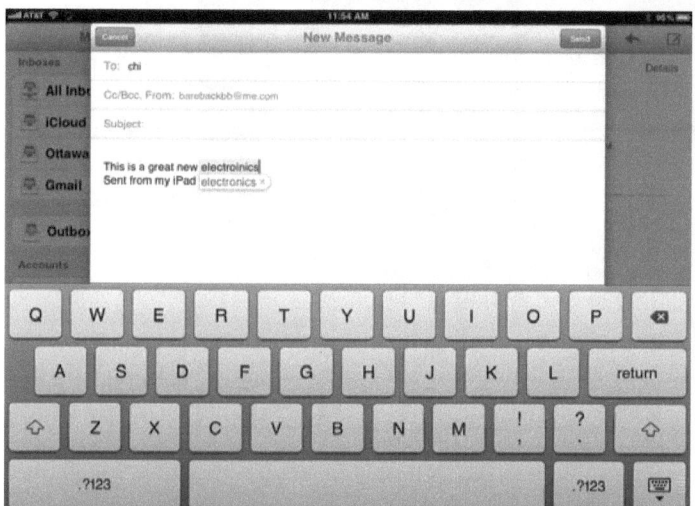

to learn words as you select the X. Using a word multiple times will cause the iPad to adapt and stop asking about the word.

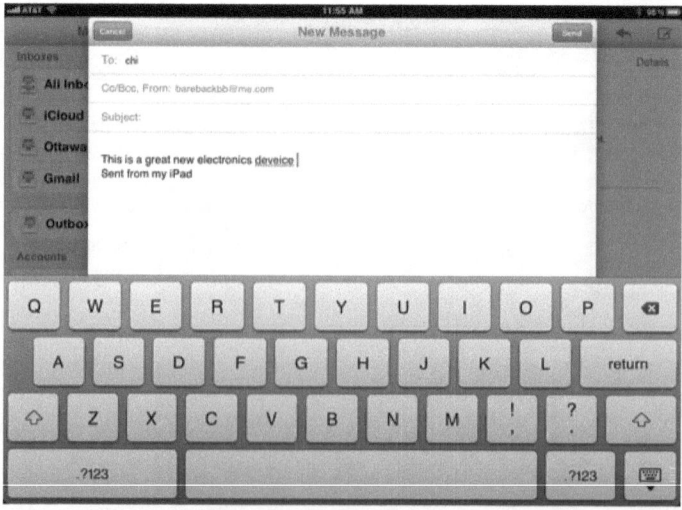

In this photo we can see that the iPad is reminding us that the word still does not look correct. Touch the word for suggested spellings.

Page 114

CONTACTS, CALENDAR, AND EMAIL

While working on an email, if you select the cancel option at the top of the email, you can either delete your draft of the email or save a copy of the draft to the draft folder in the Accounts Draft folder.

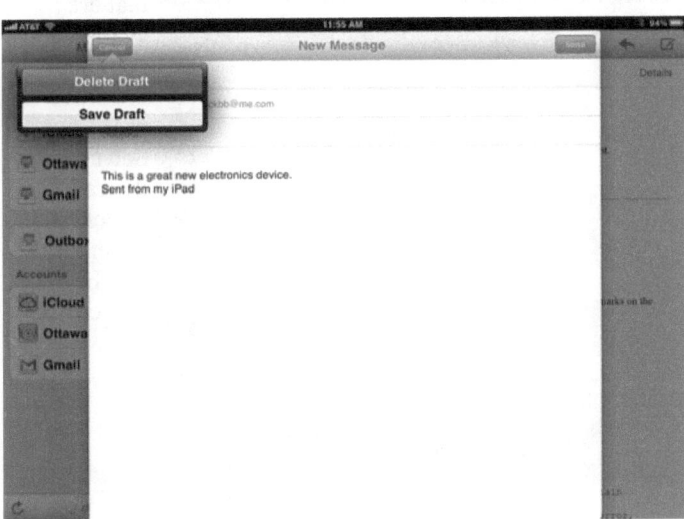

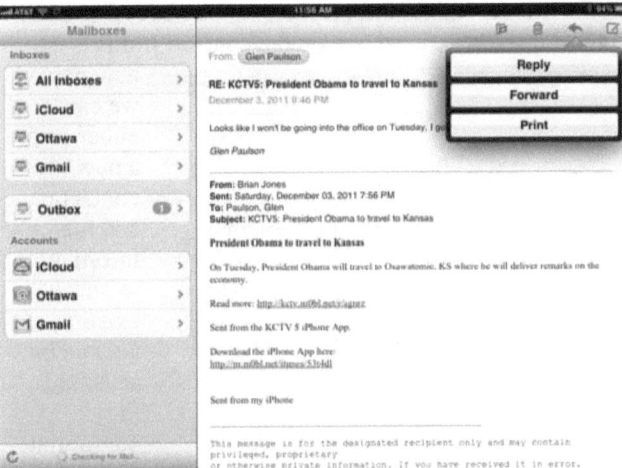

When the Reply/Forward option is selected, this is the window that will pop up. Select the option you would prefer.

Page 115

In this window, we have selected the Move button. On the left are the folders that are available to complete the move process. Select the desired folder, and the email will be moved.

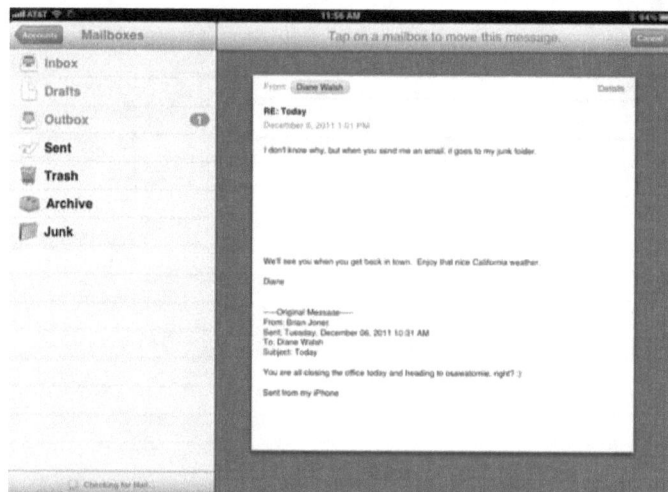

When an email is received, if you select the senders name, more details about that sender will be displayed. If the sender exists in our contacts, we will see all the information stored about that user, including a photo if we have used one on the contact. If this is a new person, we can either create a new contact or add the information to an existing contact by selecting the appropriate option in the window.

CONTACTS, CALENDAR, AND EMAIL

The arrow on the left is showing us a symbol that means this email has already been replied to. The arrow on the right is showing us that there are two additional emails related to this same matter.

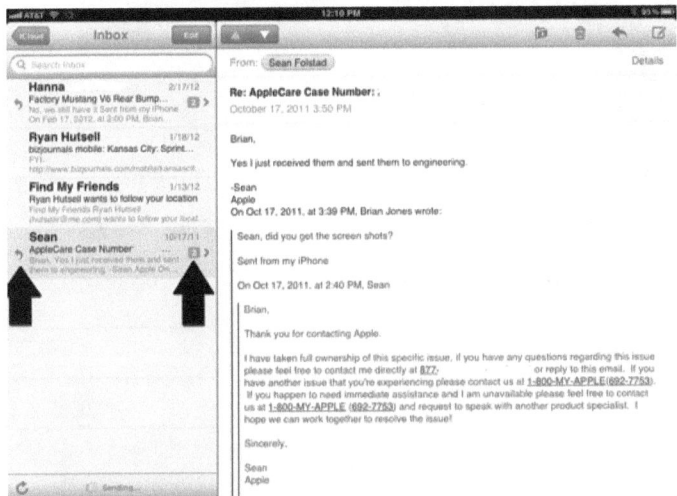

The left arrow is the button to update your email. The middle button is showing that email is currently being sent. The right arrow will allow us to hide the information in the header of the email. The header of an email will hold the information about the sender and the recipient. If the word "hide" is not there, the word

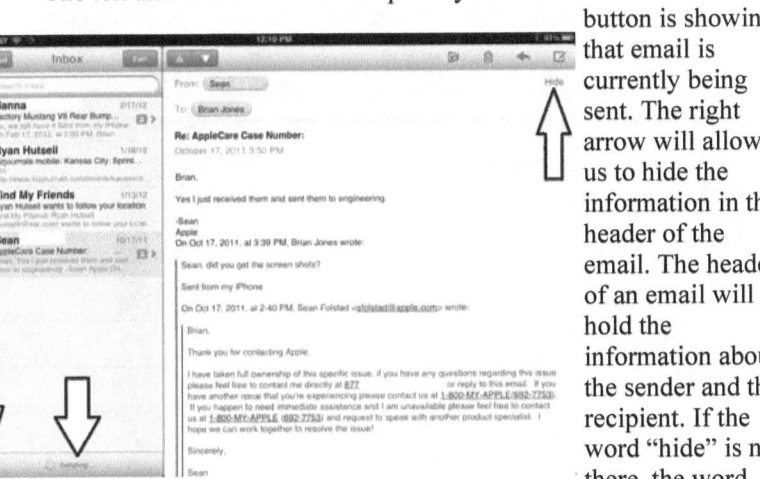

"details" should be there. Details open up the information about the header while "hide" will conceal the information.

Page 117

THE NEW USERS GUIDE TO THE IPAD

The Edit option at the top will allow us to delete, move or flag multiple messages at the same time.

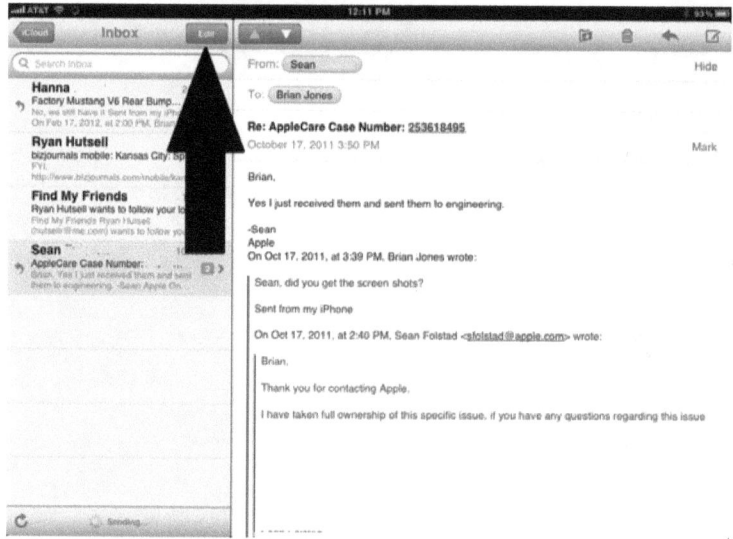

Once the edit button has been selected, there will be small circles next to each email. These circles will allow us to select as many as we would like. Once the emails are selected, click on the appropriate button to move, delete or flag all of your selections.

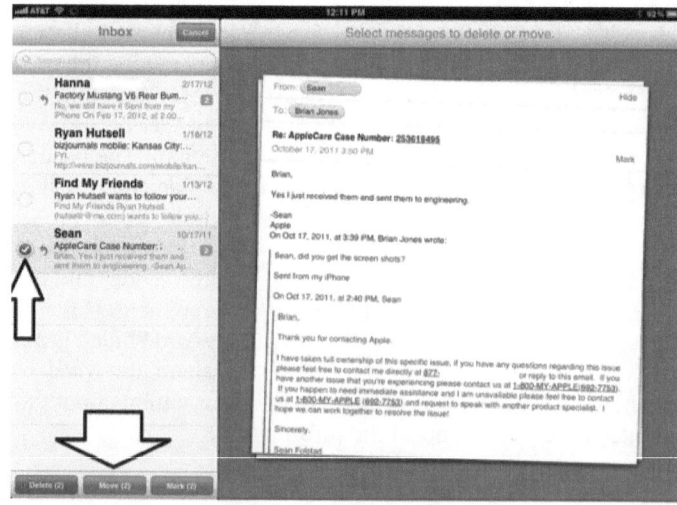

Page 118

CONTACTS, CALENDAR, AND EMAIL

In this example, we have selected one email, then we have selected the Mark option. As we can see, we can either flag the message or mark it as unread.

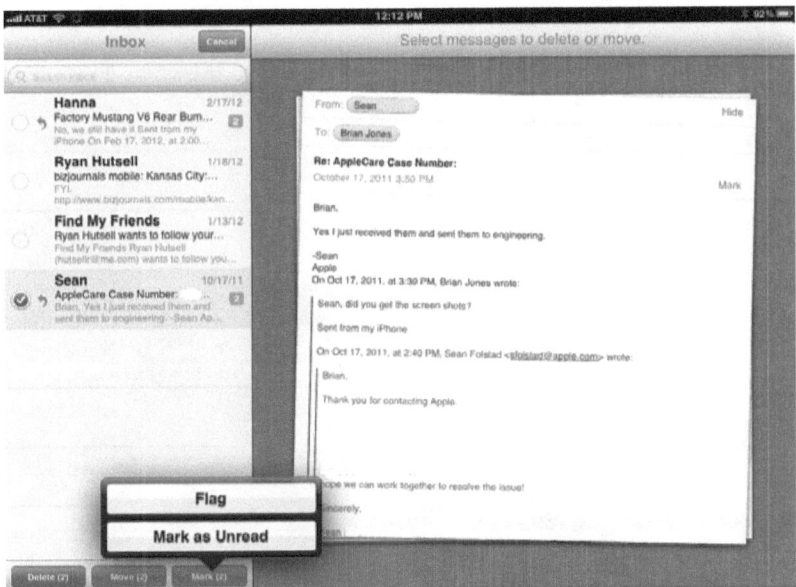

In this photo, we selected the move option on the email. When we select the folder, the email will be moved there instantaneously.

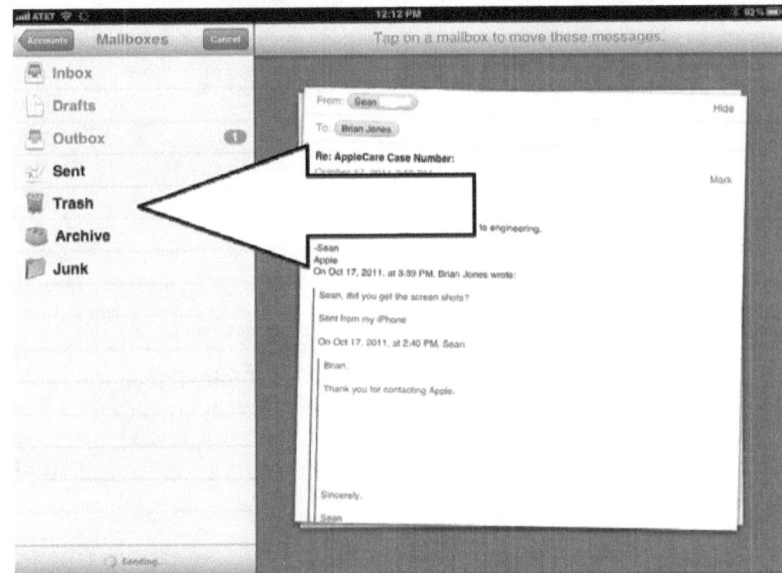

THE NEW USERS GUIDE TO THE IPAD

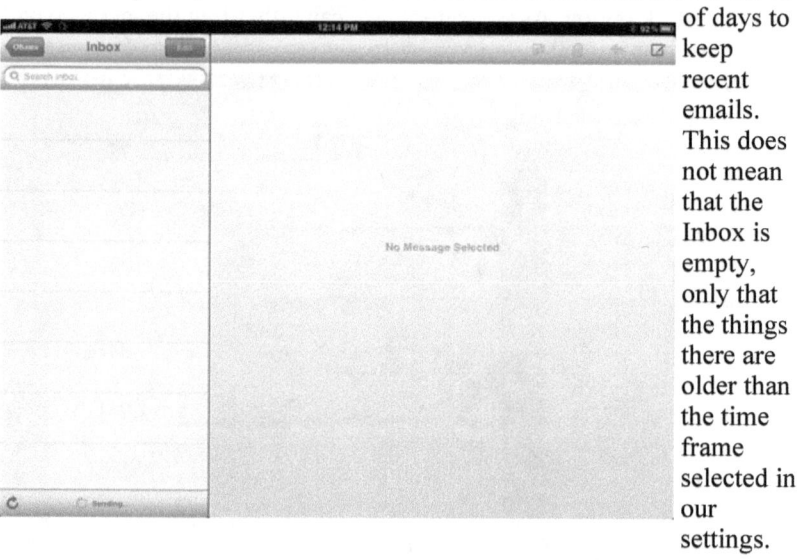

In this photo, the inbox has no recent emails that match the number of days to keep recent emails. This does not mean that the Inbox is empty, only that the things there are older than the time frame selected in our settings.

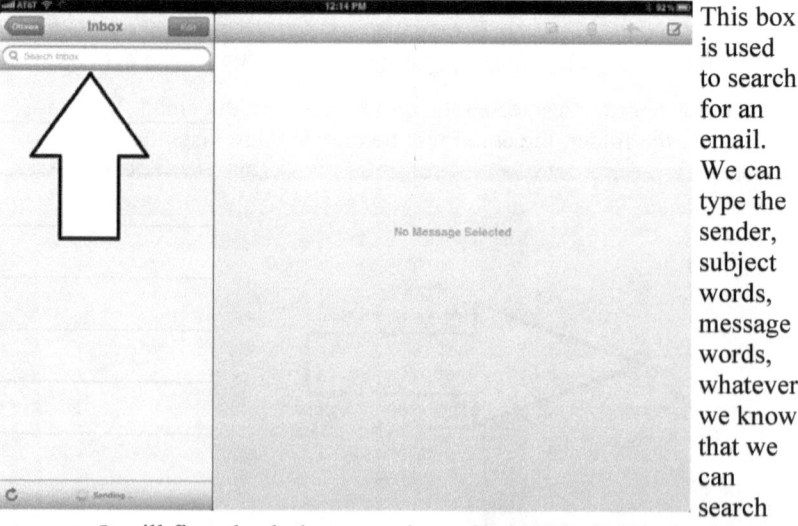

This box is used to search for an email. We can type the sender, subject words, message words, whatever we know that we can search on. It will first check the recent items in the Inbox, then it will prompt us to check the emails on the server that are older.

Page 120

CONTACTS, CALENDAR, AND EMAIL

Here we have one email in our outbox. There is an exclamation point indicating there was a problem with sending the message. It says we did not add a recipient which might be a big problem.

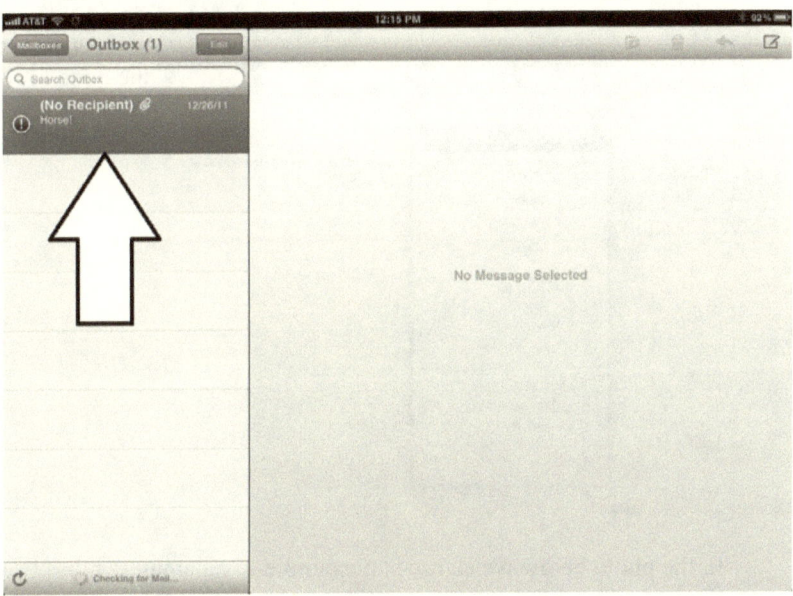

In this photo, we have selected the sender in the header to get more information on the sender. The Edit button would indicate that this person is already in our contacts. Selecting edit will allow us to edit that particular contact's information. We can also share this contact or send them a message from here.

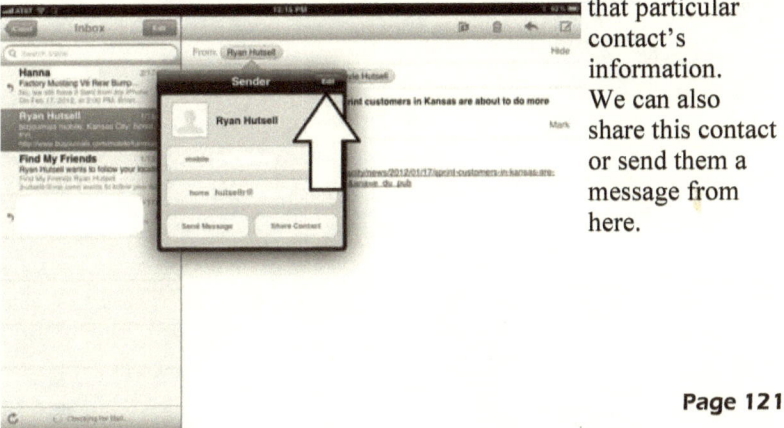

THE NEW USERS GUIDE TO THE IPAD

Here is a photo where we elected to edit an existing contact from an email sent from this person. We see all the information that is stored in the contact's record. We can change any of this information right now. When we have completed editing the contact, select the done button.

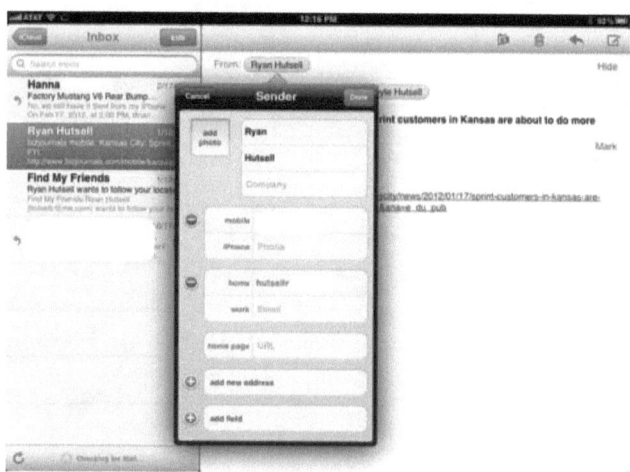

In the photo below we can see an example of an email that has been flagged by us. Flagging an email lets us know that there is something about this email that needs to stand out to us.

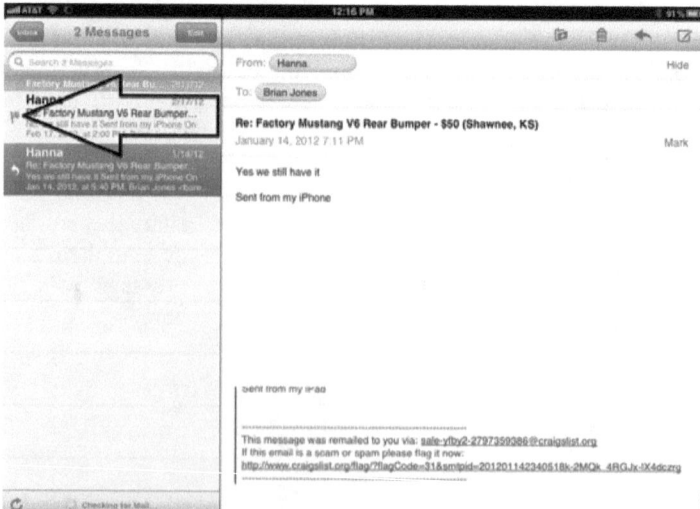

age 122

CONTACTS, CALENDAR, AND EMAIL

To create a new folder to save email into, click the edit button.

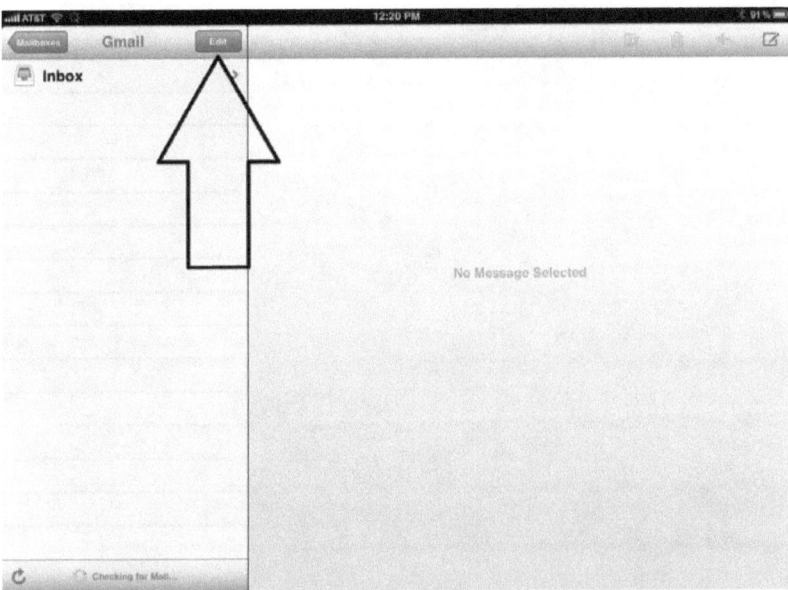

Click the New Mailbox button at the bottom of the screen.

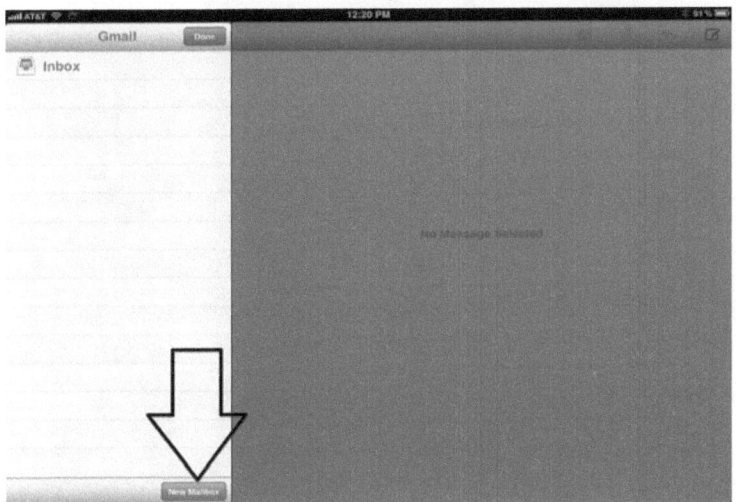

THE NEW USERS GUIDE TO THE IPAD

Give your new Mailbox a name and select save. You are done.

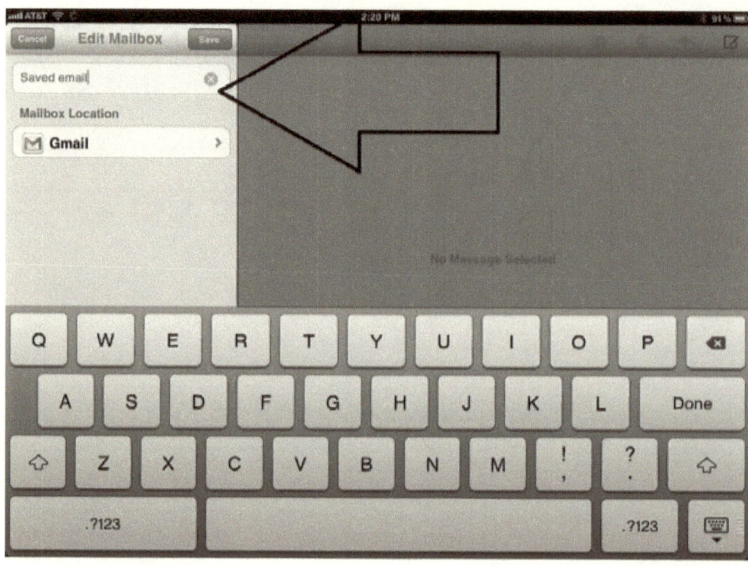

To delete an entire Email Account. Go to settings, select Mail, Contacts, Calendars. Find the account that you would like to delete and select it.

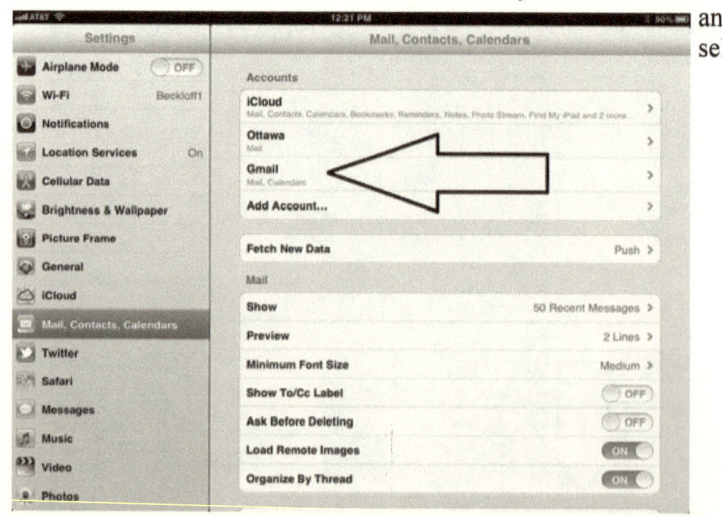

CONTACTS, CALENDAR, AND EMAIL

When an account is selected, there is a button at the bottom that will delete the entire account and all associated folders and email.

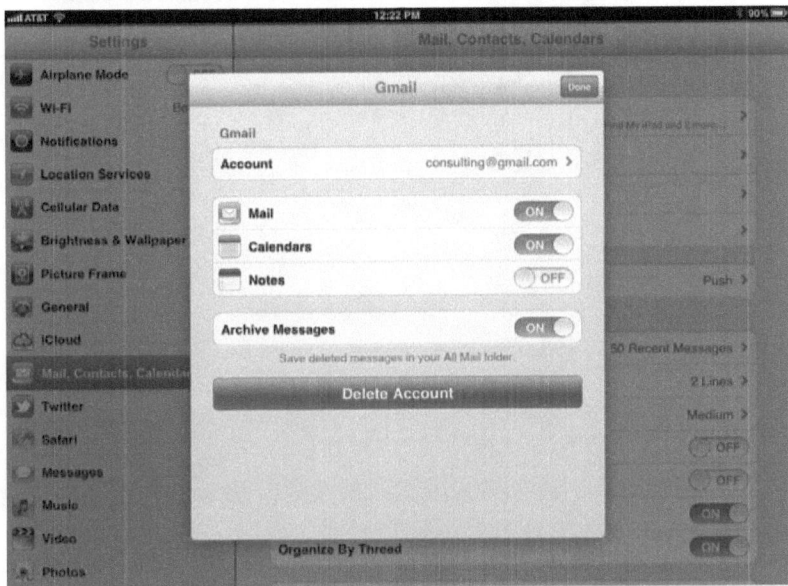

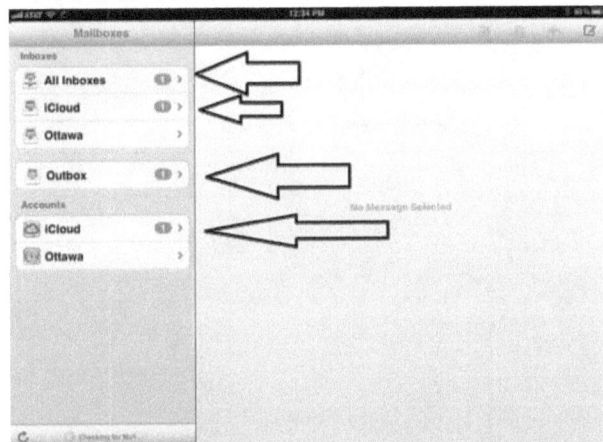

In this photo, we can see a breakdown of where our new emails are located.

Page 125

THE NEW USERS GUIDE TO THE IPAD

The Dot next to an email indicates it has not yet been read.

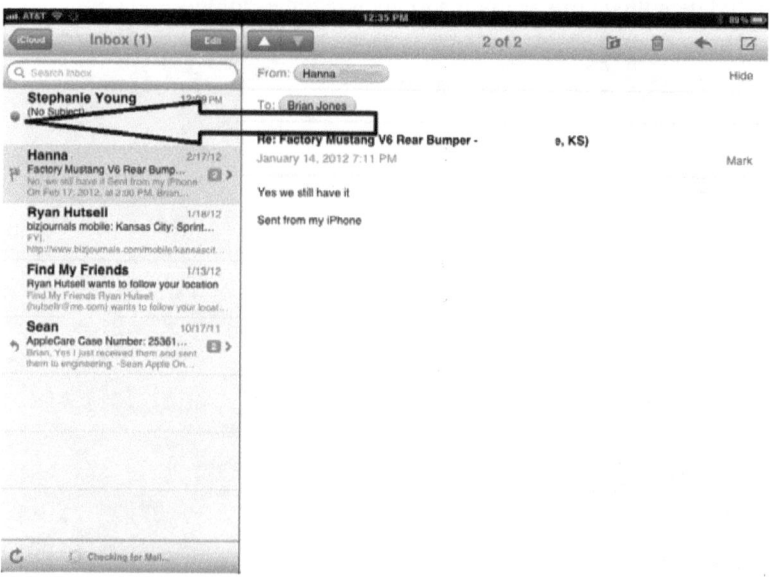

Here is another example of viewing the contact info of a person NOT in our contacts list.

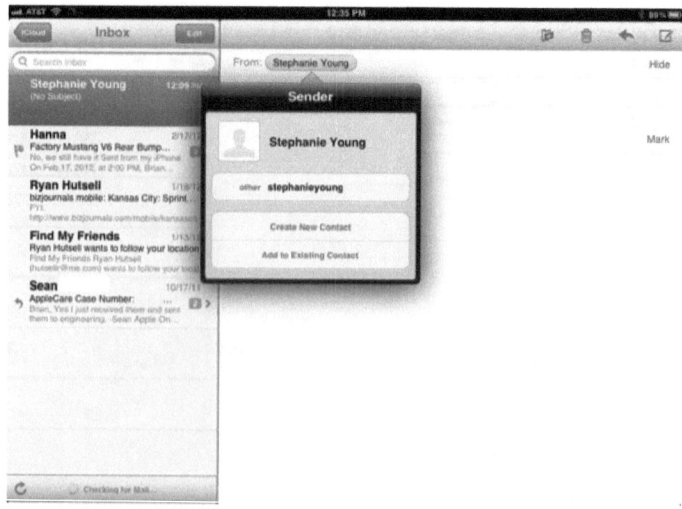

CONTACTS, CALENDAR, AND EMAIL

To send an attachment with an email, you would think that there would be a button to attach something to your email wouldn't you? Nope, it does not work that way on an iPad. To send a photo in an email, first you must locate the photo and from the photo itself there is an option to email that photo. To email a link to a website, you have to go to Safari and email the link from there. Documents and other files are done the same way. Just remember that you have to send attachments from the attachments area, not directly in an email.

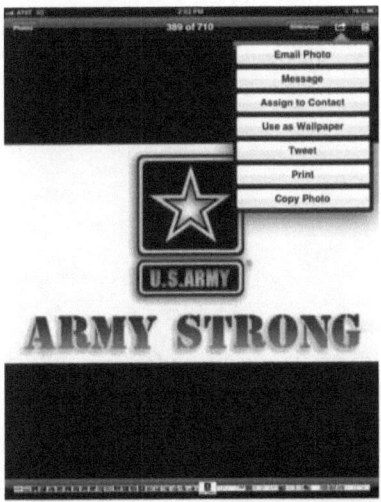
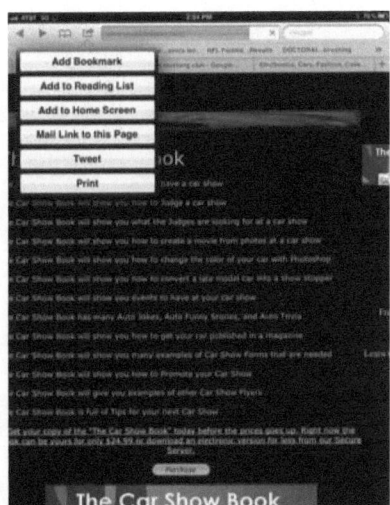
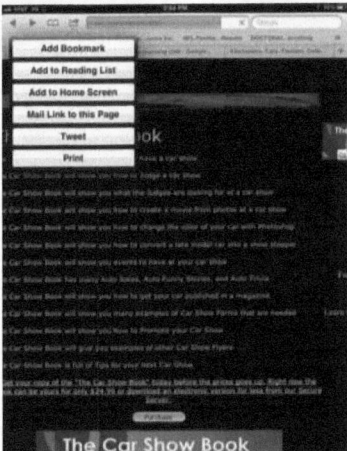

THE NEW USERS GUIDE TO THE IPAD

Email Shortcut

If you receive an email and want to forward only a portion of the email, there is a way of doing that. Highlight the portion of the email that you would like to reply with or forward. While the selected text is highlighted, click the forward or reply button.

The reply or forward will have only the text that was selected in the earlier message. This is a great way to send only a portion of the email.

CONTACTS, CALENDAR, AND EMAIL

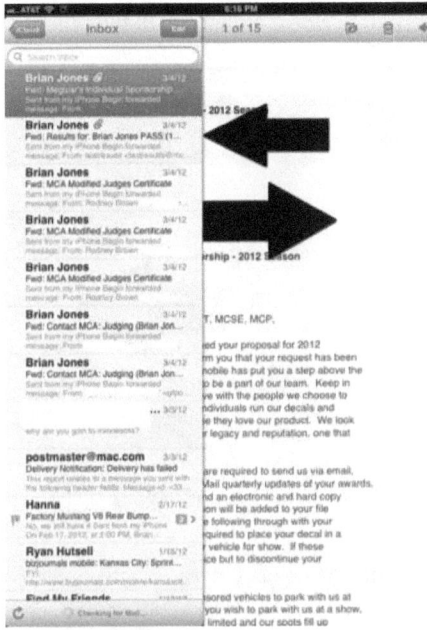

Email Trick

While the inbox is open, there is a great trick that makes reading emails much easier.

To slide the list of emails out of the way, slide the list to the left out of the way.

To view the list of emails while hidden on the left, place a finger on the left side of the Inbox and slide your finger to the right to restore the view.

THE NEW USERS GUIDE TO THE IPAD

Mark an email as unread. When the email is open, select the details then look for the "Mark" option.

After selecting the Mark option, select the "Mark as Unread" option. The email will now show as being unread.

CONTACTS, CALENDAR, AND EMAIL

How to mark multiple emails as unread.

Click the "Edit" button.

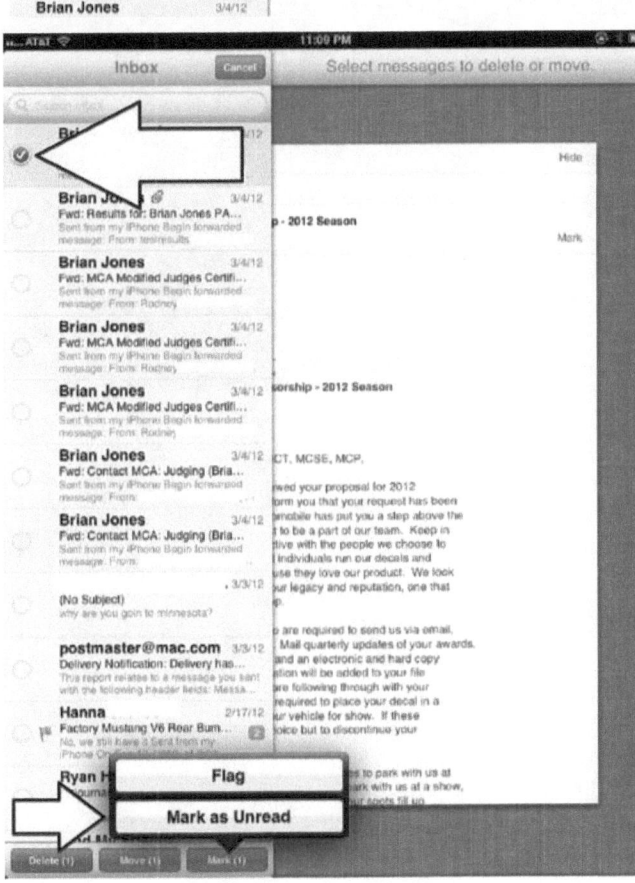

While in edit mode, place a check next to each email that you would like to mark as Unread. When all items are marked, select the "Mark" button at the bottom and then select the "Mark as Unread" button to mark all the selected emails as being unread.

Page 131

THE NEW USERS GUIDE TO THE IPAD

To search for a specific email, there is a search box. If you are in one email account, that is where the search will be performed. If you are in a unified messaging inbox with more than one account configured, the search will look through all configured accounts. Below the search box is the area to search for the information. Searches can be performed by who an email is from, to whom an email is sent, words in the subject, or on all fields in the message. The search returns will appear in the area below the criteria. In the example below, we have found three emails that match the criteria we are searching with. If the search results do not find anything, there is an option to go back to older emails that are stored on the server that may not be stored on the iPad any longer.

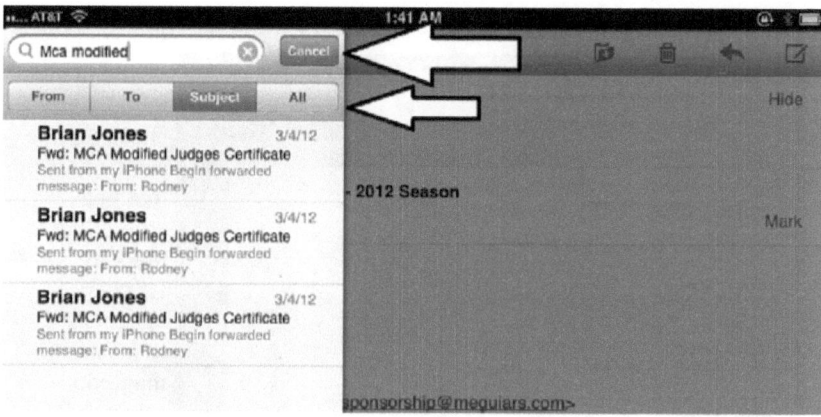

CONTACTS, CALENDAR, AND EMAIL

In the photo below, we are searching on the name "Ryan" in the from field. The results should return any emails where Ryan is in the name whether it is a last name, a first name or part of another name such as Bryan. In the example below, we have located one email that matches our criteria for our search.

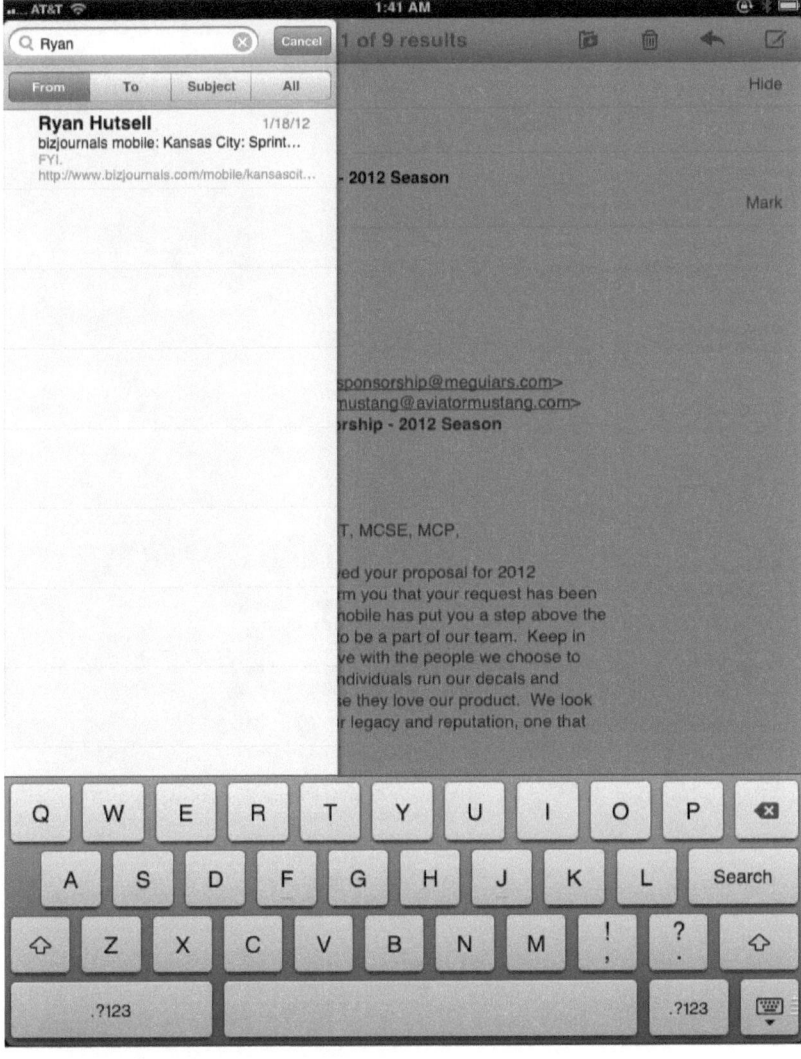

THE NEW USERS GUIDE TO THE IPAD

When an email is open, there is a Trashcan icon that will allow a user to delete that email. From the list of emails shown below, slide a finger to the right across one of the emails and Delete option will appear. Select the Delete button to remove that email.

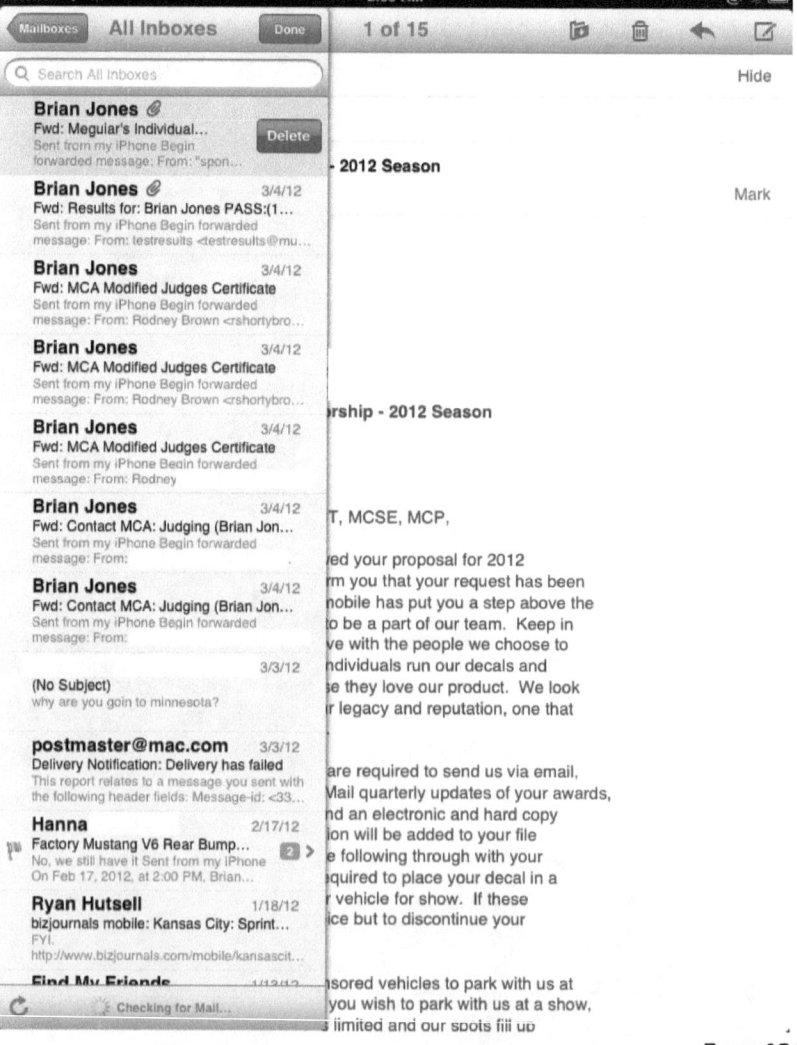

CONTACTS, CALENDAR, AND EMAIL

To delete multiple emails, select the "Edit" button. While in the edit mode, place a check next to each email that you would like to delete. When all the emails are selected, click the Delete button at the bottom of the screen.

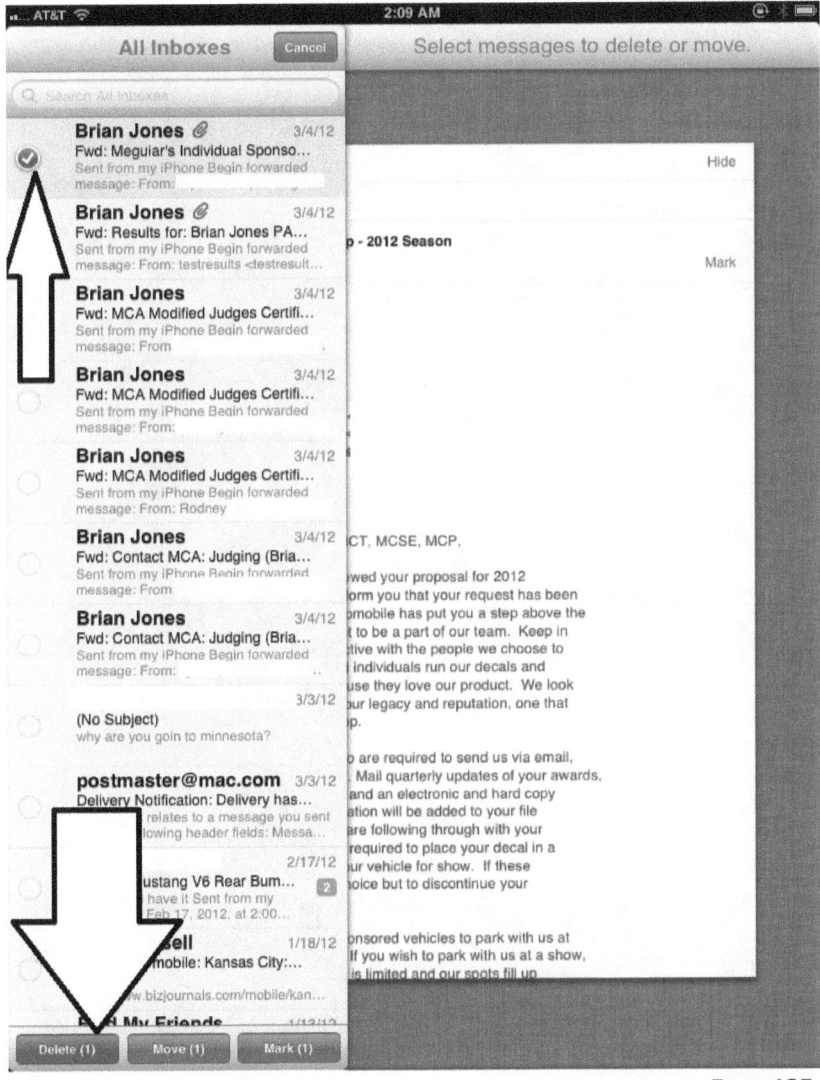

Page 135

THE NEW USERS GUIDE TO THE IPAD

App Store

The App store is where you purchase apps or programs for the iPad.

Page 136

APP STORE

 On the main screen, the icon may have a red circle with a number on it. This number in red will indicate how many of the currently installed apps have an update available to be downloaded.

When the app store opens, you will see several apps available. At the bottom of the app store are different ways to find apps for the iPad. Featured apps are those that Apple is featuring. The Genius option will look at other apps that you have downloaded and make suggestions based on previously selected apps. Top Charts will show the top apps that have been purchased or rated. You can break the tops apps down to either free or non-free. The Categories option will list the apps in a categorized list that can be used to find apps that provide a specific function.

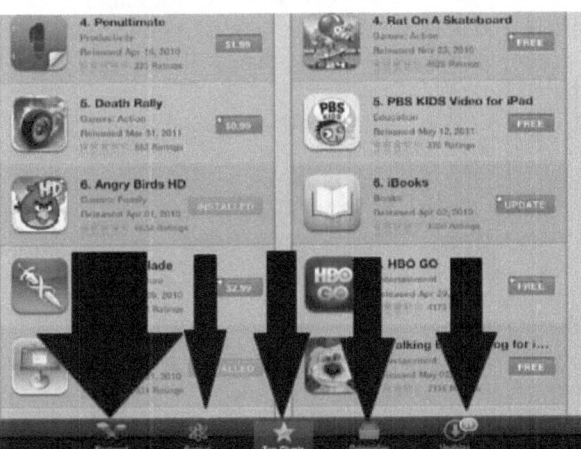

Updates on the bottom right are where all the updates for the previously installed apps will be located.

Page 137

THE NEW USERS GUIDE TO THE IPAD

Click on the price to select it for installation.

When an item is selected to purchase, you will be presented with a Log In for your Apple ID credentials. The payment for the item will process through your Apple iTunes account.

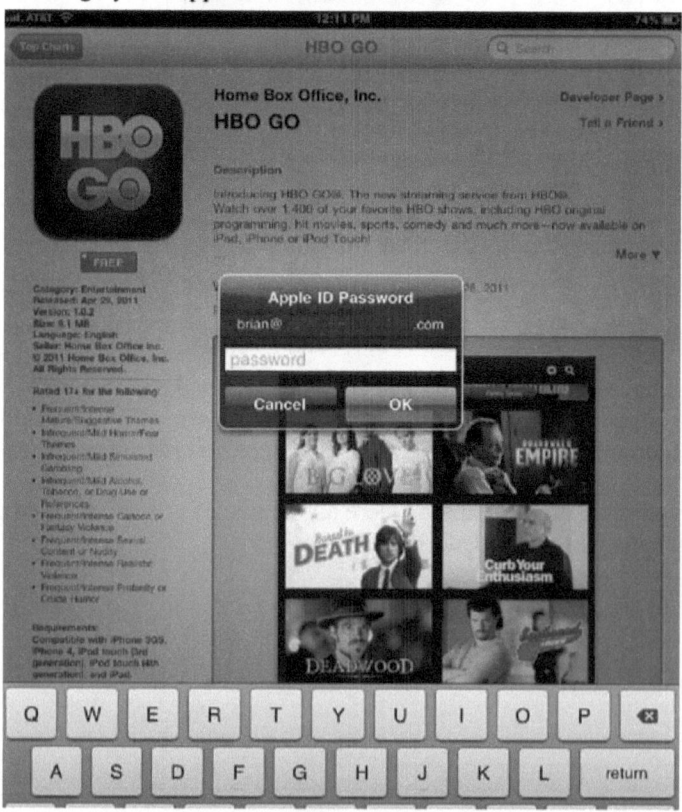

APP STORE

We selected to Install the iTunes U app. Once we select the price, we select the Install App option.

The app store will need your Apple ID and password to handle the transaction.

The new app will show up on our iPad screen waiting to download from the app store.

The app will start the installation and you should see a "Loading" screen and a progress bar on the app itself.

The download can be paused by simply touching the app while it is loading. While in a pause state, if you touch the app again it will resume loading.

Upon completion of the download and installation, the new app will be ready to use on your desktop.

THE NEW USERS GUIDE TO THE IPAD

Apps can be searched by categories. Below is a category view of the apps that are available. Select the category icon to see the items in the category.

APP STORE

At the bottom of the screen, you will see updates that are available to the apps that are installed on the iPad. Most updates are free of charge. On the right you can see the charge for the update, if there is one. To update an app, click on the button (the ones below are free) on the right. At the top of the screen is a button to update all the apps at one time.

THE NEW USERS GUIDE TO THE IPAD

Here is a view of the main page of the app store using the New option at the top of the window. At the top of the window, you can select "What's Hot" or "Release Date". The view of the apps will change based on the selection at the top.

APP STORE

Genius works through the iTunes library information--including what songs they have, play counts, and star ratings. This information is then compiled into a database of all iTunes Genius users by Apple to discover relationships between songs, artists, and musical tastes. With this huge set of data, Genius is able to automatically group and recommend music based on user preferences.

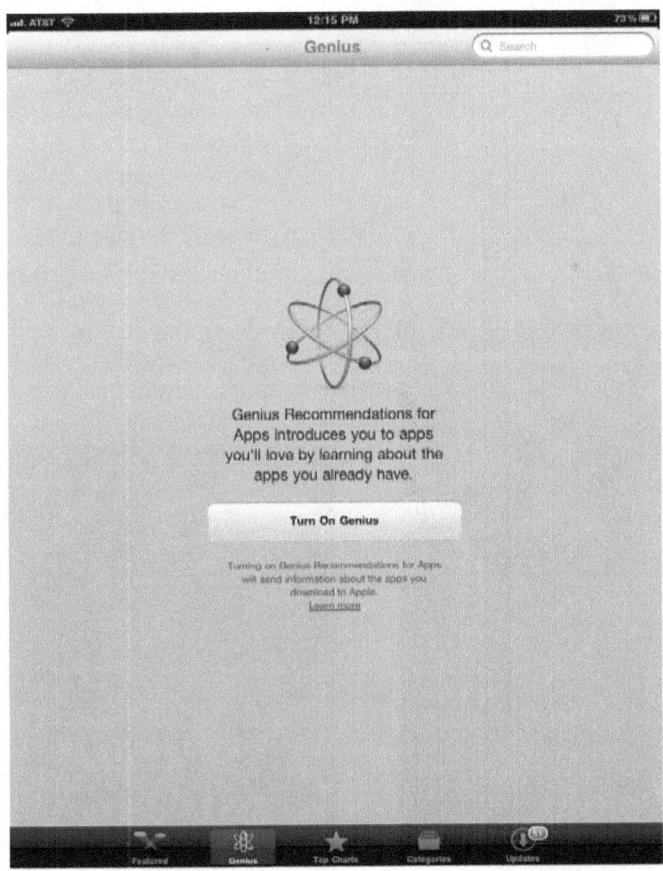

THE NEW USERS GUIDE TO THE IPAD

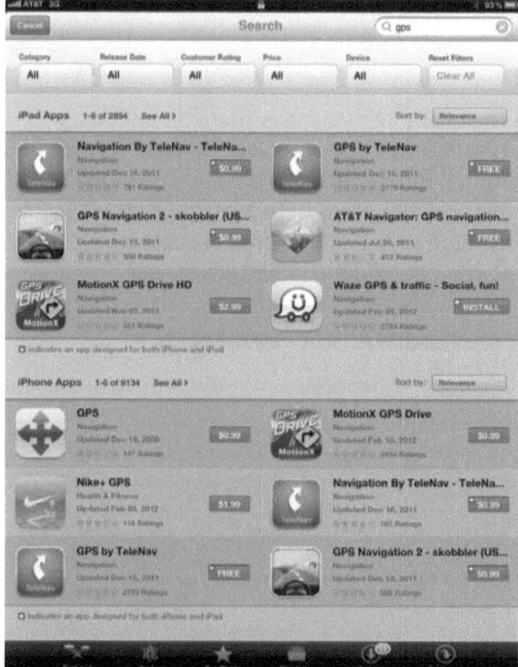

When you do a search on an app, the results will show iPad and iPhone apps in the results. Almost all iPhone apps will work on the iPad.

In the lower left hand-corner we are showing a photo of an iPhone app running on the iPad. In the photo in the lower right-hand corner an arrow is pointing to the "2X" button that will increase the size of an iPhone app to the full size iPad screen size. If the iPhone app is running in "2X" mode, there will be a "1X" button to shrink it back to a normal iPhone sized-app.

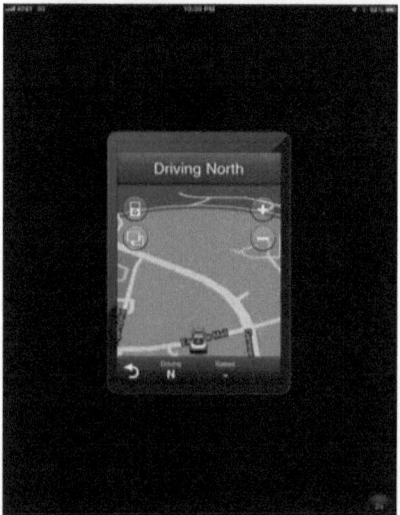
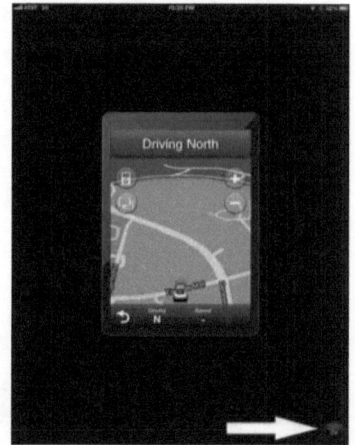

Page 144

APP STORE

THE NEW USERS GUIDE TO THE IPAD

Calendar

The Calendars option allows users to keep track of their appointments and other dates and times.

CALENDAR

Here is the default view that will open for your calendar. You will see today has been marked with a bar under the date. At the bottom are additional ways to move through the calendar.

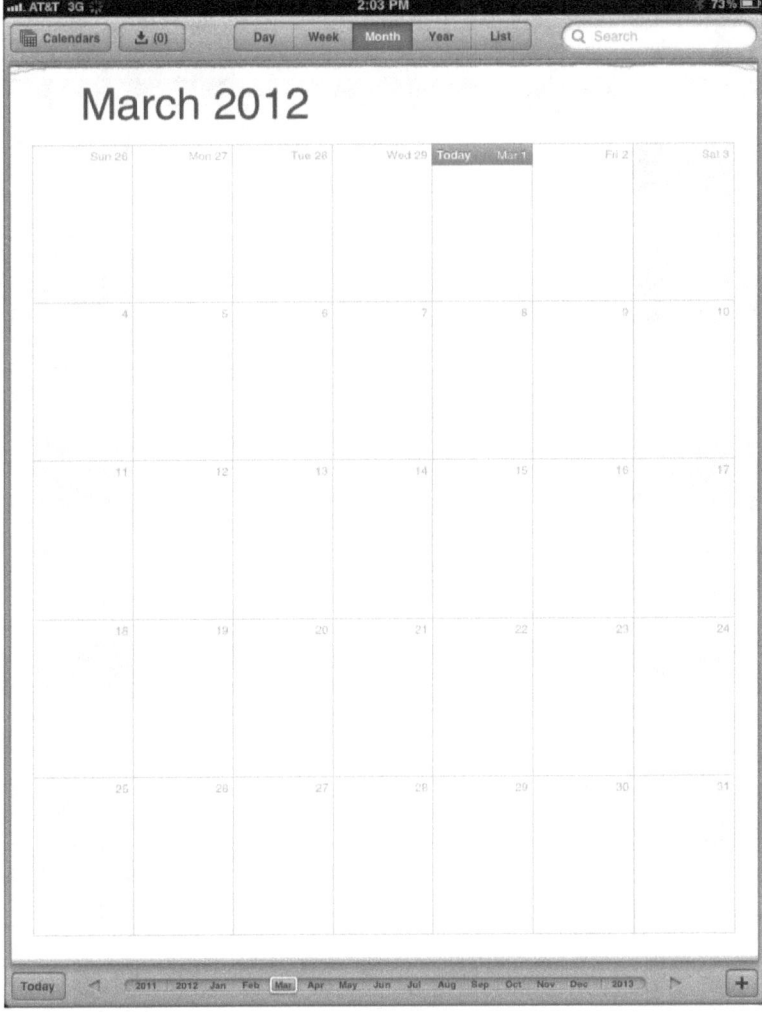

THE NEW USERS GUIDE TO THE IPAD

Most email accounts will have a separate calendar for each account. You can also create as many calendars as you would like through the settings options. In the upper left-hand corner, there is a button to look at calendars from different accounts. You can select them all to show up or only select certain calendars to show up. You can also hide all calendars.

CALENDAR

In this photo, we have elected to edit our calendars from the previous screen. At this point, we need to select the specific calendar to edit.

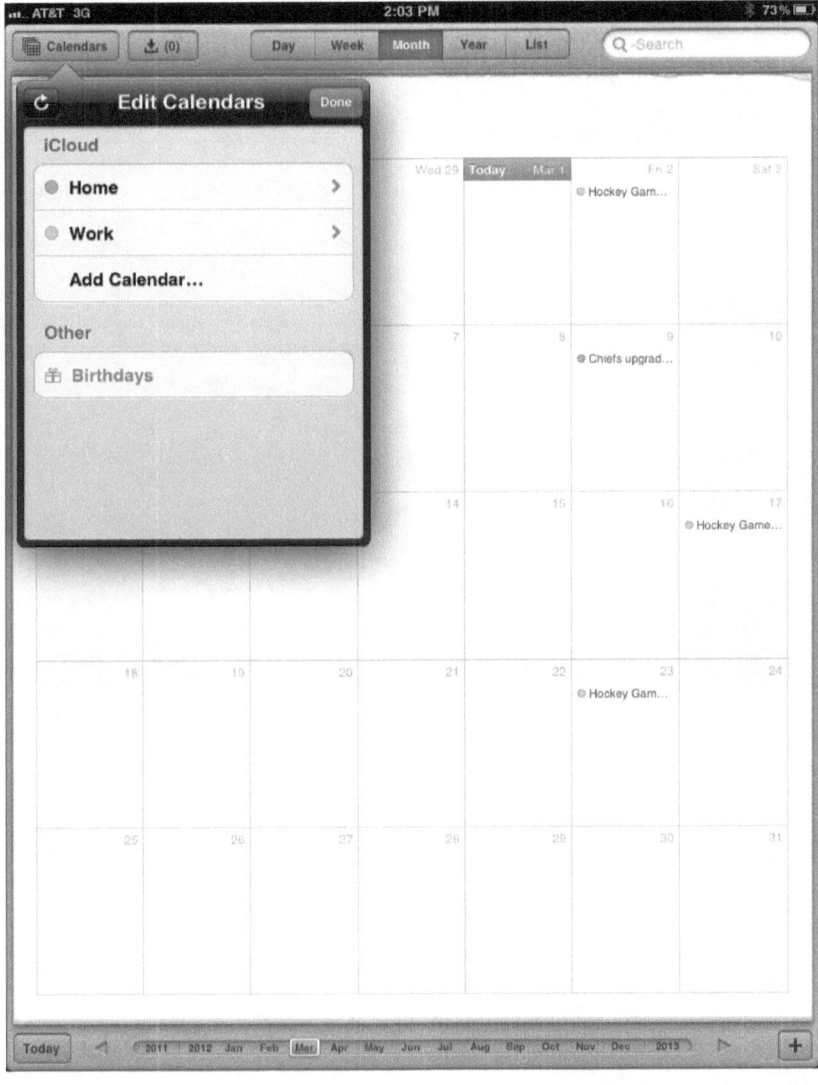

THE NEW USERS GUIDE TO THE IPAD

Here are the options to edit this calendar. We can change the colors, we can change the name of the calendar, and finally we can delete the calendar completely. When you are done editing, select the save button.

Page 150

CALENDAR

The second button over from the left is our Invitations button. This is the button where we can send invitations to meetings or other items on our calendars.

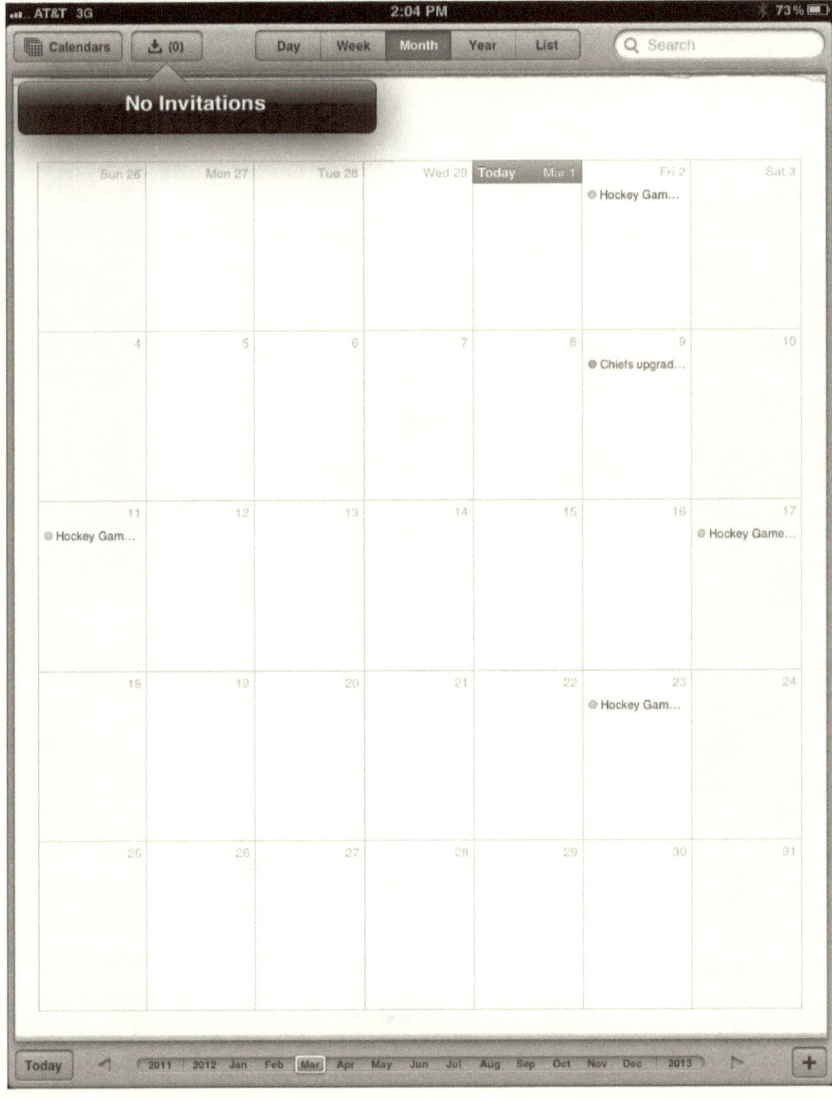

THE NEW USERS GUIDE TO THE IPAD

Here is a daily view of our calendar. To change the time-frame view of the calendar, look for the buttons in the middle bar at the

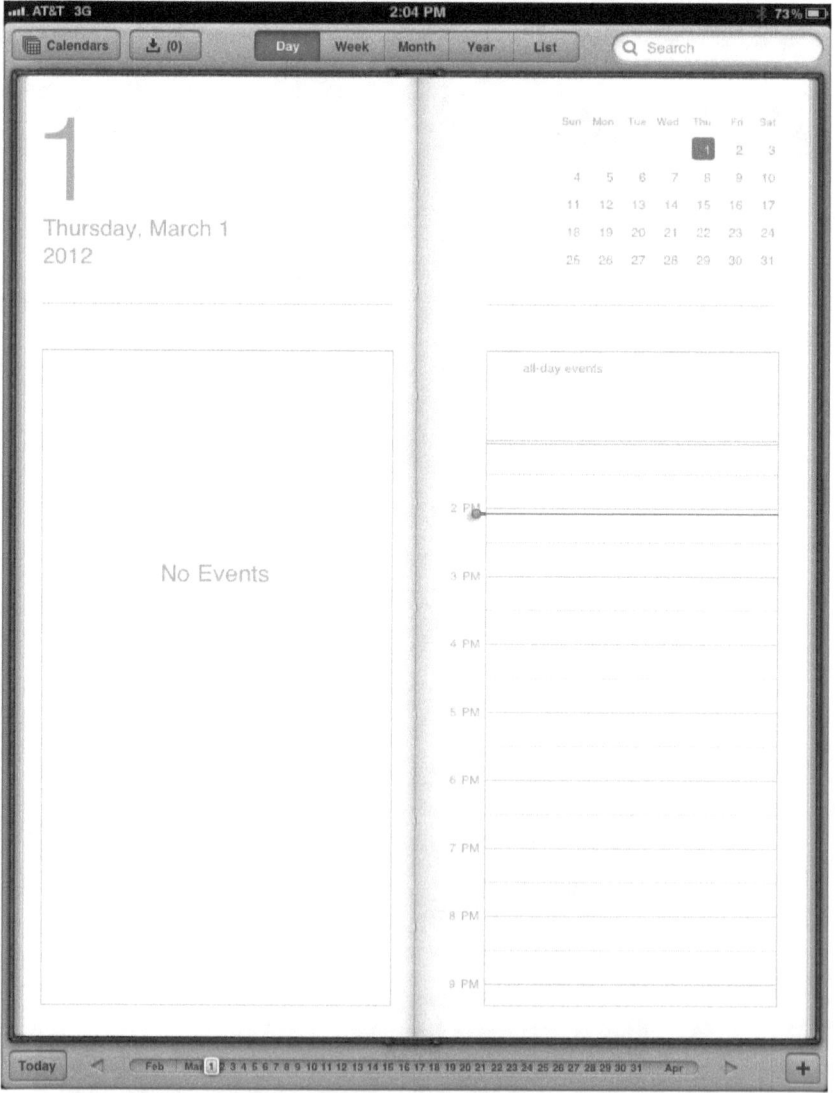

top.

CALENDAR

Here is a weekly view of our calendar.

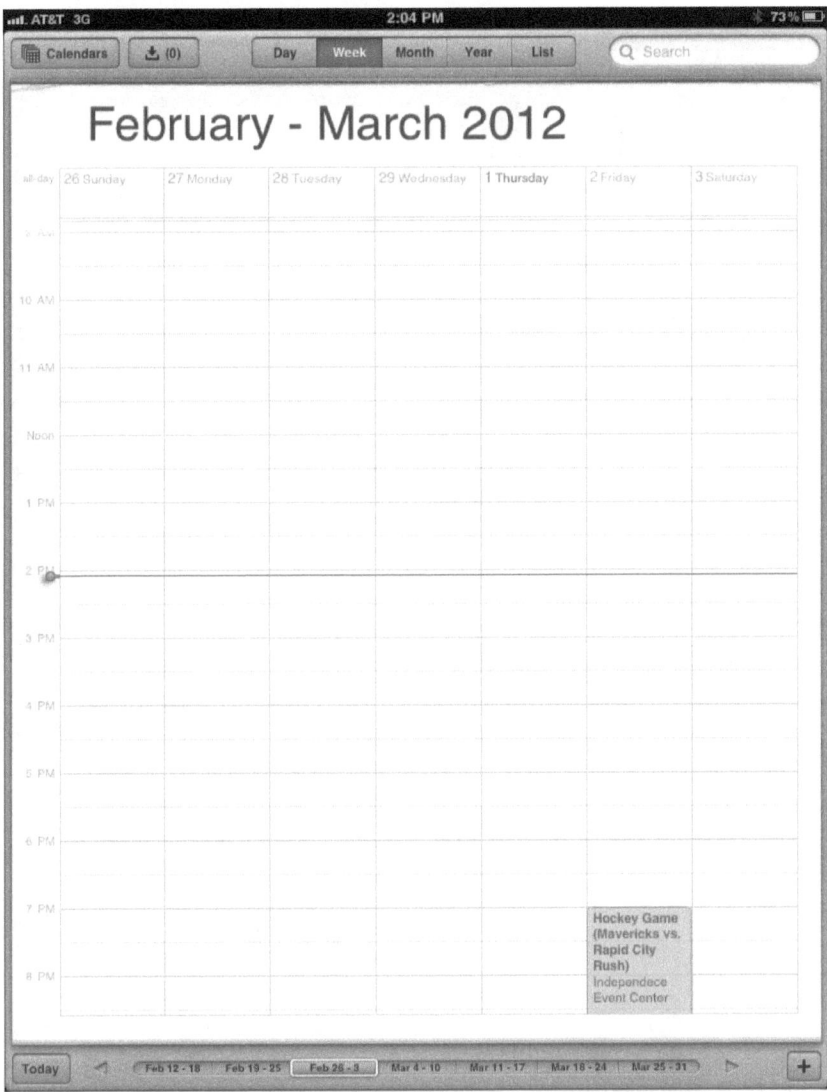

THE NEW USERS GUIDE TO THE IPAD

Here is a monthly view of our calendar.

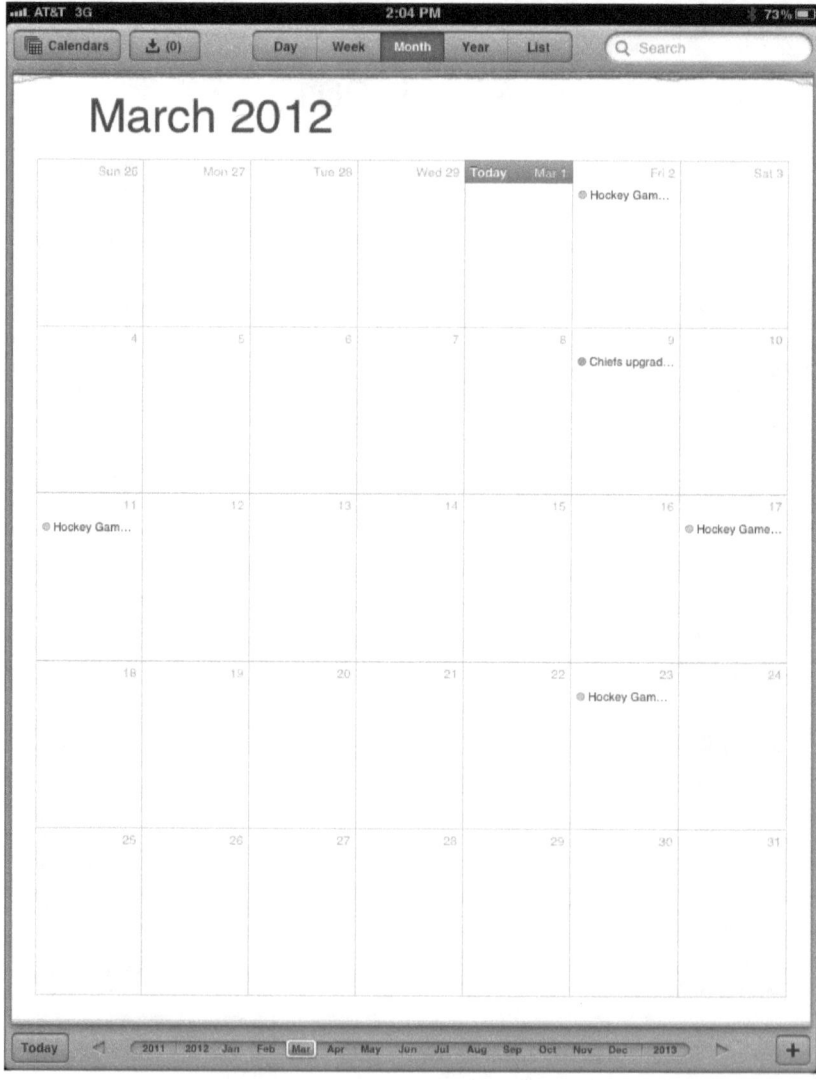

CALENDAR

Here is a yearly view of our Calendar.

THE NEW USERS GUIDE TO THE IPAD

Here is a list view of everything that is on our calendar.

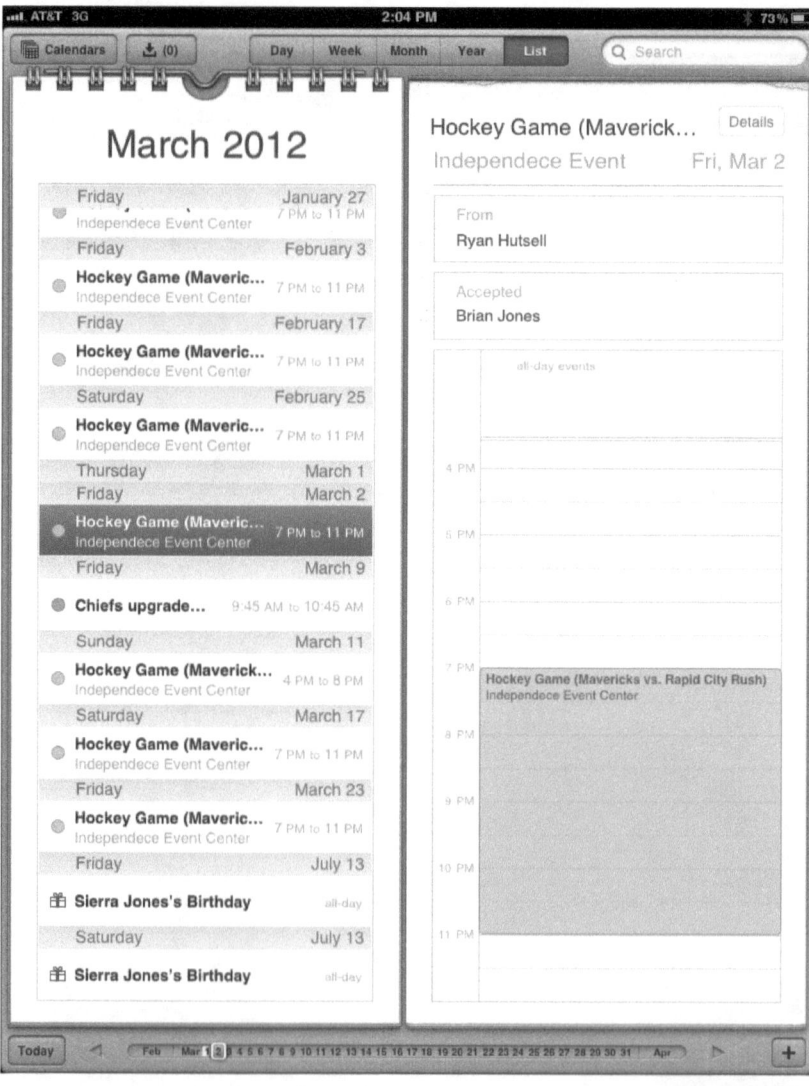

CALENDAR

In the lower right hand corner of the main screen is a plus sign. This symbol is what is used to add new items to your calendar. In this photo, we have added an event, and here are the options we have to fill out for the event and then we need to save it to our calendar.

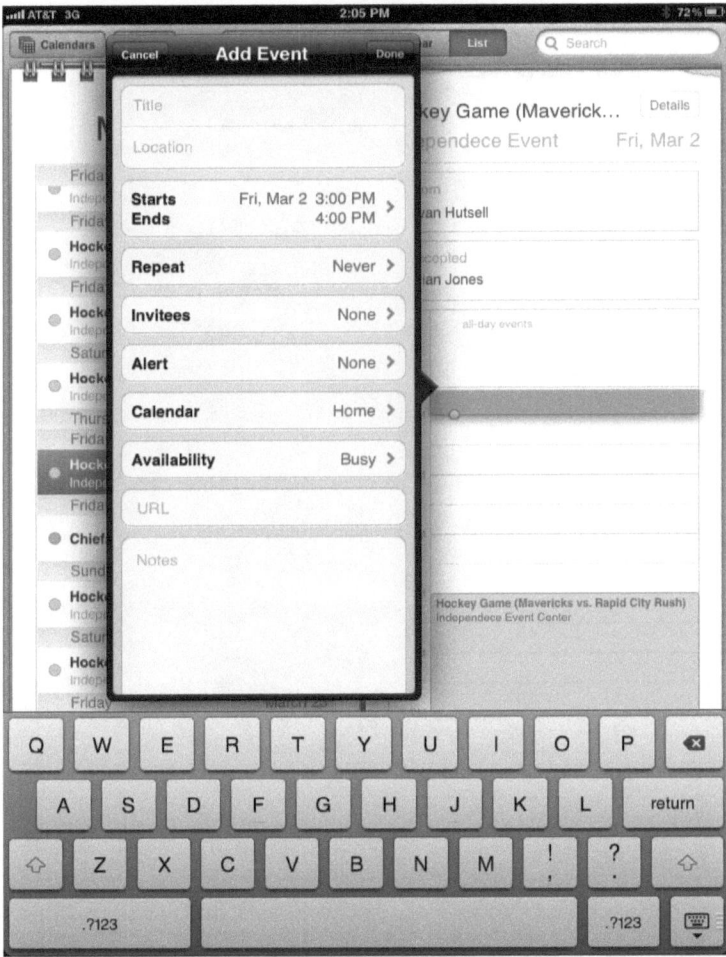

THE NEW USERS GUIDE TO THE IPAD

In the upper right-hand corner of the screen is our search box. We can type in whatever we know about an event that may be on our calendar and then search through the calendar for those events.

CALENDAR

THE NEW USERS GUIDE TO THE IPAD

Contacts

Contacts contain the information about your friends and family.

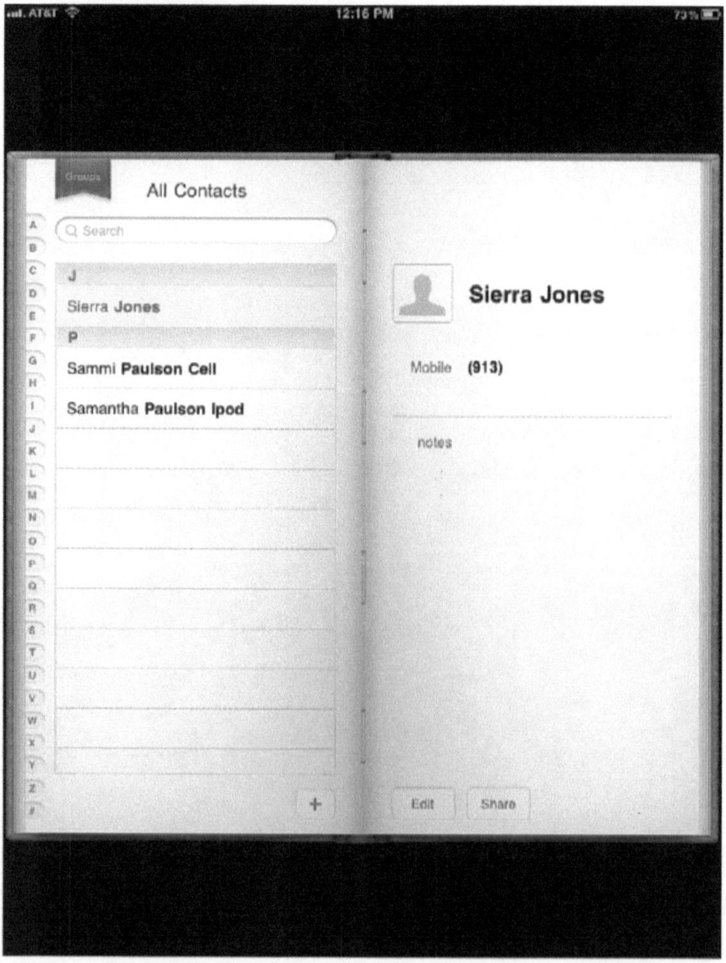

CONTACTS

The contacts list has an alphabetical list along the left side to make locating contacts easy. Select a record and you will see its content on the right side. There is an option on each record to share that contact with others. The plus sign at the bottom is used to add new contacts. The edit button will allow us to edit the selected record. The circle with an arrow is our refresh button.

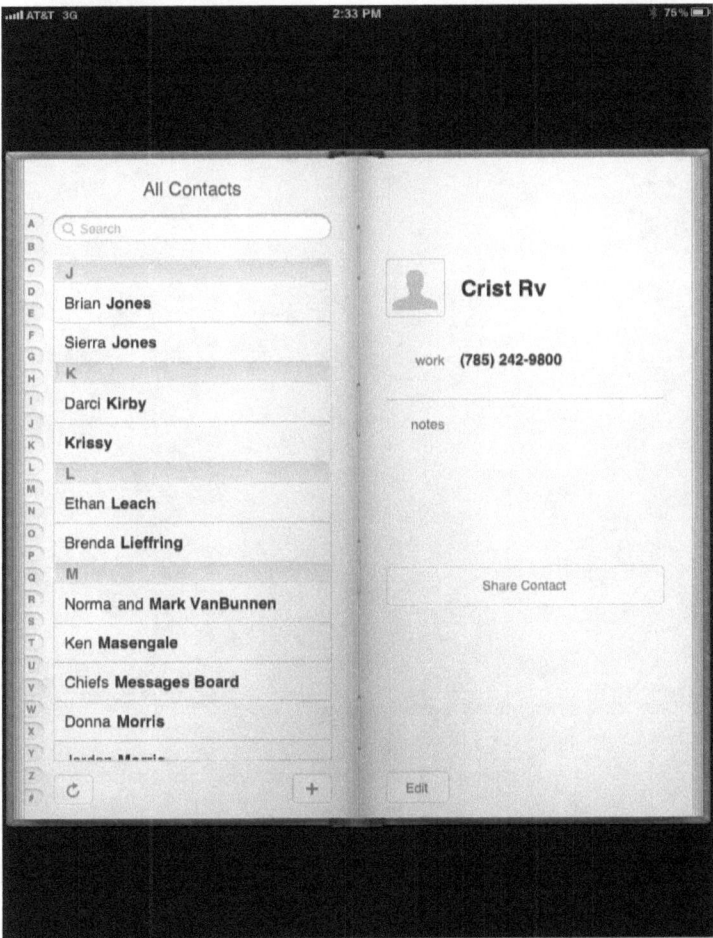

THE NEW USERS GUIDE TO THE IPAD

In this photo we are adding a new contact. There are fields for many things and you only need to fill in the ones you need. If you have a photo on your iPad, you can select the "add photo", and that photo will be associated with this contact.

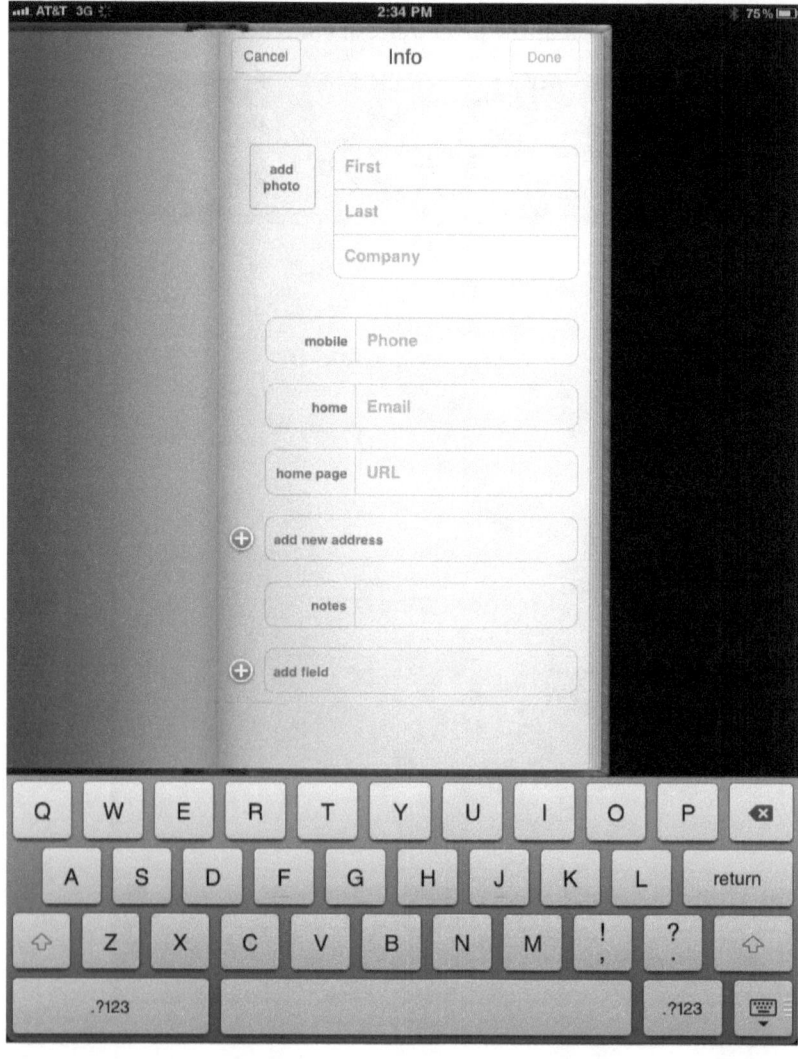

CONTACTS

In this photo we are editing an existing record. The circles with the minus sign allow you to delete information rather than updating. The plus sign will allow you to add additional information.

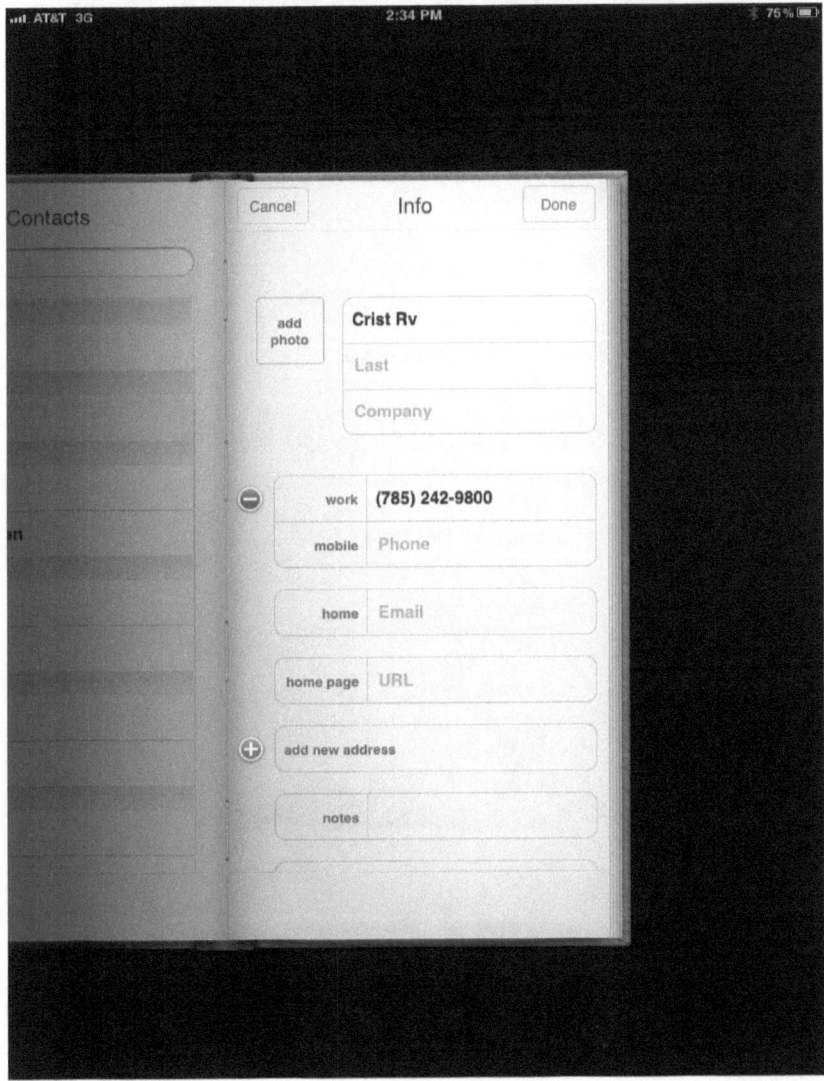

THE NEW USERS GUIDE TO THE IPAD

While not always visible, if you scroll to the bottom of the edit record screen, you will see the option to delete the contact record.

CONTACTS

THE NEW USERS GUIDE TO THE IPAD

Notes

Notes are electronic documents that are kept on the iPad.

NOTES

Notes has the look of a yellow legal pad. This application is designed to let a user write notes, documents, lists and more. These documents can be set up to not only be on the iPad but also on the iCloud so that they are always available. Notes can be set up so that when a new note is created, not only is it on the iPad but by being in the cloud, it becomes available on your iPhones.

Let's start with something new and cool in notes. Did you know that you can split your keyboard into two parts. By splitting the keyboard, you can actually see more of the documents. To split the keyboard, place one finger on each side of the space bar. With both fingers on the spacebar slide your fingers apart in an outward motion. This motion should split the keyboard into two parts.

NOTES

To rejoin the keyboard, place a finger on each keyboard space bar and slide your fingers toward the middle or toward each other. This motion will rejoin the keyboard into one solid piece again.

THE NEW USERS GUIDE TO THE IPAD

In the upper left-hand corner is a notes button. This is the button used to access the different notes. Notes can also be stored in different accounts. These are also accessed via the notes button. In the photo below we can see the different notes that are stored on this iPad. To change to a different note, just select the one you want from the list.

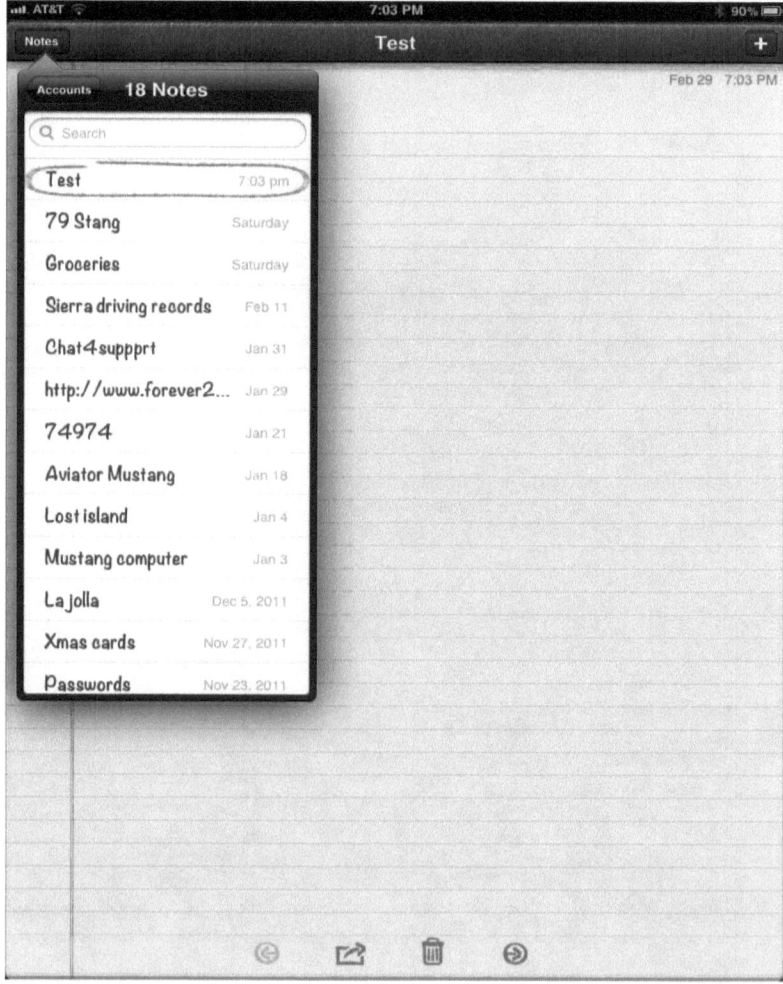

NOTES

In this photo, we can see the different accounts used on this iPad.

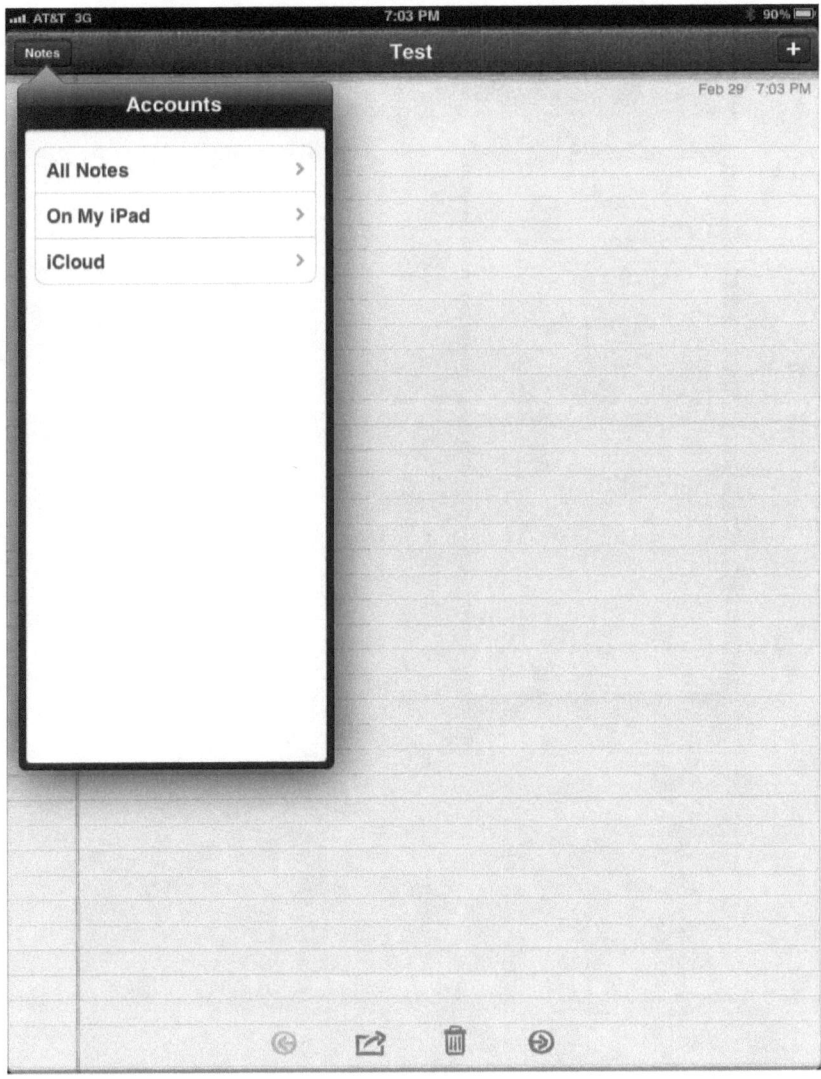

THE NEW USERS GUIDE TO THE IPAD

In this example, we can see that there are two notes in this account.

NOTES

At the bottom of the page, the second icon from the left is the link button. Using this button, we can email our notes to anyone.

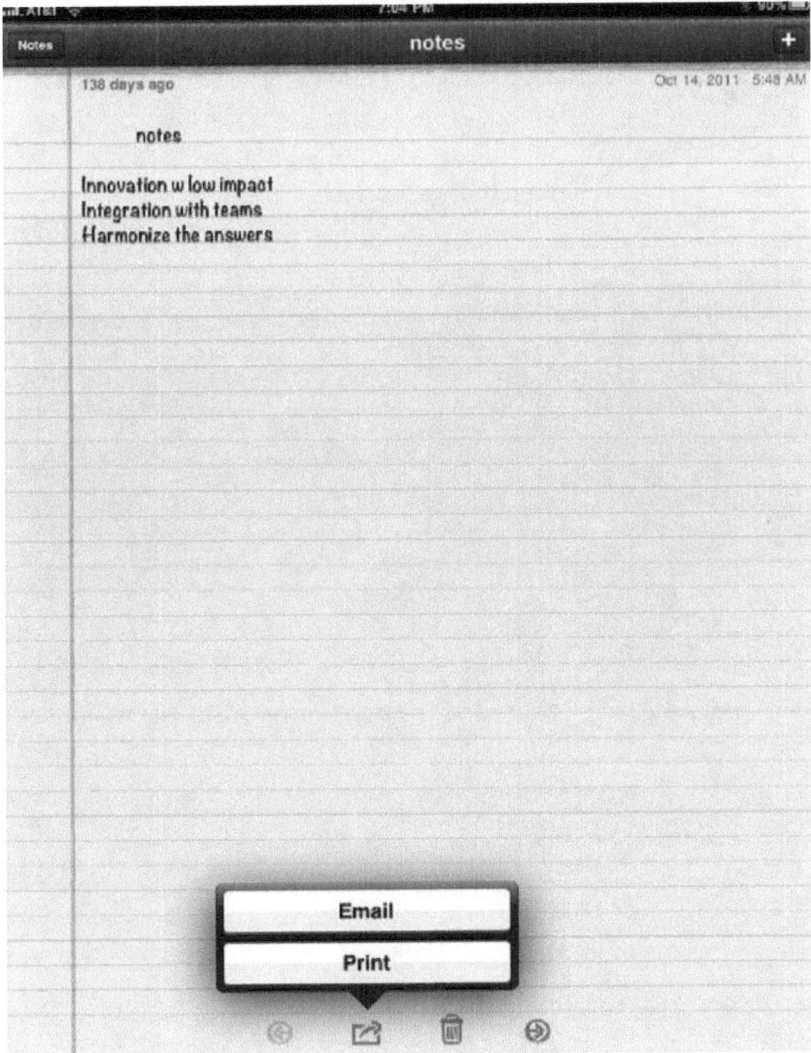

THE NEW USERS GUIDE TO THE IPAD

At the bottom of the page, there are two arrow keys, one to the left and one to the right. These arrow keys allow you to navigate through the different documents. The Trashcan button will delete the active note. In the upper right-hand corner is a plus sign. This button is used to create new notes.

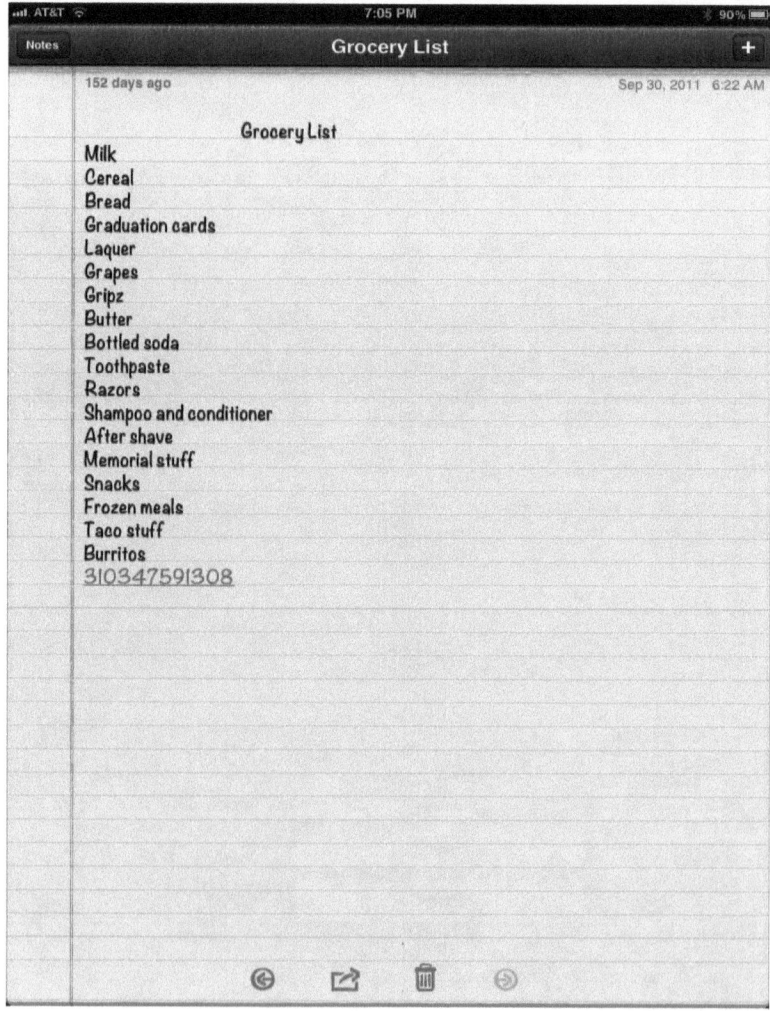

NOTES

When you click into the body of the note, the keyboard will activate and allow you to start typing. The name of a note is usually the first line in the body of the note.

THE NEW USERS GUIDE TO THE IPAD

Maps

Maps is an electronic version of the old paper maps from the past. With Maps and a 3G iPad, you can use your current geographical location on the Map.

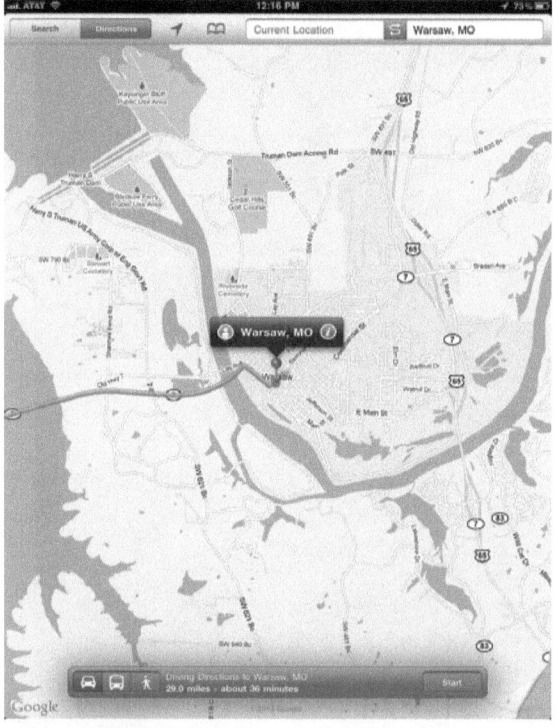

If Maps has a problem receiving a signal, the error message to the left may appear. If this window appears, try moving to a different location by a few feet. If all else fails, take the iPad and rotate the device in a figure eight motion to allow for recalibration.

MAPS

The iPad with 3G has the ability be located geographically anywhere there is cellular signal. Maps uses this information to show your exact location on the map.

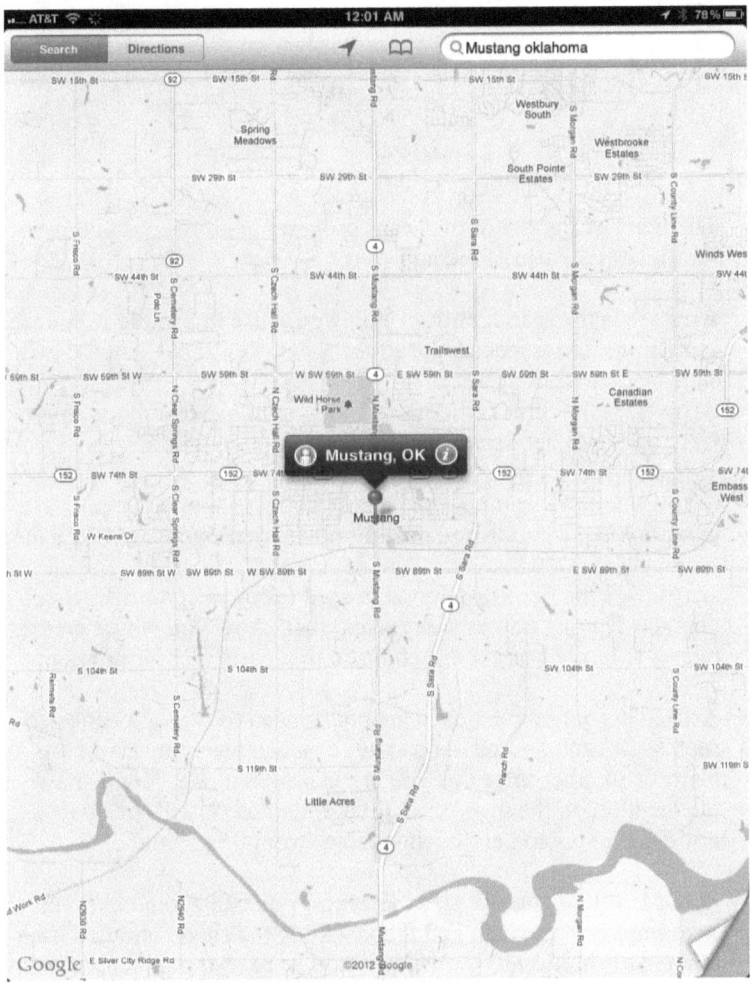

THE NEW USERS GUIDE TO THE IPAD

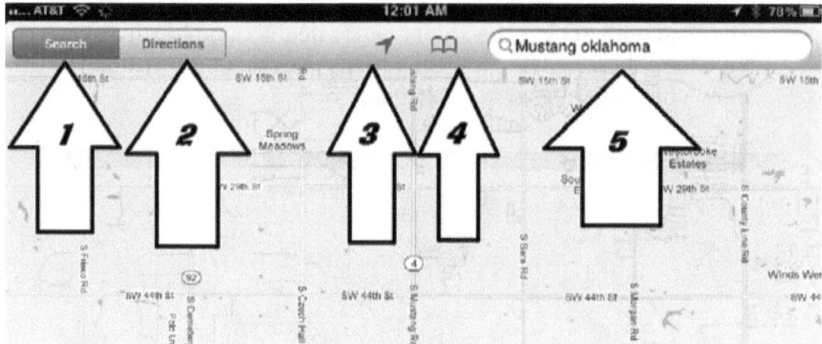

The items at the top of the Maps program are the icons you use throughout the use of the app.

Arrow 1 is the search option. You would use this mode if you were looking to find a specific location.

Arrow 2 is the direction option. You would use this mode if you were trying to get directions from one point to another.

Arrow 3 is the locator point. This button will look at your geographical location and then pinpoint where you are on the map.

Arrow 4 is the book. The book is used to find a contact in your contacts list that has an address and then show you where on the map it is located or get directions to that particular destination.

Arrow 5 is the search box. This box is used to type a location to search for such as a city and state. You can also type landmark names and other things. If you are in search mode, it will show you the location on the map. If in direction mode, it will give you options on how to get directions to or from this point.

ZOOM: While you are viewing Maps, you can zoom out by placing two fingers on the map and then swiping the fingers toward each other. This motion would be as if you were trying pick up a small object by pinching your fingers together. To zoom in, use two fingers and push the fingers apart. This motion is used throughout the iPad to zoom in and zoom out. To move around the map, use one finger and drag in one direction at a time.

MAPS

In this photo, we are in Directions mode. We have asked for directions from our current location to Mustang, Oklahoma. Maps determines the best options for the route and then gives us several options. The button between the location and the destination will reverse the route. The letter "i" next to our destination stands for information. If you select that option, it will give you more information about the destination of Mustang, Oklahoma. At the bottom of the screen are the route types. Route types are car travel, public transportation or transit travel, and finally travel by foot. Maps will also show the time frame associated with each travel type.

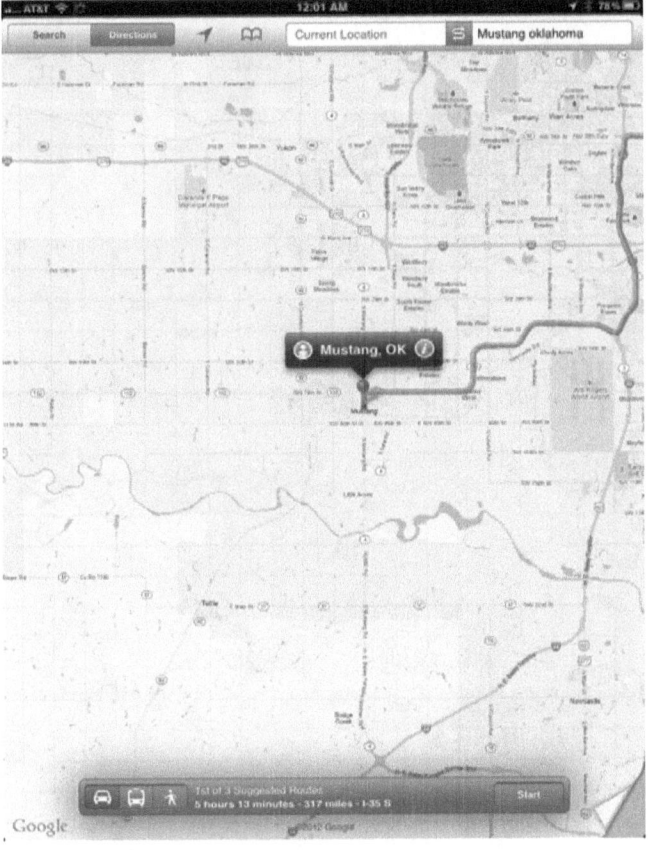

THE NEW USERS GUIDE TO THE IPAD

Maps has several options available for use. To access the options, look at the lower right-hand corner for what looks like a curl in the paper. Use one finger and drag the curl towards the middle of the page. Under the curl, you will see options such as Satellite view, Hybrid (which is satellite with roads identified), and Terrain. Traffic view can be turned on or off.

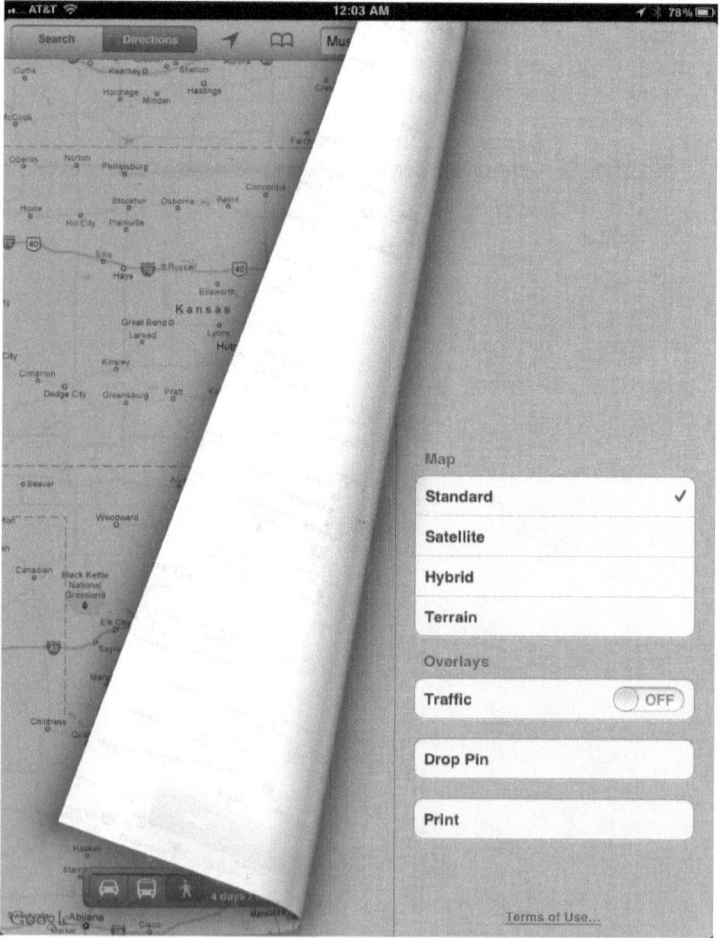

MAPS

When you have your map directions determined, there will be a start button at the bottom. Click the start button to start the first leg of your journey. Once the first leg is completed, you can select to go to the second leg of the journey and continue until you reach the destination.

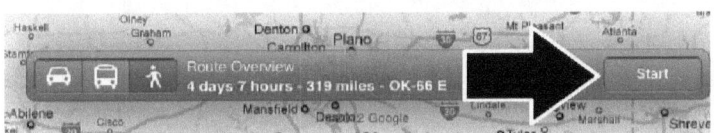

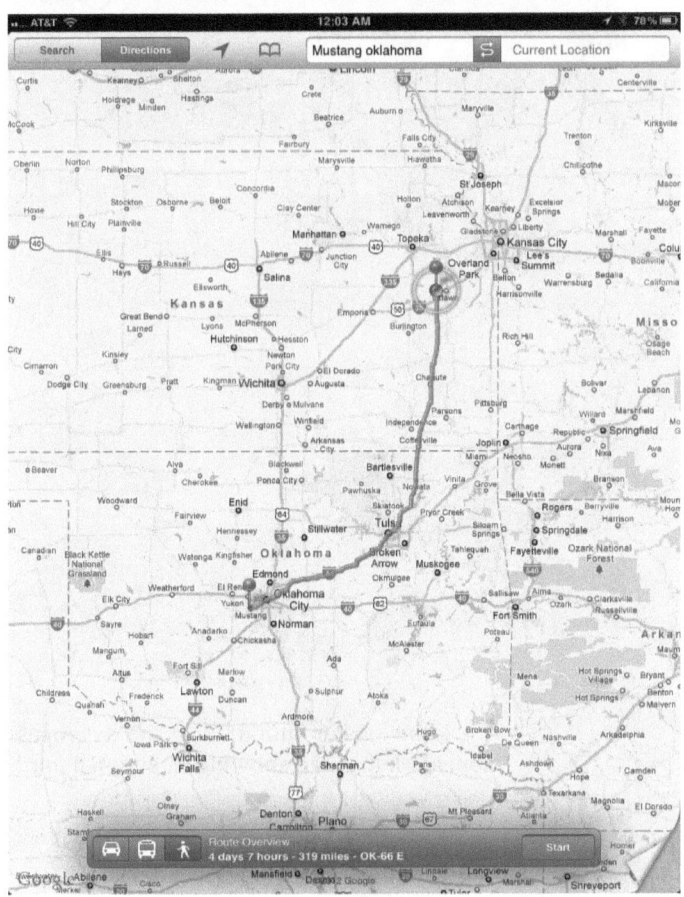

Page 181

THE NEW USERS GUIDE TO THE IPAD

We can find specific places or landmarks by searching on their name. In this example, we have done a search for the Worlds of Fun amusement park.

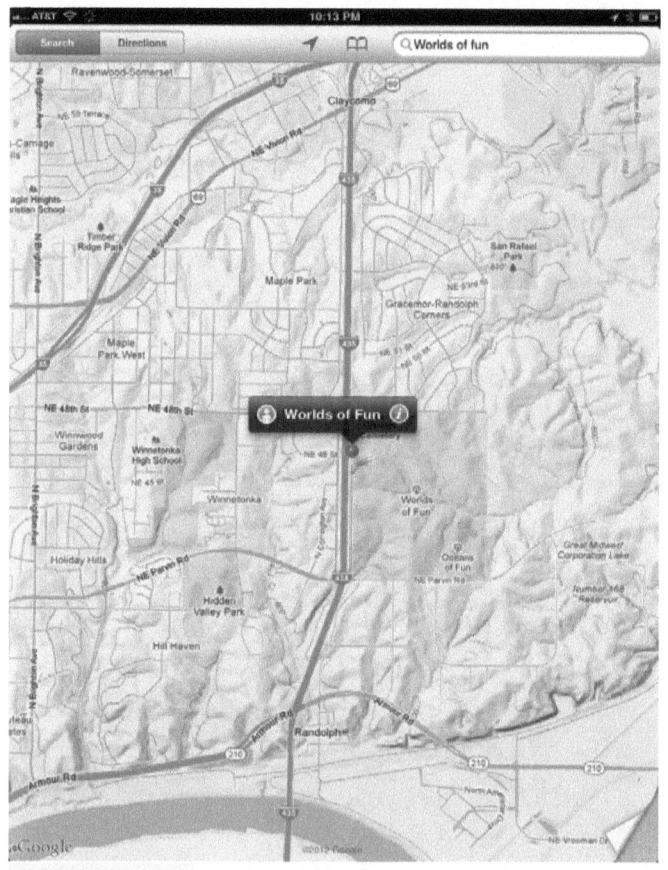

 Click the locator button twice and a compass will appear on the map showing directional north.

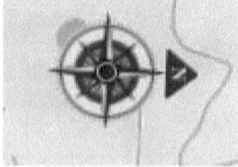

Page 182

MAPS

The "i" button will display more information about that object.

The details on the information screen allow us to get directions to/from this location. Information about the spot, such as address or phone number, are displayed.

Add to contacts will allow us to create a contact with the address and phone number of this spot.

Add to bookmarks will allow us to create a shortcut to return to the spot.

The Share Location will email a locator to another Apple device user, and they will be able to find this exact spot in Maps. When a location is shared, a pin is sent to the other Apple user via email or Messenger. When the other Apple user, clicks on the pin, the iPad will take them directly to the exact spot which was sent to them. If a great spot is found for fishing, bonfire, or a party, the location can be sent to one or many Apple users which have an iPhone or an iPad.

THE NEW USERS GUIDE TO THE IPAD

To share a location, get the detail of the location.

 Click the "Share Location" button.

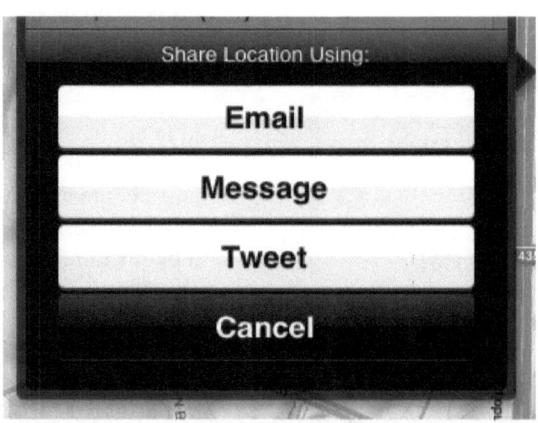 The location pin for the spot can be sent to other Apple users by Email, Message, or Tweet. Select the option to send the pin.

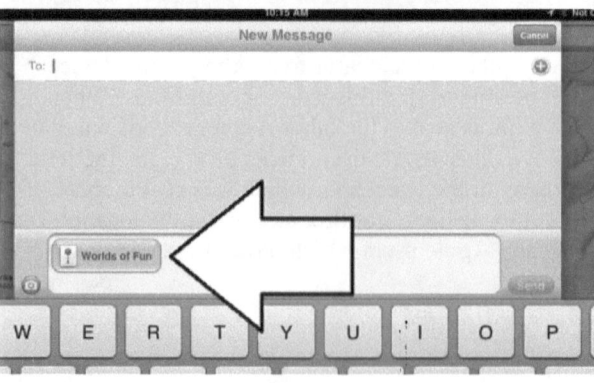 In the message will be a mobile pin that other users will be able to open directly in their Maps app. Just think if the pirates of old would have had this technology!!

MAPS

This button will show a street level view of the spot.

The street level view can be moved by placing a finger on the photo and dragging left or right as well as up or down.

The icon below will show the direction of the view.

THE NEW USERS GUIDE TO THE IPAD

A pin is a point that can be located on a map by dropping a pin. Place a finger on a spot on the map and hold it there until a pin drops on the map.

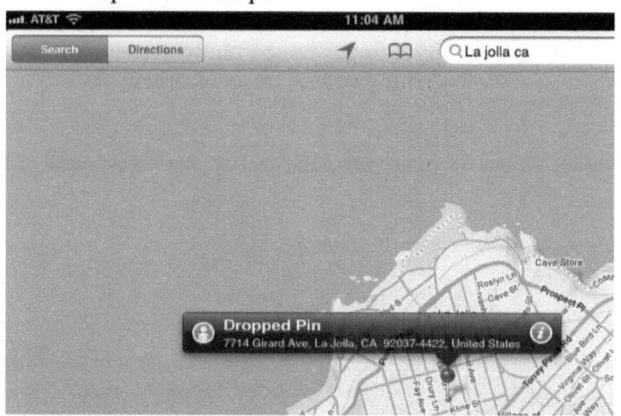

 Select the "i" button for more information on where the pin was exactly dropped.

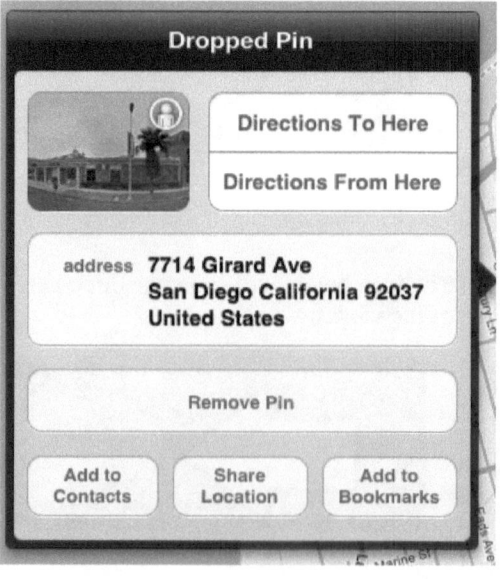

The detail screen about the pin allows for direction to and from the pin. The address and phone number will be displayed if known.

To remove the pin from the map, select the "Remove Pin" button.

This location can be added to a contact, shared with other Apple device users, or added as a favorite for later reference.

A small photo of the pin location may appear.

MAPS

Click the street level button on the dropped pin to see a view of what the streets around that spot look like. With street view, a 360 degree view of the spot can usually be seen. Navigation around the spot is done by touching the screen and moving the finger around the screen.

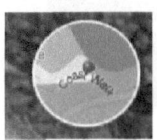

To exit street view on a pin, select the icon in the lower right hand corner of the photo.

THE NEW USERS GUIDE TO THE IPAD

Video

The video library will be shown when you select the Video icon.

VIDEO

Open the Video app and the gallery of movies and videos will open. The gallery view will show a thumbnail of the files that are listed in the folder. The Store button in the upper left-hand corner will take the user to the iTunes store. The "Edit" button in the upper right-hand corner will allow you to delete video files.

THE NEW USERS GUIDE TO THE IPAD

From the gallery view, there is an "Edit" button in the upper right-hand corner. When the view is in edit mode, video files can be deleted. Select the Red "X" in the corner of the video file to delete that file. Once deletions are completed, select the "Done" button.

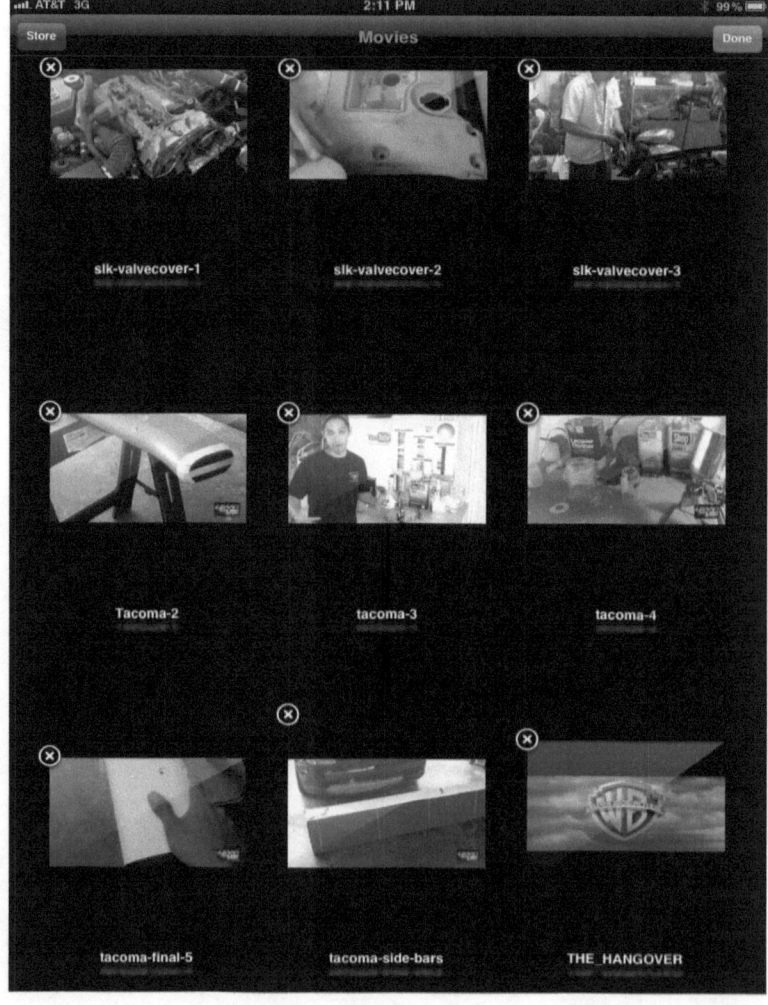

VIDEO

When you select a video from the library, the window that opens will show information about the video with a Play button at the top right on the screen.

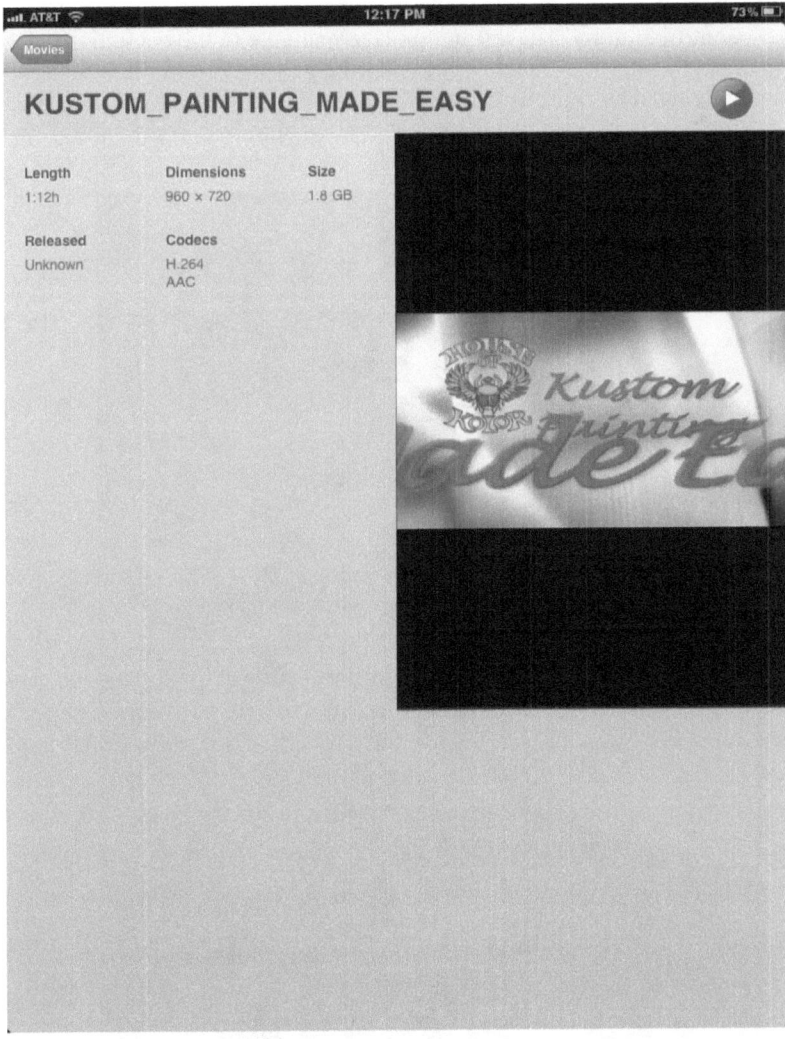

THE NEW USERS GUIDE TO THE IPAD

When the video is playing, there are several options that are available. At the top, the "Done" button will take you back to the video library. The timeline in the middle at the top shows the video length and current location. You can select an area in the timeline to navigate to that instance in the video. At the bottom are the control buttons. The left button is to navigate to the beginning. The middle button is the play button or the pause button if the video is playing. The right button will take you to the end of the video. If the iPad is rotated, the view will change between portrait and landscape views.

VIDEO

Video files stored on the iPad will automatically play in full screen mode. Rotating the iPad from portrait to landscape will change the display format.

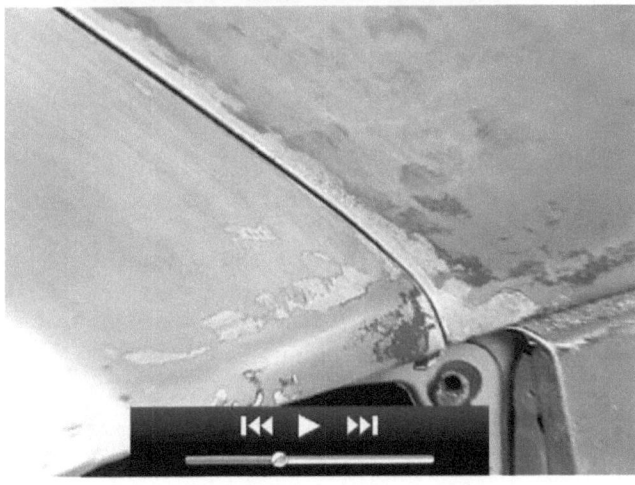

THE NEW USERS GUIDE TO THE IPAD

YouTube

There is a built in YouTube video player to watch the millions of videos that are hosted on YouTube.com

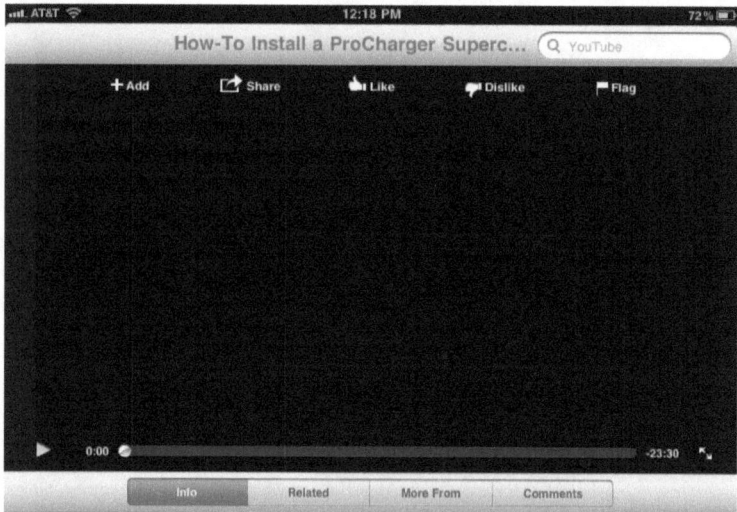

How-To Install a ProCharger Supercharger
November 18, 2010
motorztv
20,400 views

Chris Duke from Motorz TV http://www.motorz.tv/ shows you how to install an ATI ProCharger supercharger on a 2008 Ford Mustang GT. Special appearance from ATI ProCharger's Nick Schmidt.
Show notes: http://www.motorz.tv/mustang-supercharger/
Website: http://www.motorz.tv/
Facebook: http://www.facebook.com/motorz
Twitter: http://twitter.com/motorz

category: Autos & Vehicles

tags: supercharger, blower, procharger, ati, accessible technologies, s197, mustang, v8, ford, installation, diy, how-to, centrifugal, roots, intercooler, kit, p-1sc-1, intercooled, torque, horsepower, performance, nick schmidt, enigne, jba racing, dyno dynamics, dynamometer, diablosport

YOUTUBE

The YouTube videos can be displayed in several different formats. The screen below shows the videos that were featured on YouTube on this day. At the bottom of the screen are the different view options.

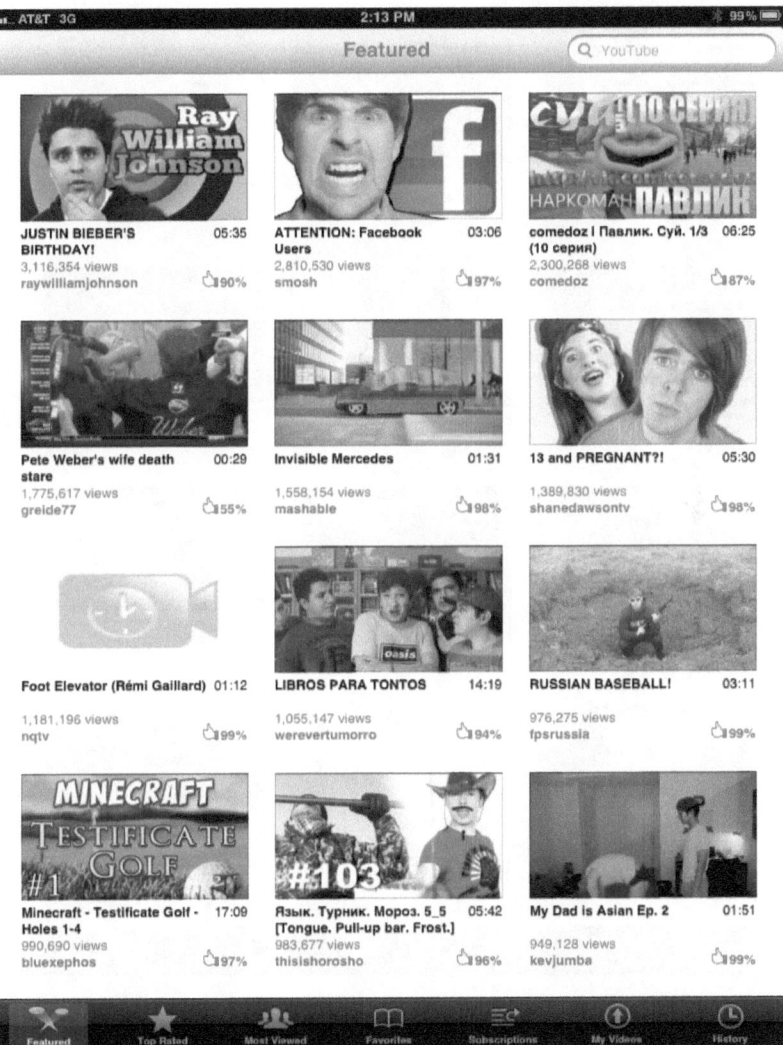

THE NEW USERS GUIDE TO THE IPAD

This photo shows the top-rated videos for the site on this date.

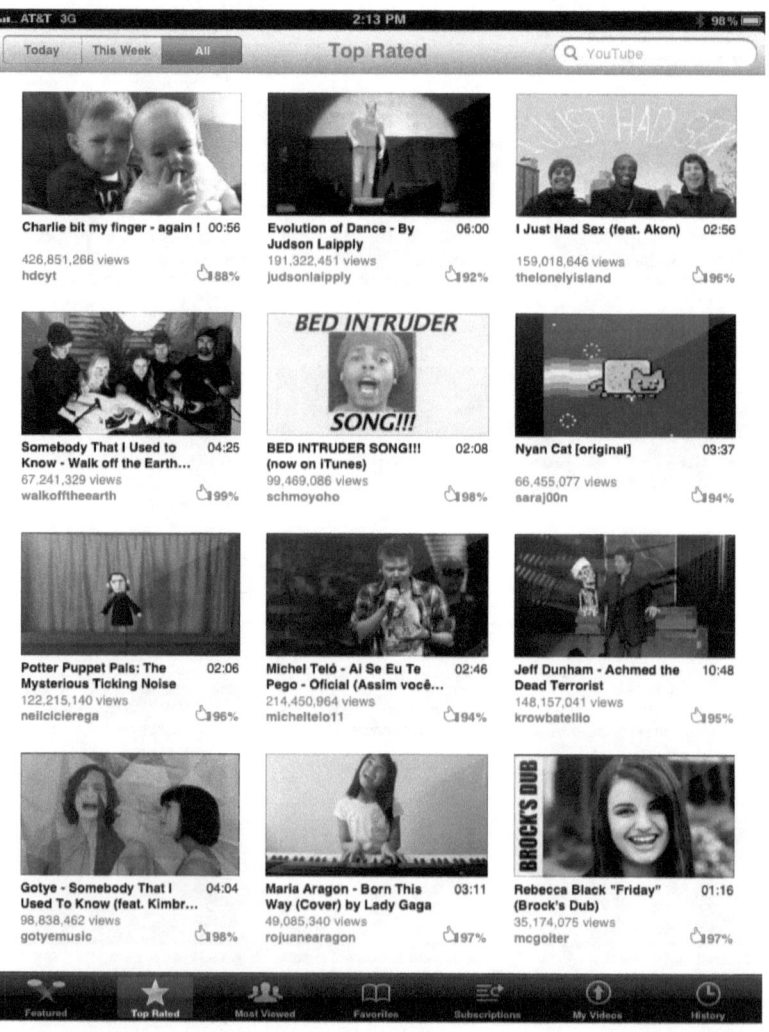

Page 196

YOUTUBE

This photo shows a screen shot of the most viewed videos on YouTube on this date. At the top right are some additional ways to view the most viewed for the week or other options.

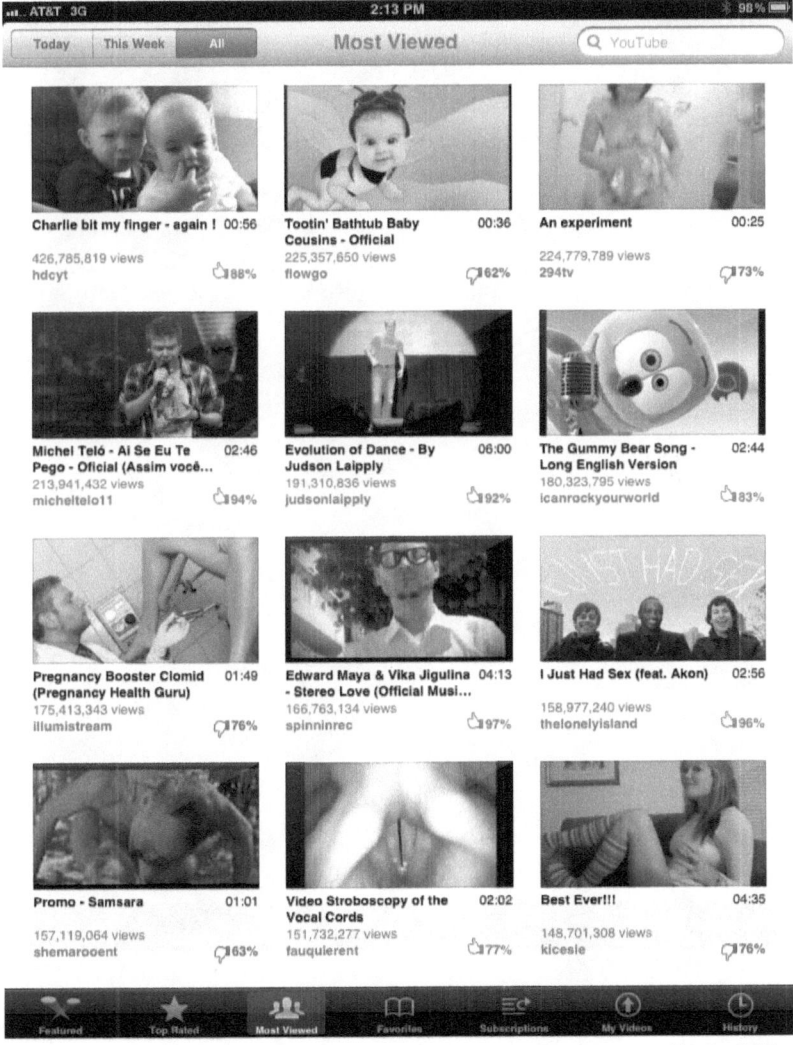

THE NEW USERS GUIDE TO THE IPAD

If you find a video that you enjoy, it can be saved as a favorite. On this screen, we see three videos that have been marked as a favorite.

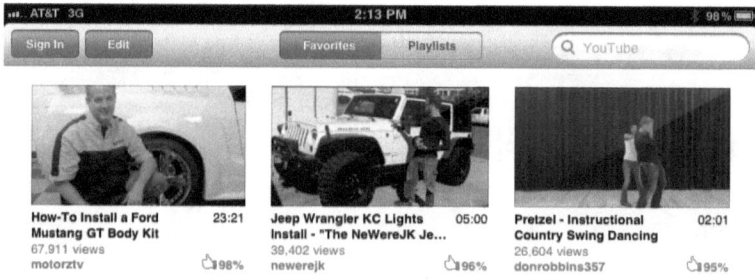

YOUTUBE

YouTube has the ability to create subscriptions to users that post videos. To access subscriptions, you will need a user account on YouTube.

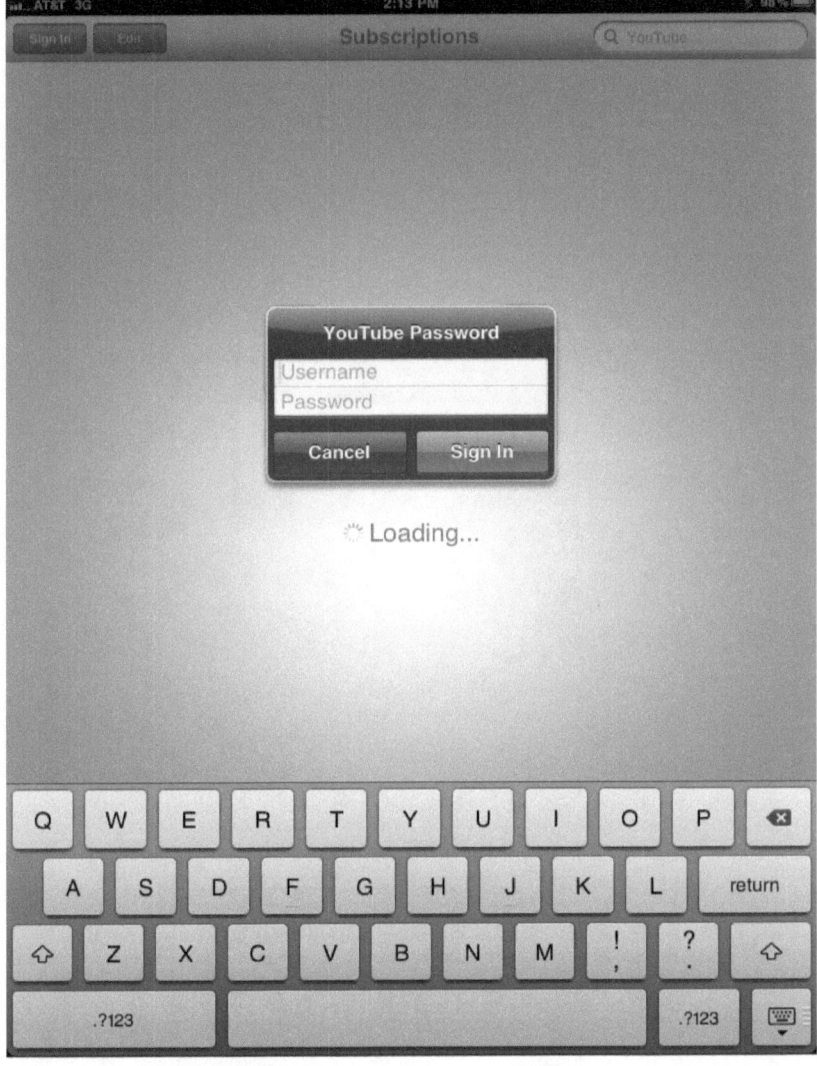

THE NEW USERS GUIDE TO THE IPAD

If you have an account on YouTube, you can post videos under your account. This screen will show the videos that you personally have uploaded to YouTube. You will have to log in to YouTube to view these files.

YOUTUBE

In this photo, we see the details about one specific video. This video can be added to favorites. The video can be shared with others. Users can like, dislike or flag the video from here. Below the video are some options to see other videos by this user.

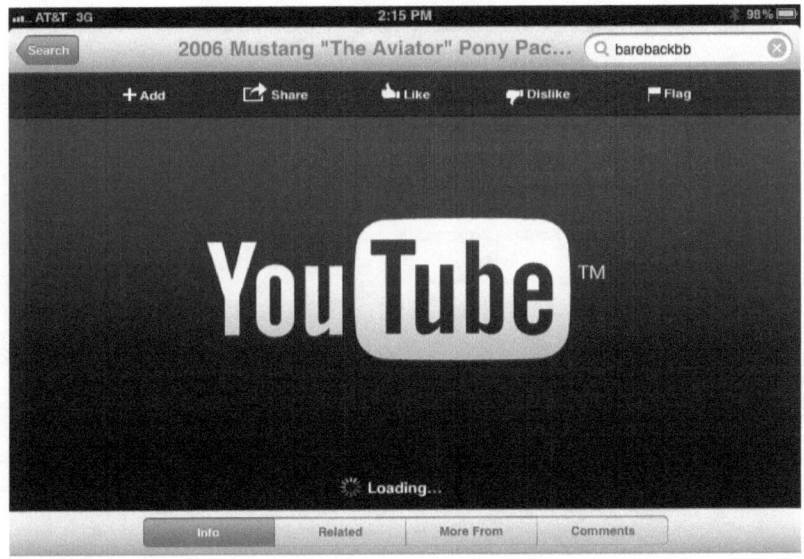

2006 Mustang "The Aviator" Pony Package V6
August 31, 2008
barebackbb

8,753 views

www.aviatormustang.com 2006 redfire mustang convertible with Cervini C500 front fascia. Car is personally signed by Carroll Shelby, Chip Foose, George Barris, Gen. Chuck Yeager, and CE "Bud" Anderson. Car is called "The Aviator" and nicknamed Amelia. The site for this car is www.aviatormustang.com

category: Autos & Vehicles

tags: mustang, cervini, foose, redfire, shelby, amelia, the aviator, car sponsors, sponsor, www.aviatormustang.com, sponsorship, sponsorships

THE NEW USERS GUIDE TO THE IPAD

A video can be shared via an email link. If you are a Twitter user, you can tweet this video. This video can be added to your favorites from this screen.

2006 Mustang "The Aviator" Pony Package V6
August 31, 2008
barebackbb

8,753 views

www.aviatormustang.com 2006 redfire mustang convertible with Cervini C500 front fascia. Car is personally signed by Carroll Shelby, Chip Foose, George Barris, Gen. Chuck Yeager, and CE "Bud" Anderson. Car is called "The Aviator" and nicknamed Amelia. The site for this car is www.aviatormustang.com

category: Autos & Vehicles

tags: mustang, cervini, foose, redfire, shelby, amelia, the aviator, car sponsors, sponsor, www.aviatormustang.com, sponsorship, sponsorships

YOUTUBE

When the video plays, there are controls at the bottom to control the playback. The two arrows allow the video to be played in full screen mode. At the top is a timeline for the video. Touch the "Done" button to return to the video detail page.

THE NEW USERS GUIDE TO THE IPAD

Game Center

Game Center lets a user expand their game play into a social gaming network.

GAME CENTER

Log into the Game Center with your Apple ID and password. Your Apple ID will be the account that Game Center uses to track play and points.

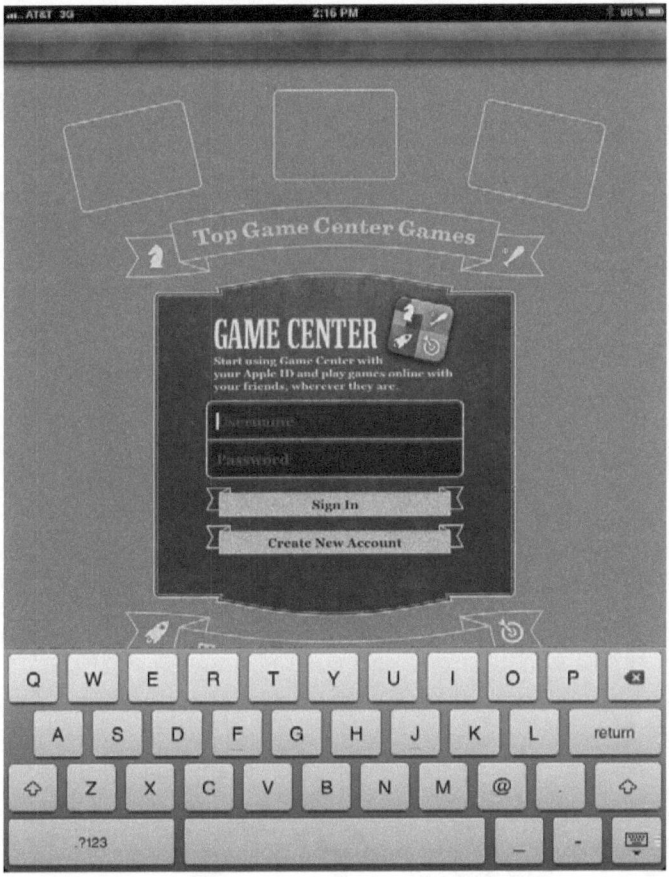

THE NEW USERS GUIDE TO THE IPAD

When a user is logged into Game Center, they will see their nickname, points, and games played on the "Me" page.

GAME CENTER

A photo can be added to your account so that other gamers can see your photo when working with you in Game Center. To add a photo, click the button that says "Change Photo".

THE NEW USERS GUIDE TO THE IPAD

Locate a photo to use on your account.

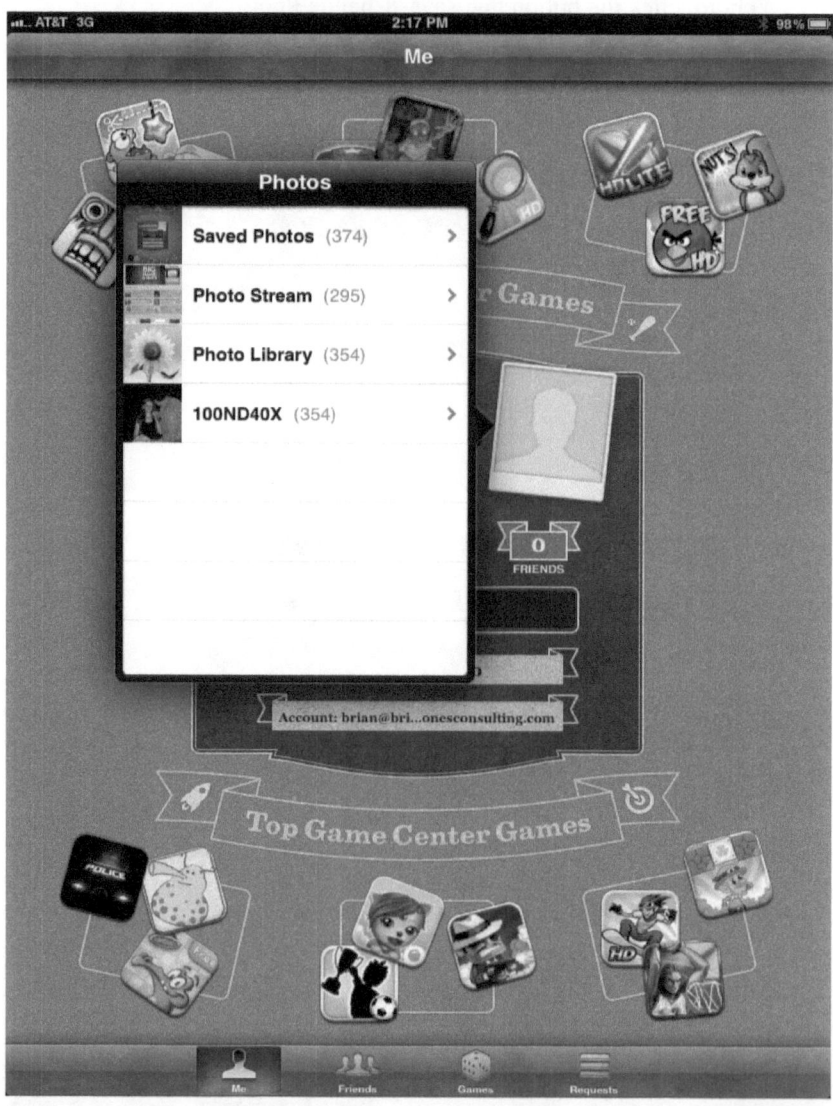

GAME CENTER

The "My Friends" view will show friends that you have authorized to work with you in the Game Center.

THE NEW USERS GUIDE TO THE IPAD

The "Games" view will show the games that have been played by this user.

GAME CENTER

The "Requests" view will show other users that have requested authorization to work with you in Game Center.

iTunes

iTunes is the store where a user can buy music, movies, or more for their iPad.

At the top of every page in the iTunes store is a button for featured items or for items that are top in the charts.

ITUNES

Inside the iTunes app, there are areas along the bottom of the screen to choose. This screen is the downloads screen. Downloads will show the items that we have downloaded from iTunes in the past.

THE NEW USERS GUIDE TO THE IPAD

In the photo below, we see the music options available to us from iTunes. In the upper left corner there is a Genres button to narrow our music choice by genre. In the middle, at the top, we can view featured music, music in the top charts, or use Genius to help us find similar music to what we have already purchased. In the upper right-hand is a box for searching for specific music or artists.

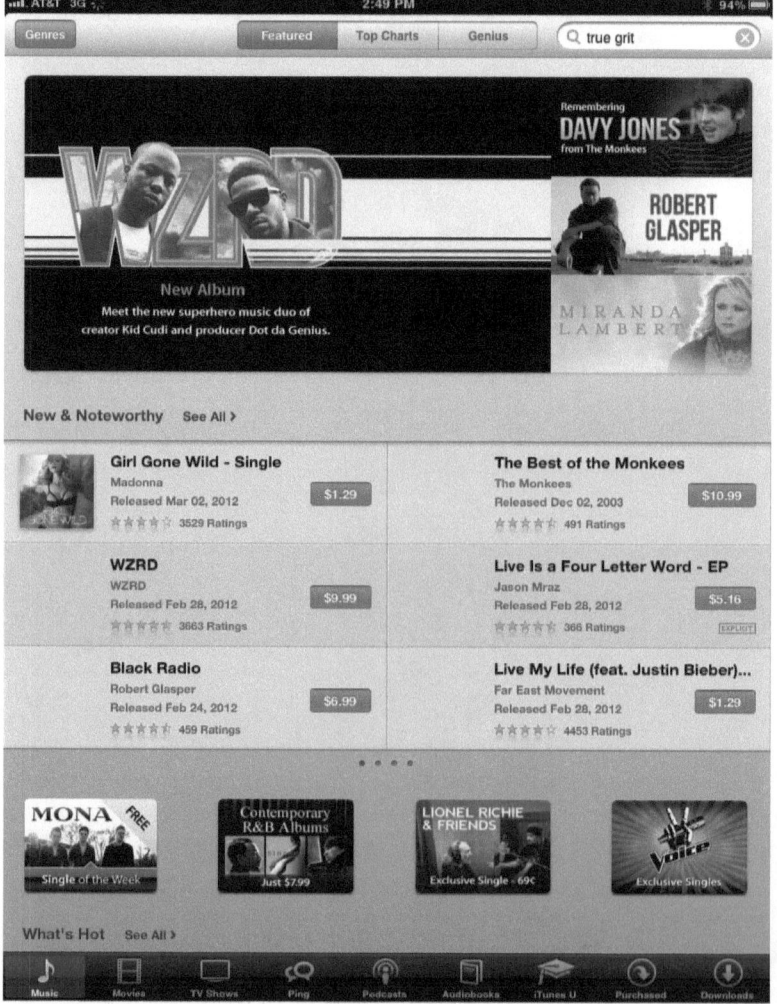

ITUNES

The iTunes movies screen has the same options as the music screen. Movies rented on iTunes are different in some ways than music. Music that is purchased is always available to the customer. Movie rentals, however, have a timeframe for their use. Once a movie has been rented, there is a 30 day period to watch the movie before it disappears. Once the movie watching has started, a consumer has 24 hours to complete watching of the movie and then it disappears. If a movie rental is not watched during the 30 day period, it will disappear from the library. Movies can be purchased for a larger amount, and they will always be available for your viewing.

Television shows purchased on iTunes work the same way as the movies that are purchased on iTunes. Television show episodes or complete seasons can be purchased. Currently, Apple does not rent television shows.

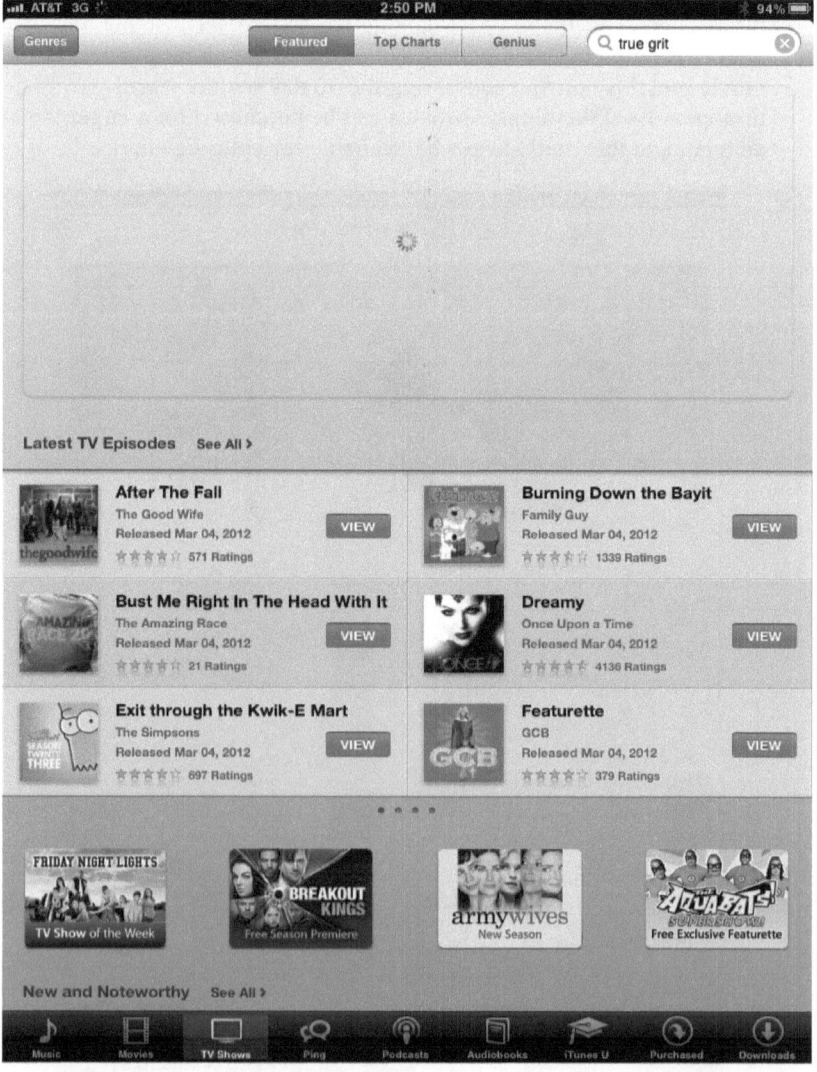

ITUNES

iTunes Ping, also known simply as Ping, is a software-based, music-oriented social networking and recommender system service.

The service allows users to follow artists and see short timely postings by both friends and artists.

A podcast is a type of digital media consisting of an episodic series of files (either audio or video) subscribed to and downloaded through the web. The word is a neologism derived from "broadcast" and "pod" from the success of the iPod.

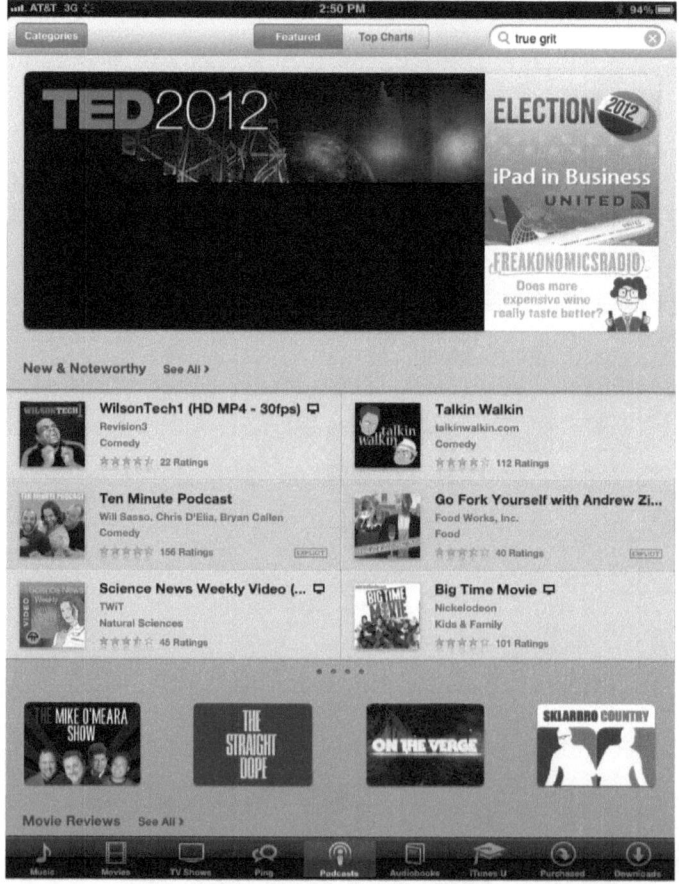

ITUNES

The audio book section in iTunes works the same way as the music purchases. These are books that have narration accompanying them. The print version is there along with the audio portion.

THE NEW USERS GUIDE TO THE IPAD

iTunes U is a section of the iTunes store where users can download free educational course content from many colleges and universities, non-profit educational institutions, and K-12 organizations.

ITUNES

The purchase screen will list those items that were previously purchased on iTunes.

Here we have selected a TV show season. On this screen, we can purchase the entire season. There is a High Definition or a Standard Definition version for sale. Individual episodes from this season may be purchased.

ITUNES

At the top of the page, we can select a specific genres of types. In the middle at the top, we can look at featured shows, the top shows in the charts, or allow genius to help us find selections.

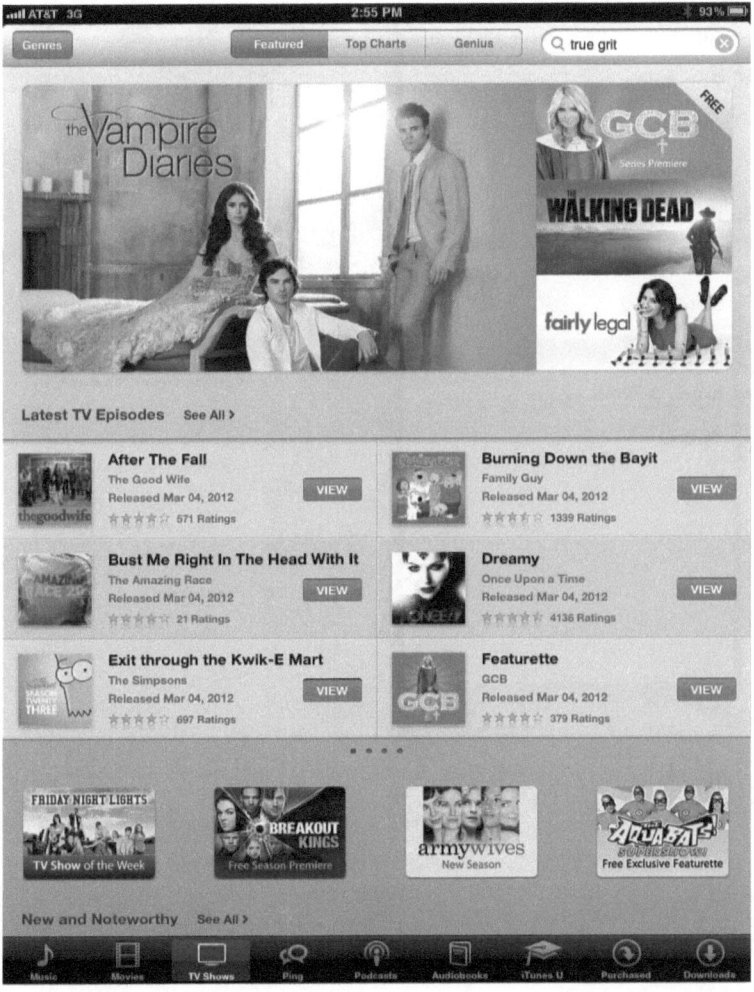

THE NEW USERS GUIDE TO THE IPAD

The Genres button in the upper left of the screen, will allow a user to filter their selections by selecting a specific genres of files.

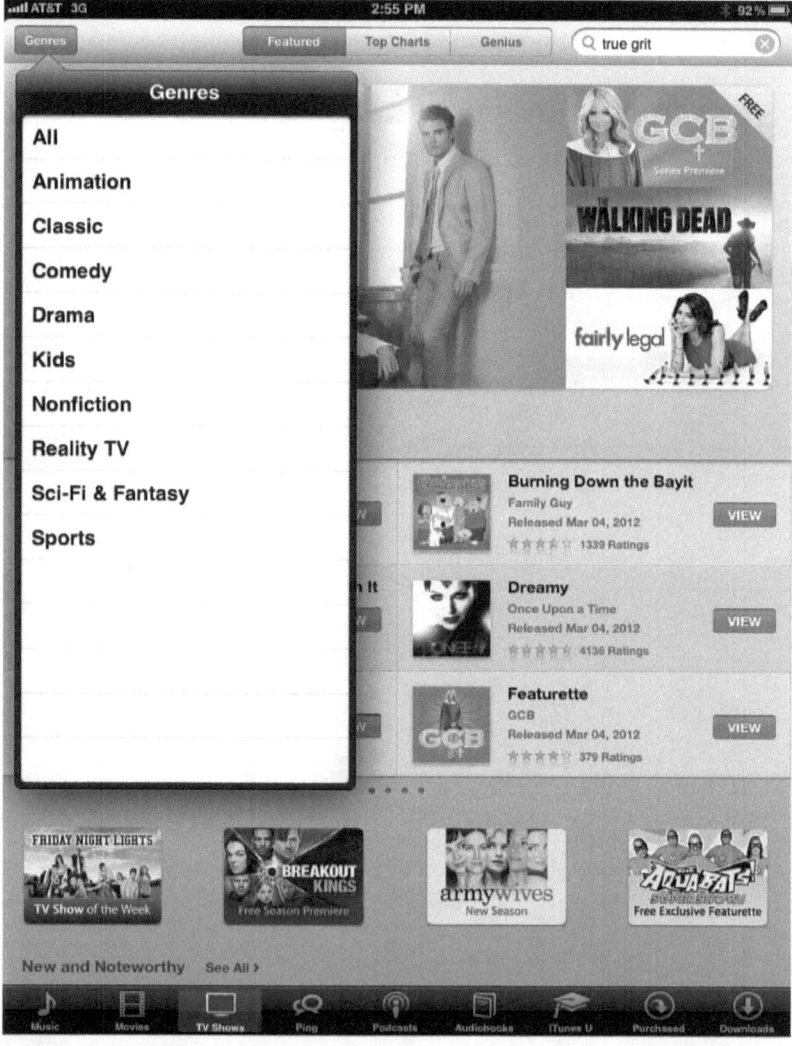

ITUNES

A computer can be used to sync music, books, apps, and other files from the iPad. If the iPad is in sync with the computer, files are backed up and can be restored if needed. Items can be purchased on the iPad or on the PC through iTunes and then the sync will copy them to the iPad. iTunes is a free program available for download from the Apple web site. Today a sync can be done with the USB charging cable plugged into the PC or done wirelessly when attached to the same wireless network. Before a wireless sync can be imitated, a wired sync has to happen first. There are some settings that also need to be set during that first wired sync. We will discuss all those in this chapter.

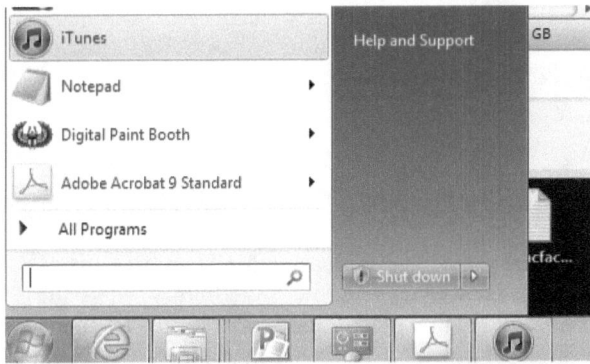

To start iTunes on a computer, locate the icon and select the program. The iTunes application on the PC can be started first and then have the iPad plugged into the computer, or as soon as the iPad is sensed attached to the PC, iTunes will start automatically.

If you do not want iTunes to start automatically each time the iPad is plugged into the computer, there is an option to stop that from happening. On the computer, look for Edit at the top, and then look for preferences. When the preferences open, select the device tab. Place a check mark next to the option to prevent automatic sync.

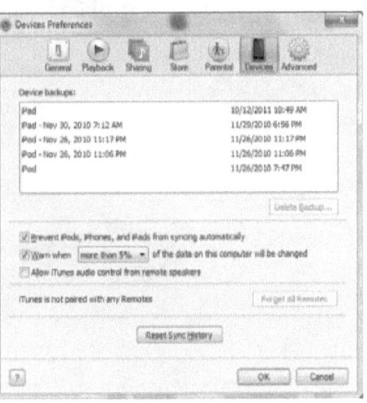

THE NEW USERS GUIDE TO THE IPAD

Here is what iTunes will look like on a computer. The arrow is pointing to the iPad once it has been recognized and this is where it will appear. At the top left of the screen are music controls to play the music or other files on the computer.

Along the left side are the different areas within iTunes on the computer. At the top left above the arrow is the library where the files and folder hold the data. Select a folder in the library, such as music, and the different music files that are in the library will show up on the right-hand side. Below the arrow are the different playlists, genius lists as well as the online iTunes store. If you have music on the computer and would like to add either one song or a folder full of songs, we do that from the top of iTunes. Click on the word file at the top, there are two options, add files to library and add folder to library. This can be done for music, movies, or even books. Once they are added to the library, they can then be transferred to the iPad.

ITUNES

Select the iPad device in the list and the information about and stored on the iPad will appear. There are two areas that we will discuss on this screen. Below the iPad, on the left, are the folders that are stored on the iPad and the files that are stored in those folders. Across the top, there are options for each of the sync options on the iPad as well as information about the iPad. On this screen, we can see that we have the summary selected at the top. On the

summary screen, we can see the name of the iPad, the total capacity of the iPad, the software version and also the serial number for our device. There is a button to check for software updates online. There is a button to restore the iPad to a previous date when a sync was performed. Along the very bottom, there is a graphical display of items stored on the iPad. This is a great way to quickly see where all your space is being used on the device itself.

Page 227

THE NEW USERS GUIDE TO THE IPAD

Scrolling down on the Summary screen, we see the additional options that are available.

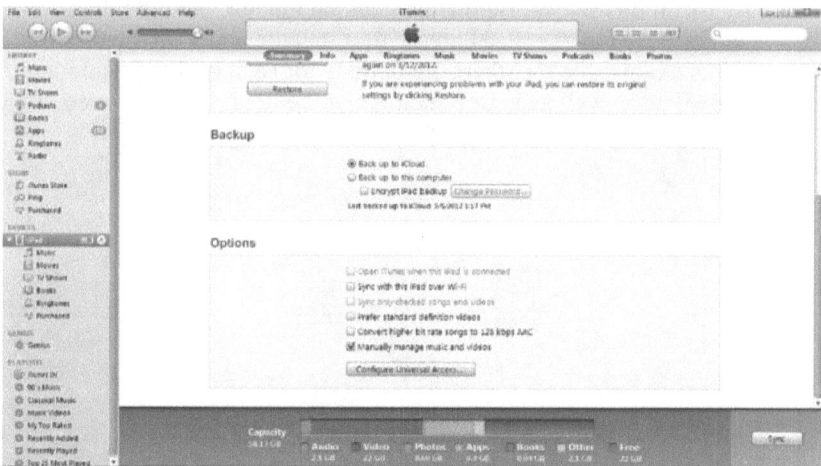

The backup options allow us to use the iCloud (a place on the Apple servers where information can be stored over the internet). Backups can also be stored on the computer. For security reasons, the backup data can also be encrypted with a password. This screen will also show when the last backup was performed.

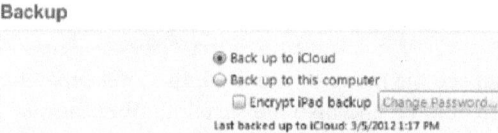

The Options screen is where we can set up the iPad to sync wirelessly. There is an option to open iTunes each time the iPad is detected. "Convert higher bit rate songs", if selected can save on space. Higher bit rate songs require more storage. The option to manually manage music and videos will allow you to drag and drop the songs and movies you want.

Page 228

ITUNES

On the top option list, we have selected the Info option. This is the area where we can sync such information as contacts, calendars, email and more. Select the items that you would like to sync. If your email and information is stored on a corporate email server such as

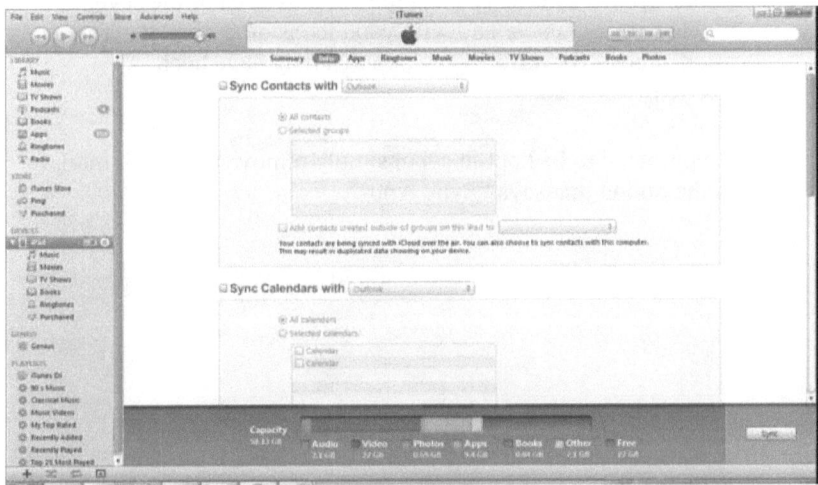

Exchange server, this step would not be necessary since the information is already stored inside of its database. If you are not sure, check with your IT Administrator. The same is true for email services such as Gmail, Hotmail, and others.

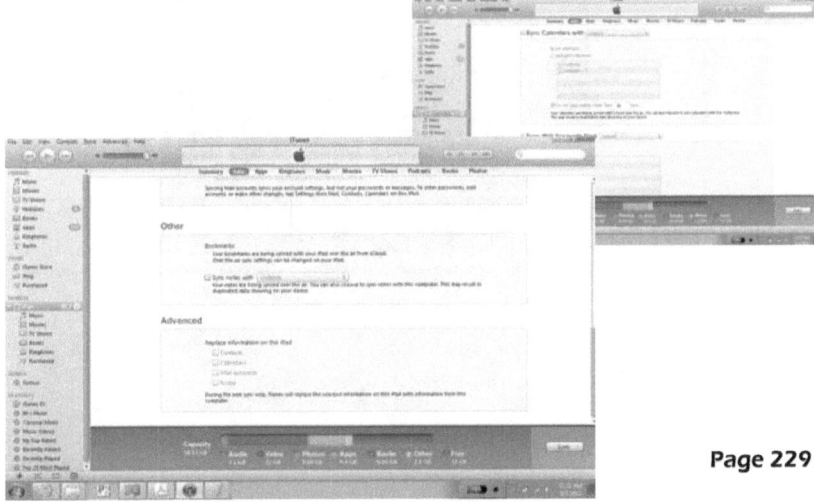

THE NEW USERS GUIDE TO THE IPAD

Apps are the programs that are used on the iPad. When the Apps option is selected, the apps that are on the iPad will be displayed. Individual apps can be checked or unchecked. There is a photo of the iPad and below it are the individual screens that are configured on the iPad. On this screen, you can look at how each of the seven available screens appear and with what icons on each page. This location is great for restoring an app that may have been inadvertently deleted.

If no apps need to be kept in sync, simply remove the check mark from the option that says "Sync Apps".

ITUNES

The ringtone option was primarily used for iPhones. Since the iPad does not use ringtones, I would recommend not using it.

The Sync Music options allow a user to sync all music or just a folder with music stored in it.

THE NEW USERS GUIDE TO THE IPAD

The Sync Movie options allow a user to sync an entire movie library or just individual movies. A word of caution here, movie files can be very large, and as such, will use up your memory quickly on the iPad.

TV show options are where you can sync individual episodes or full seasons, as well as all TV shows.

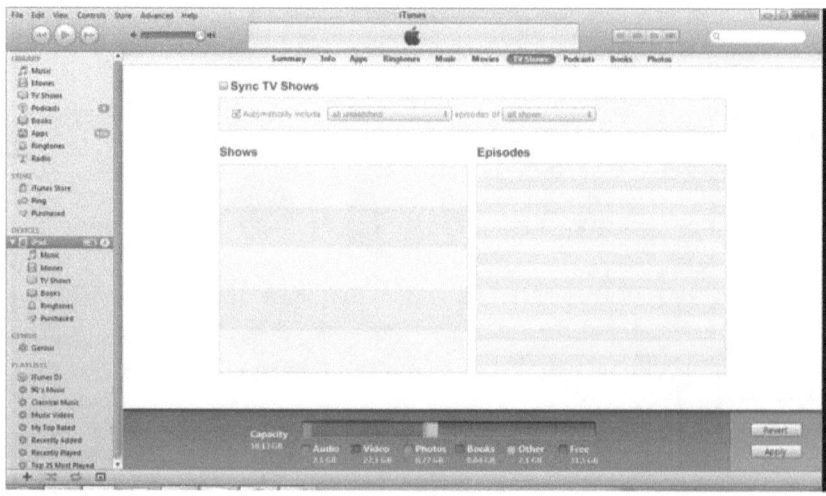

ITUNES

Podcasts are similar to TV shows. Podcasts are broadcast in episode format. Using the Sync options, everything or just certain episodes can be kept in sync.

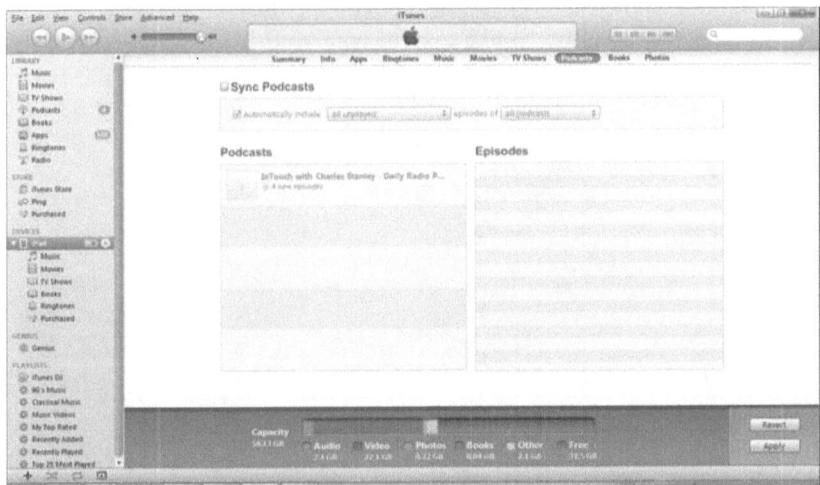

Sync options for books can be set for all books or only individual books. This is great for books that have already been read that may not need to stay on the iPad.

THE NEW USERS GUIDE TO THE IPAD

The Sync options on photos can be set for an entire library of photos or simply one folder where photos can be kept that you would like to have on the iPad. Photos can also be large so before you sync a bazillion photos and run out of room on the iPad, think ahead about what photos you would like to have with you.

If you use the right mouse button on the iPad itself in the list, you will be presented with some additional options. Eject will safety disconnect the iPad so that it can be disconnected cleanly. New Playlist will create playlists of songs. Sync can be performed from this menu. A sync can also be performed using the Sync button at the bottom of the different screens. Transfer Purchases will copy data that was purchased on the iPad and copy it to the computer. Back Up will perform a back up of the device. Restore will allow you to restore the device to a previous back up. Reset Warning will clear any error or warning messages that have shown up.

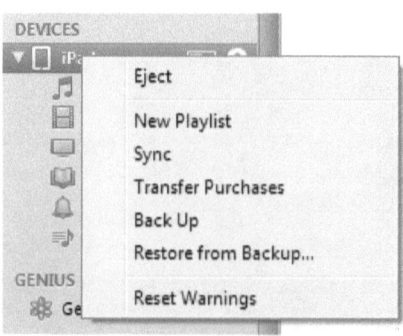

ITUNES

In this screen, we have gone into our music library on the computer, located a song we wanted on the iPad and dragged it over to the iPad and dropped the song onto the iPad. This is an example of manually managing songs. The option to manually manage media was listed on the summary page. Checkmark the option to manually manage media, and you drag new things into the iPad and drag existing items off of it.

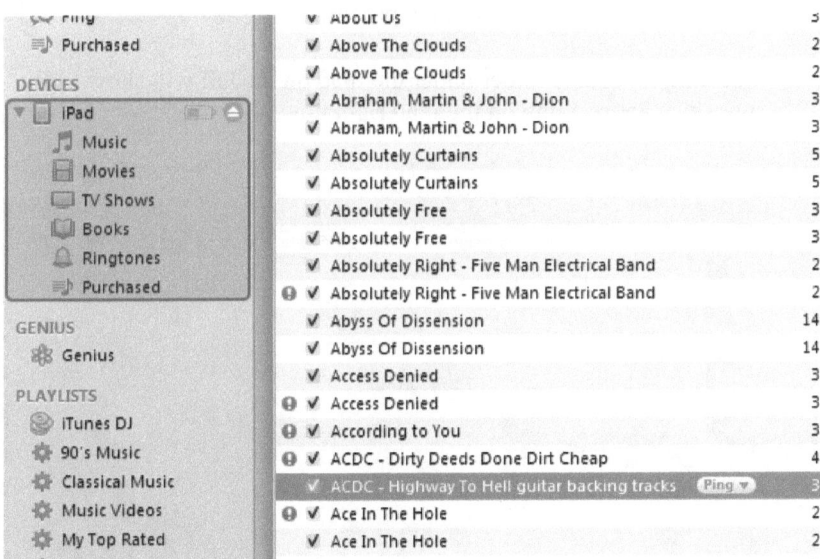

While a copy is being formed or a sync is being performed, the top of the screen will show an update in progress and it will show complete when done.

Page 235

THE NEW USERS GUIDE TO THE IPAD

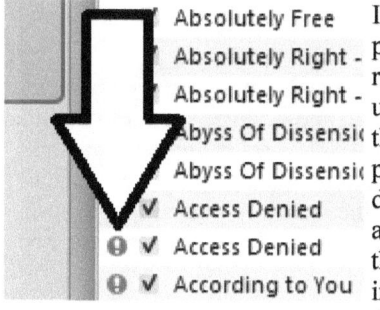 If one of the songs in the library has a problem such as it was deleted or renamed, the exclamation mark will let us know that there is a problem with this song. Another way to tell about a problem, would be when you try to drag and drop the item onto the iPad and you see a circle with a line through it. A circle with a line will indicate that there is a problem with the process.

Selecting the music folder under the iPad on the left will show us the songs that are residing on the iPad right now.

Page 236

ITUNES

Right click on a specific item in the iPad library and there will be additional actions that can be performed on an individual item. More information about an item can be displayed. A rating can be given to an item to let others know what we thought of this item. These ratings are used by the genius program. This item can be copied or deleted from this location from the menu. The items can be sorted to several different orders.

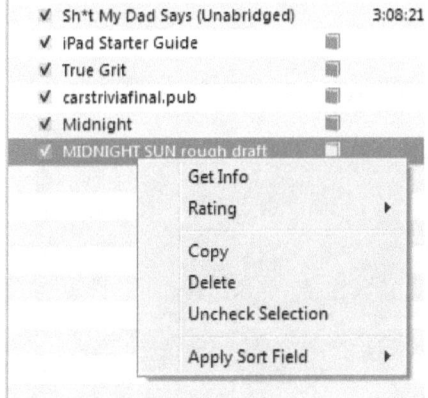

It is advisable to always eject the iPad before disconnecting it from the computer. Right click on the iPad and select eject or hit the Eject button next to the iPad.

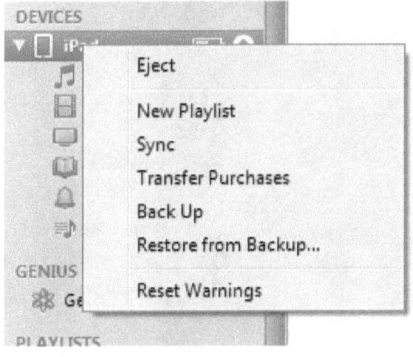

THE NEW USERS GUIDE TO THE IPAD

Safari

Safari is the internet browser used to access web pages on the internet.

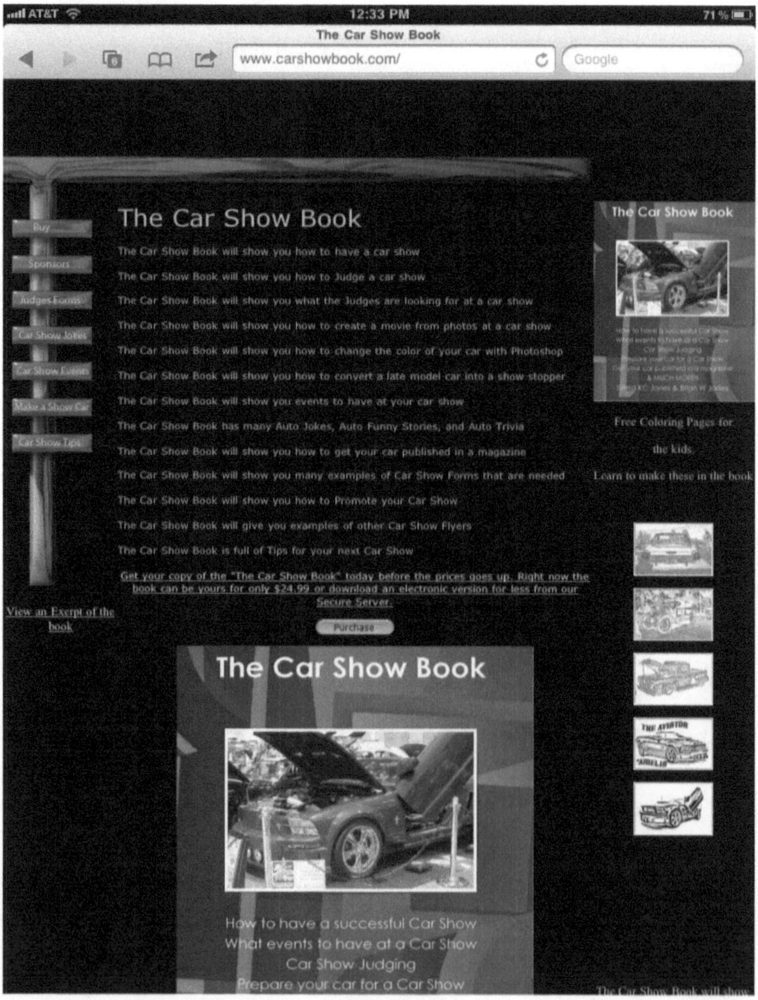

SAFARI

To go to a website, type in the address such as www.me.com

It is not necessary to type the www or the .com, simply type yahoo

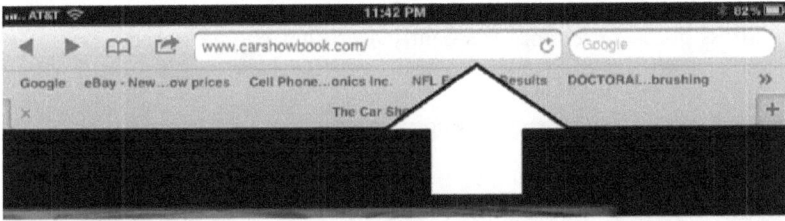

In the figure below:

Arrow 1—navigate forward and backward on pages.

Arrow 2—bookmarks or favorite websites that we have saved.

Arrow 3—The action button. These actions are detailed later in the chapter.

Arrow 4—Search Dialog. This box will use your default search engine (set in the settings) to search for key words.

Arrow 5—This is the button to add another tab for additional sites.

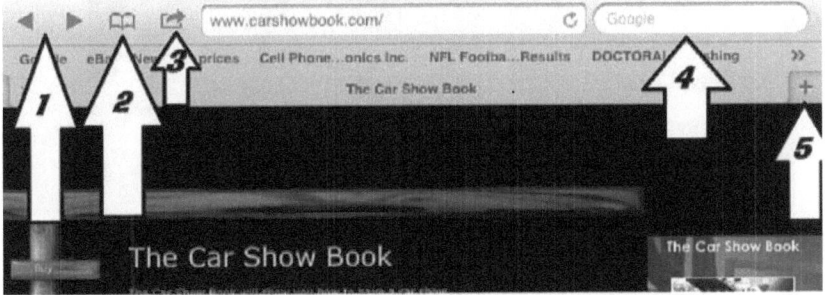

THE NEW USERS GUIDE TO THE IPAD

The Bookmarks are websites that we have marked with a bookmark as a favorite site. The Reading List is a grouping of sites that contain mostly text for reading. The History folder will contain a list of sites previously visited. The Bookmarks Bar is the bar right below the search box and address box, where more frequently used sites can be stored. The other items in this list are websites that we will frequently visit.

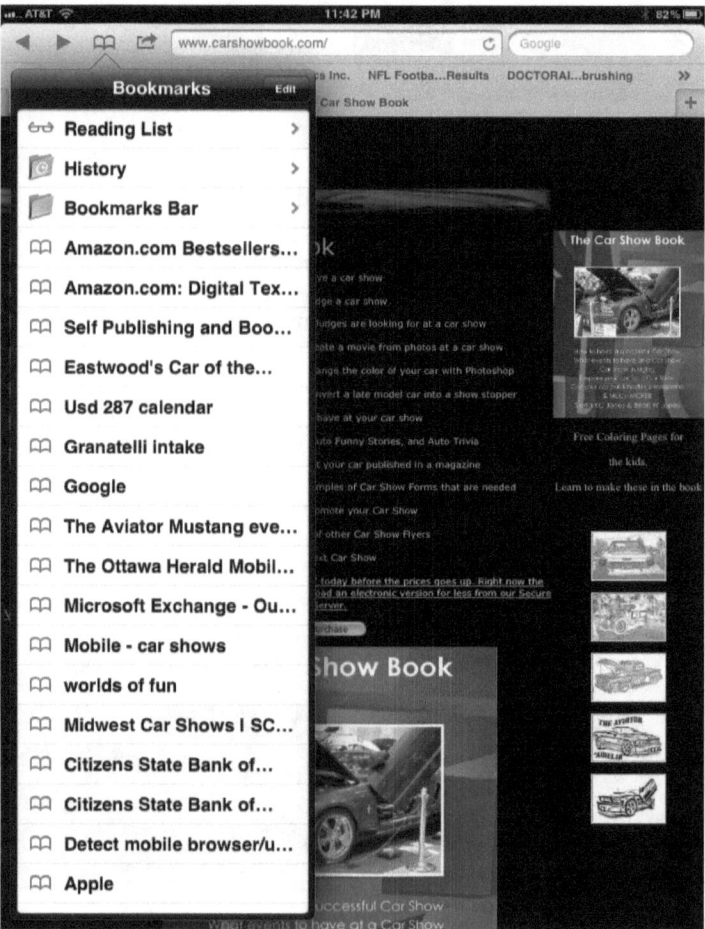

SAFARI

The action button has several functions that can be performed on the current website.

Add Bookmark—this option will create a favorite or bookmark in the bookmarks lists that is available when you click the open book icon.

Add to Reading List—this option will create a listing for this website in the reading list, available when you select the open book icon and then select the glasses icon.

Add to Home Screen—this option will create a favorite or a bookmark for the site, but rather than add it to the bookmark list, it will create a shortcut to the website and put an icon on the main screen of the iPad. This allows a user to get to a site using an icon rather than opening safari and then opening the bookmark.

Mail Link to this Page—this option will take the address of the website we are currently on, then add the web address to a new email to allow us to send a link to the site to someone else.

Tweet—this option will allow us to create a tweet in Twitter about this web site.

Print—using the AirPrint option on a printer, the print action will print a hard copy of the web page. The printer must have AirPrint option built into it. For a complete list of printers that support AirPrint, consult the Apple web site.

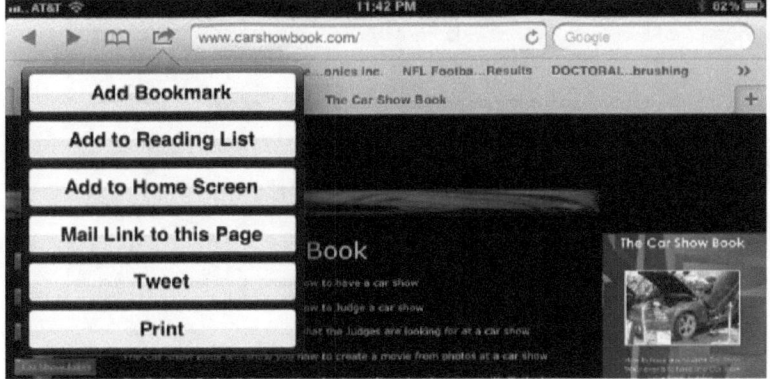

THE NEW USERS GUIDE TO THE IPAD

When you elect to save a bookmark, the window below will open. The address of the site will be listed. There is an option to change the name of the bookmark to make it more descriptive and easier to remember. There is an option to add the link to the bookmarks bar as well as listing it in the bookmarks as a favorite site.

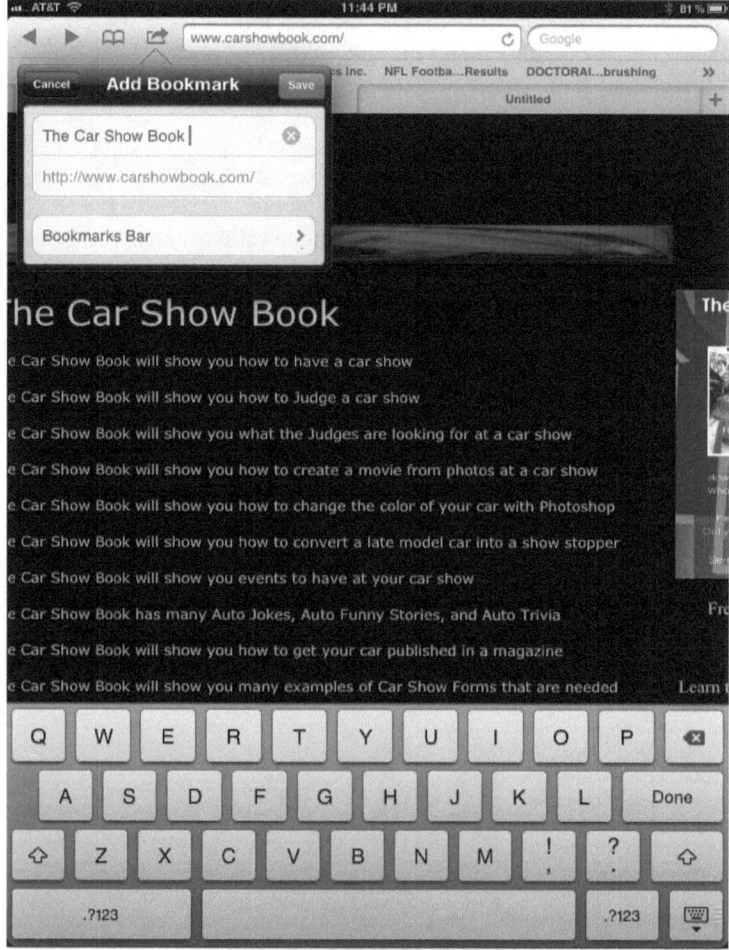

SAFARI

When the "Add to Home" option is selected from the actions icon, the following window will pop up. On this screen, there needs to be a name to describe the shortcut. This will be the name that will appear under the icon on the main page. The picture to the left of the name will be the icon that will show up on the main page. These are great for web sites that are visited regularly.

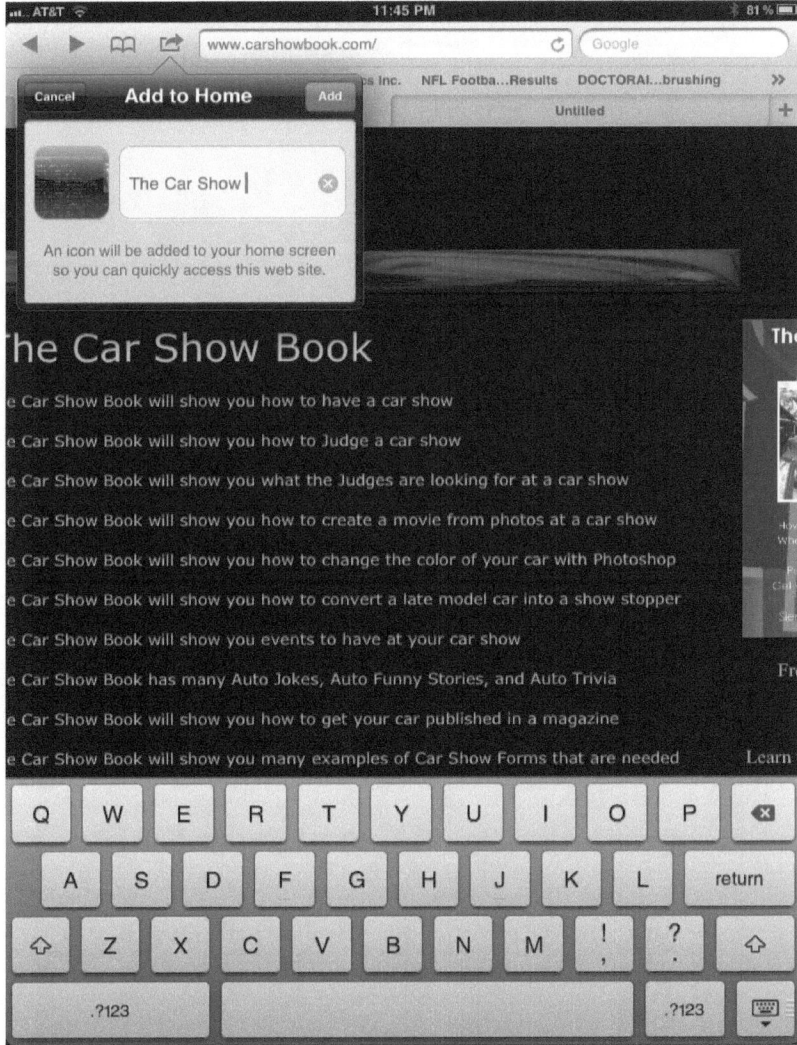

THE NEW USERS GUIDE TO THE IPAD

From the actions menu, the screen below will demonstrate what the "Send Link" email will look like. At this point, the subject can be changed and information entered into the body of the message. Other recipients can be added at this time. Select the send button once the email is composed and ready to send.

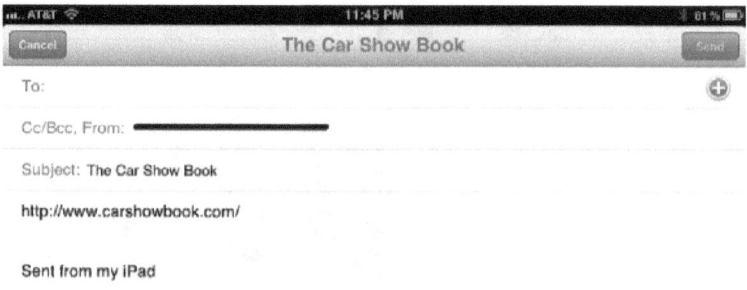

Page 244

SAFARI

If your printer has AirPrint capabilities, select print from the action button and the number of copies. When ready to print, select the print button. AirPrint is a specific capability and option that is only available on some printers.

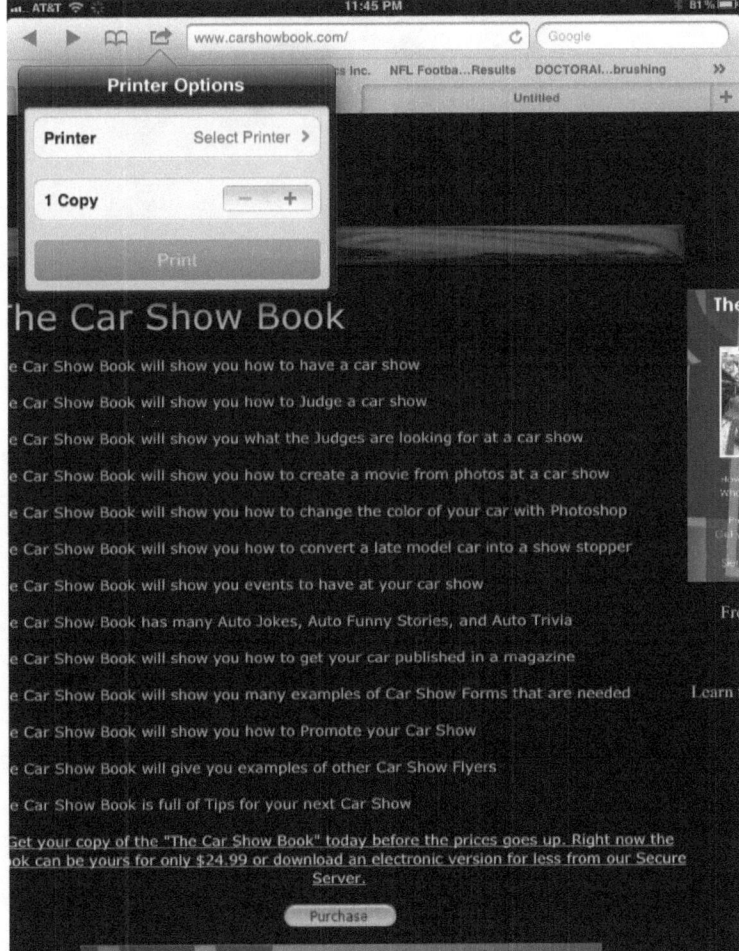

THE NEW USERS GUIDE TO THE IPAD

The search box, in the upper right hand corner, will allow a user to search for specific key words. The search engine that will be used will be the one that was selected in the settings area. Past search words and phrases will show in the drop down.

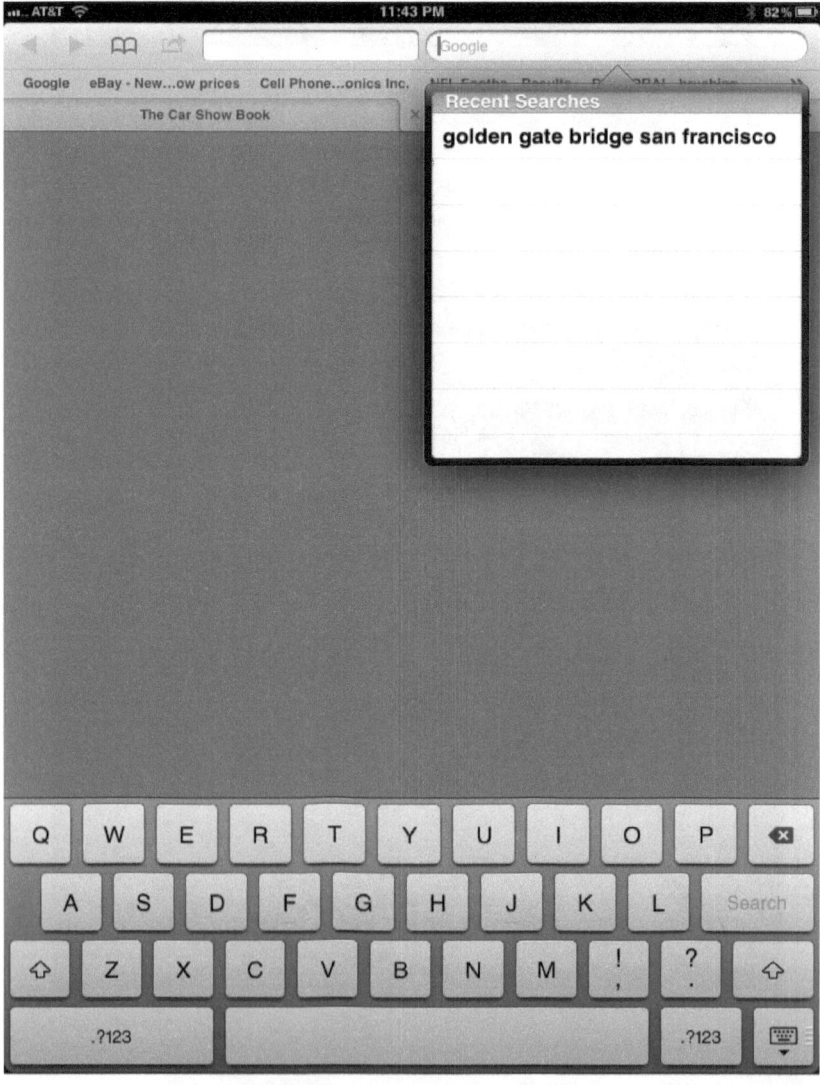

SAFARI

Safari supports tab browsing. A tab is just a new instance of a web browser. Using tabs, a user can have multiple websites open at the same time and switch between them. In the diagram below, we see that there are three tabs open with different sites. The plus sign to the right of the tabs will allow additional tabs to be opened.

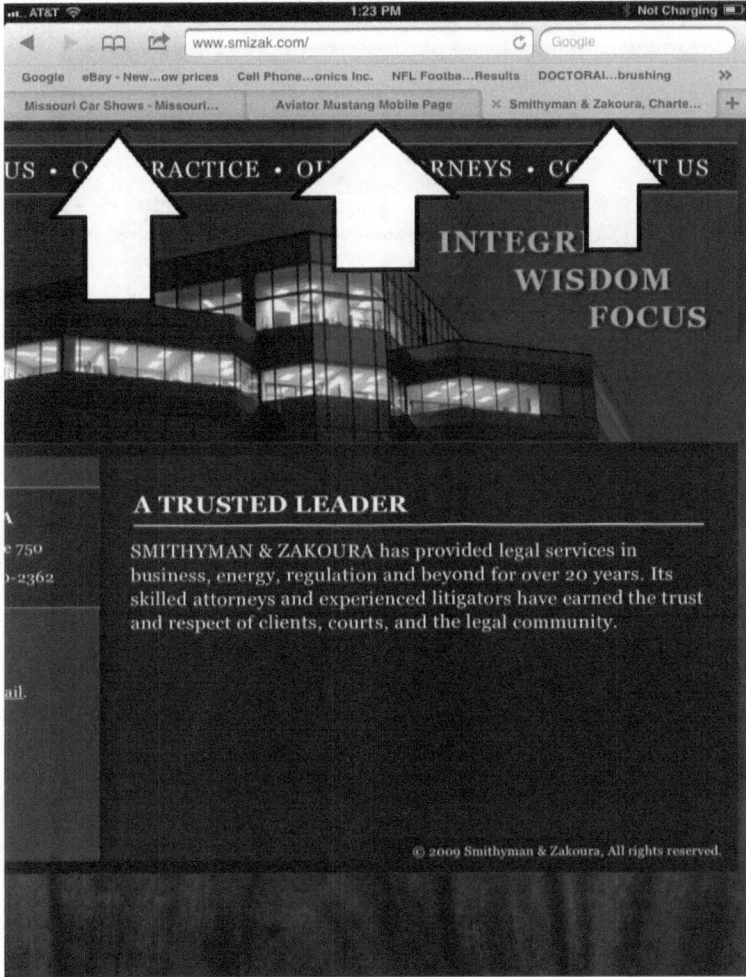

THE NEW USERS GUIDE TO THE IPAD

If you find a photo on a website that you would like to save to your photo library, hold a finger on the photo until the menu below opens. Select "Save Image" to save a copy of the photo into your photo library. The copy option will copy the photo to the clipboard so that it can be pasted into another application.

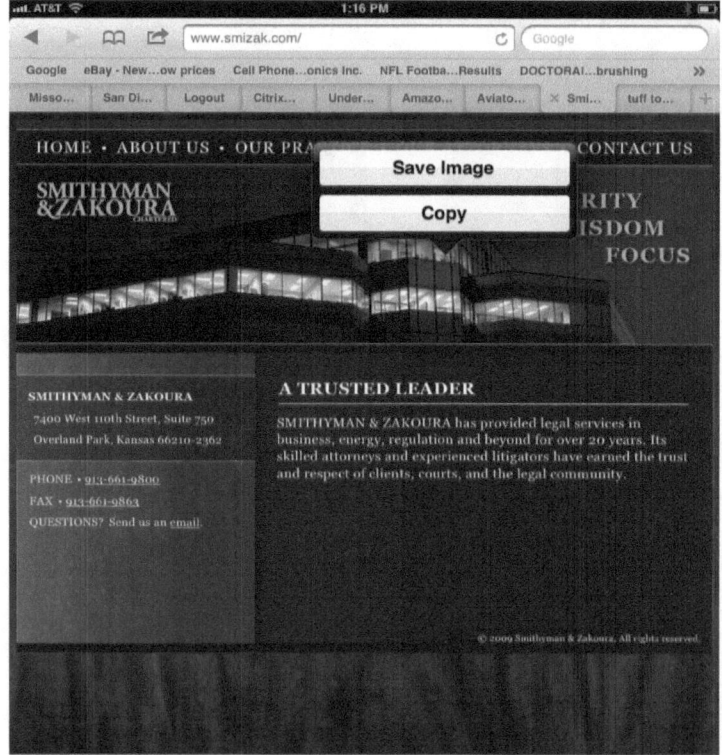

SAFARI

When there is a link on a web page, tapping it will cause the Safari browser to navigate to that page. If you hold your finger on a link for a few seconds, you will get a menu. At the top, the arrow is pointing to the exact location the link is going to. There is a great way to verify where the destination is. Click Open to open the link in the existing tab. Open in New Tab will add a tab to the Safari with the new destination on that new tab. The Copy button will allow you to copy the link into an email or a document. The reading list is a listing of sites where there is content to read, these are typically text articles on webpages.

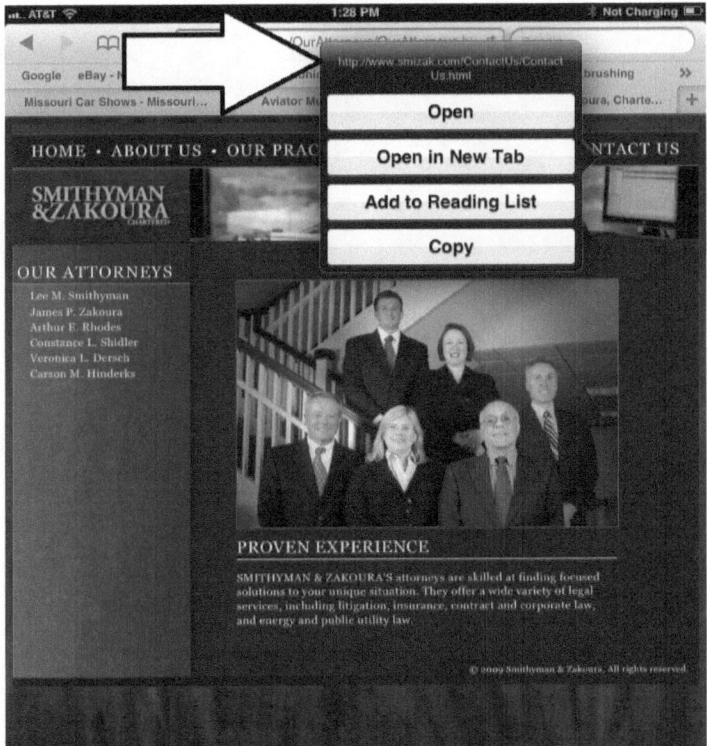

THE NEW USERS GUIDE TO THE IPAD

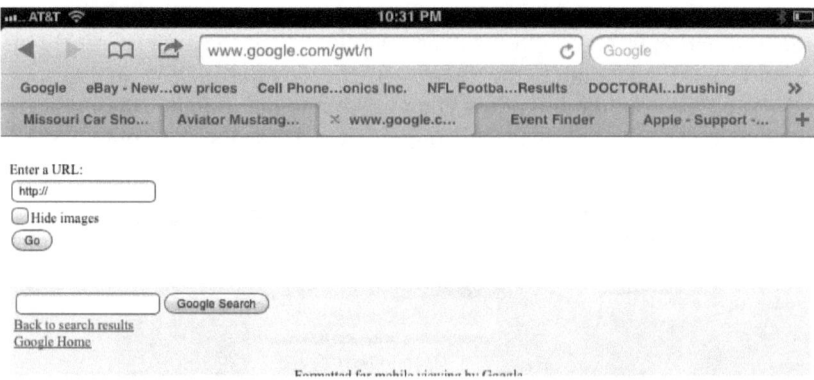

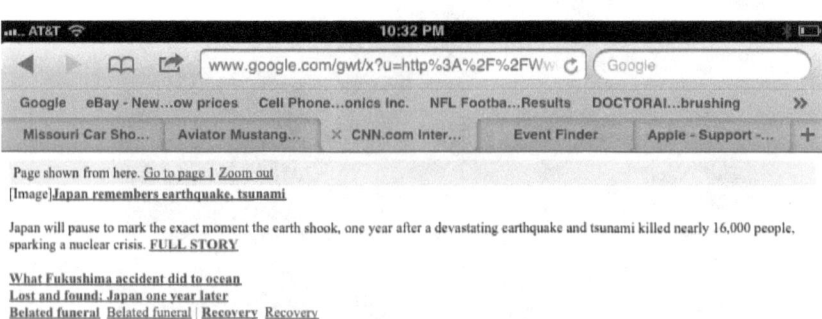

SAFARI

Tap to center and expand.

When you tap twice on a photo on a website, Safari will attempt to center the image and expand it to a larger view. Double tap while it is expanded and the item will return to normal size.

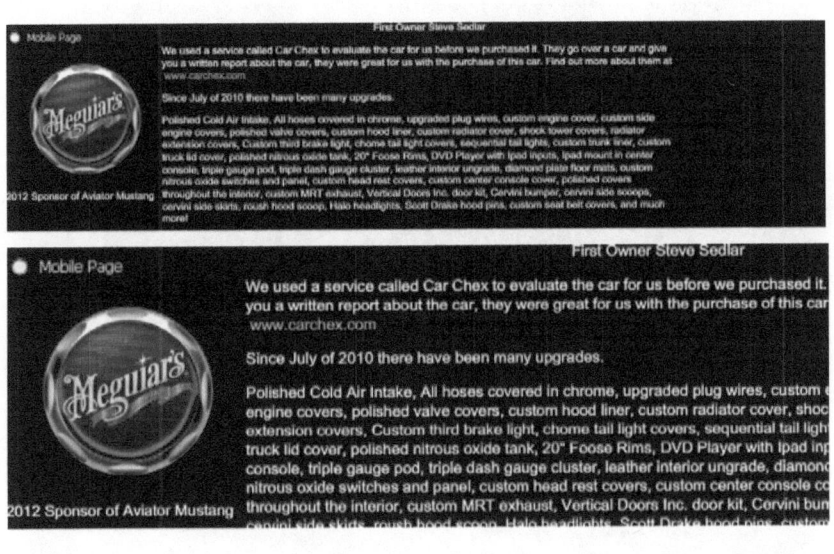

THE NEW USERS GUIDE TO THE IPAD

Tap to bottom center and go down exactly one page and center.

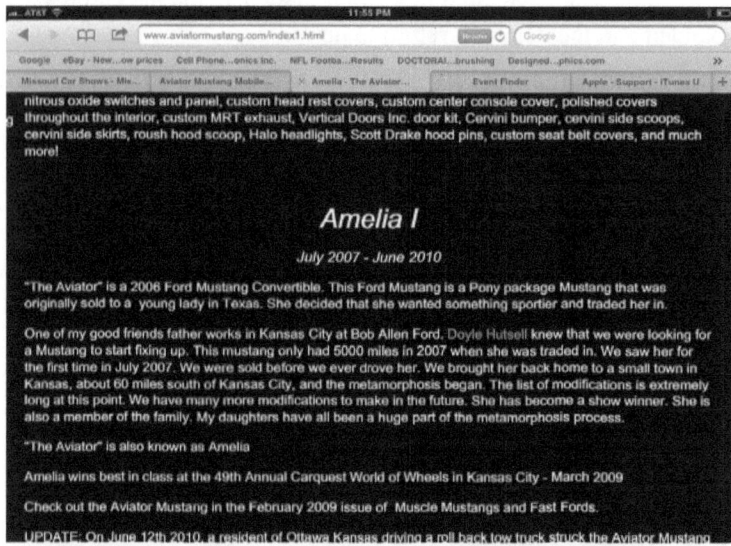

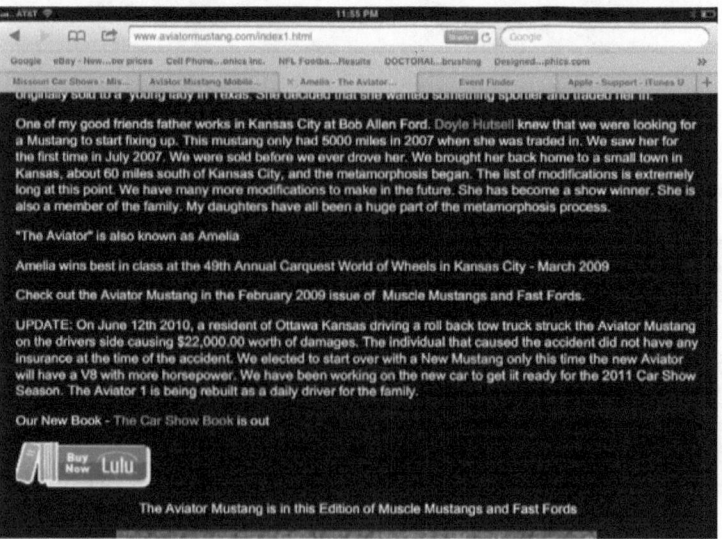

SAFARI

In the upper right-hand corner, type the search criteria desired. Below the list of suggested search terms is the box to search on the current page.

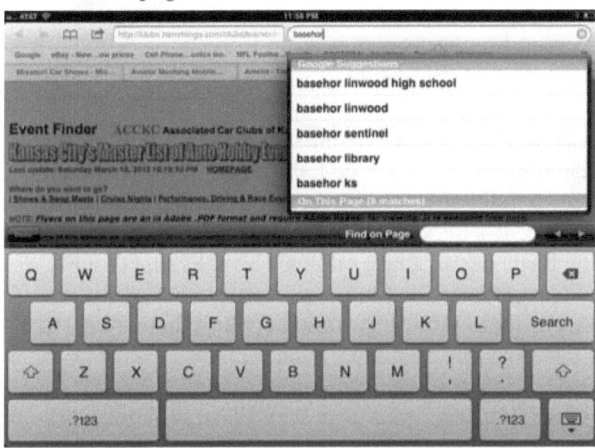

In this example, we can tell that our search word was listed a total of eight times on the existing page. Using the arrows to the right of the search box, we can go through each instance of the word.

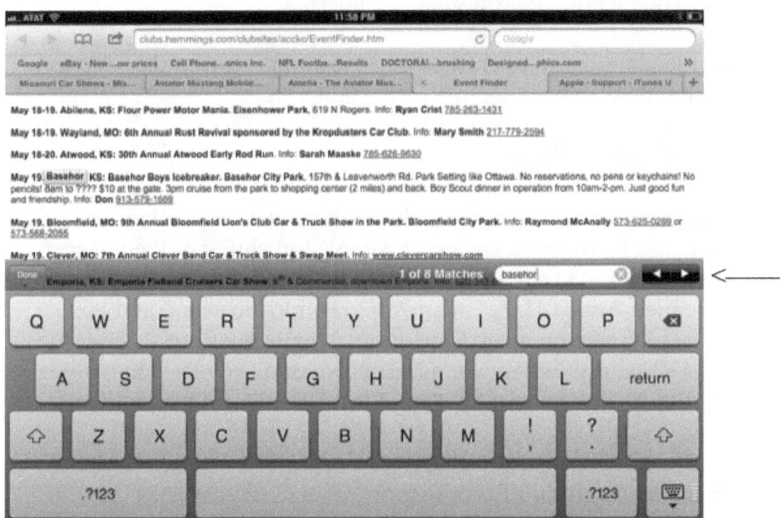

Flash and why it will not work on an iPad.

One developer states that:

It's not because of slow mobile performance, battery drain or crashes. It's because of the hover or mouse over problem.

Many (if not most) current Flash games, menus, and even video players require a visible mouse pointer. They are coded to rely on the difference between hovering over something (mouse over) vs. actually clicking. This distinction is not rare. It's pervasive, fundamental to interactive design, and vital to the basic use of Flash content. New Flash content designed just for touchscreens can be done, but people want existing Flash sites to work. All of them—not just some here and there—and in a usable manner. That's impossible no matter what.

The more common things that were said as to why Flash will not work on an iPad are:

Slow Mobile Performance. Poor Battery Performance.

Arguments between Apple and Adobe regarding one having an open standard and one having a proprietary standard.

Flash is the leading cause of crashes on Mac computers, so they were kept from the iPads to keep the platform stable.

Other words regarding Flash:

The iPad launch served as a sore reminder that, yeah, if you buy one of these, you better be ready to say goodbye to a big chunk of the internet. But Apple isn't sad to see it go. According to Wired, Steve Jobs reportedly called Adobe "lazy" at an Apple employee event, and then went on to explain the company's position: "Apple does not support Flash because it is so buggy. Whenever a Mac crashes, more often than not it's because of Flash. No one will be using Flash. The world is moving to HTML5."

Whatever the reason for no Flash support, iPad users just need to understand the limitation in their tablets.

SAFARI

Web Video Viewing

Some internet video sites have a button to view the video in full-screen mode; however, if they do not, you can use two fingers on the iPad screen and move the fingers outward to go full screen. Bring the fingers together to go away from full-screen mode.

The photo in the lower left corner shows a full screen view of a video. While the video is playing, tap the screen twice and the playing video will zoom in as shown in the photo in the lower right. To zoom back out, double tap the screen again.

THE NEW USERS GUIDE TO THE IPAD

Reminders

Reminders are simple to-dos that will remind you about things that need to be done or have been completed.

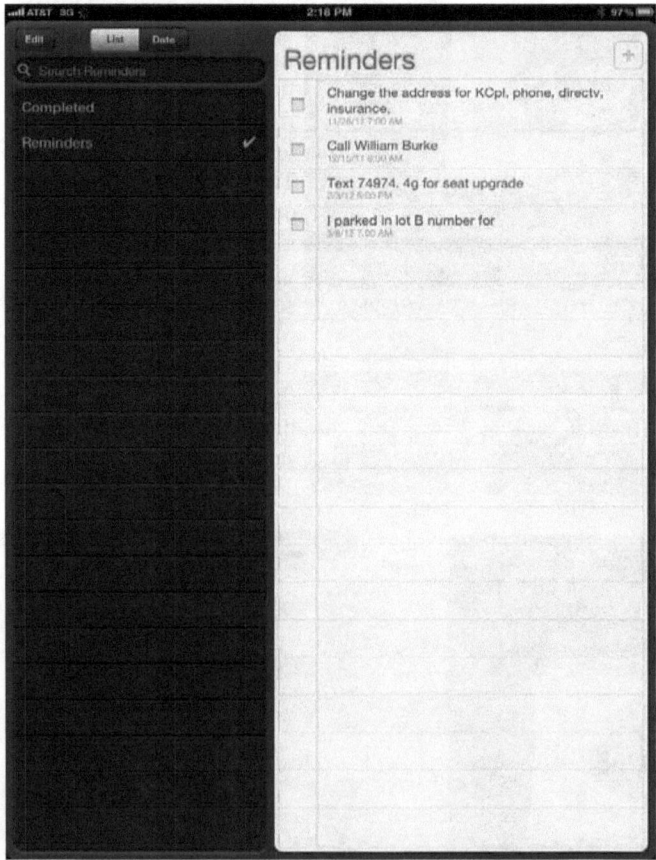

REMINDERS

Reminders are to-do's or tasks that are scheduled on the iPad to remind you about items. If you have an appointment at a certain time, reminders will flash a reminder on the screen about the appointment. In the photo below, we are showing reminders that are still outstanding. On the left, we are showing the reminders by date. Select a specific date on the calendar to view the appointments on that date.

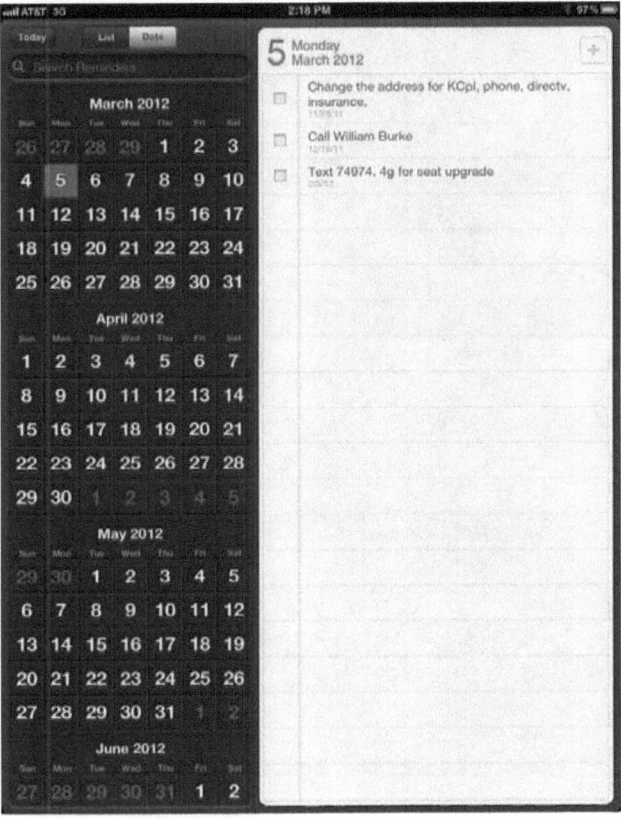

We have changed the view of the reminders to a List format. We have also changed to the completed reminders. Select completed or reminders to switch between current or past reminders. A completed reminder will have a check mark in it. Place a checkmark next to a reminder to complete that reminder. This action will move the reminder to the completed list.

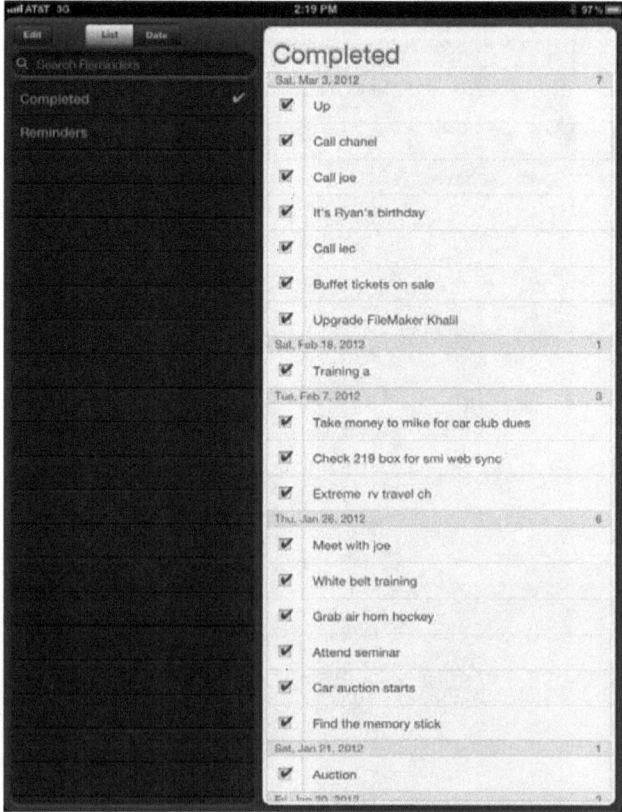

REMINDERS

To create a new reminder, select the open area under the last reminder. Type the reminder text on the area below the past reminder. On this screen, we are showing all the reminders in date format. Below each reminder is the date when the original reminder was scheduled. Since there are no checks, these overdue reminders continue to show up every day until a checkmark is used to complete them.

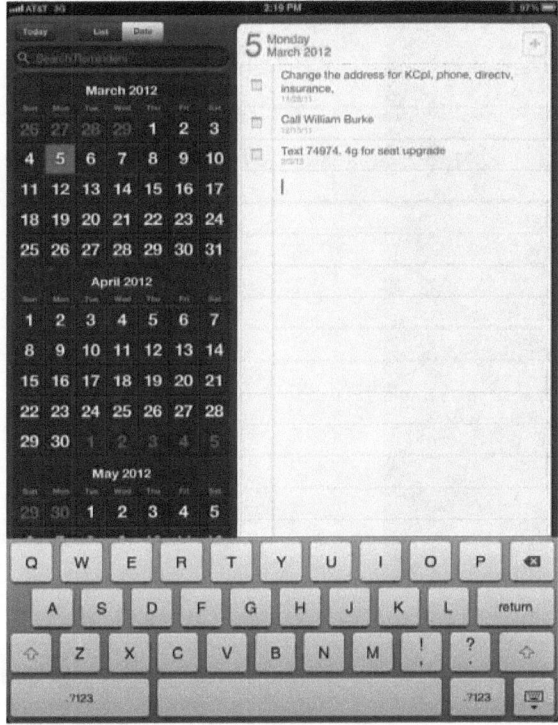

THE NEW USERS GUIDE TO THE IPAD

In the photo below, we have added a new reminder to remind us to "Publish iPad book." As you can tell there is no date associated with the reminder. This is a basic reminder.

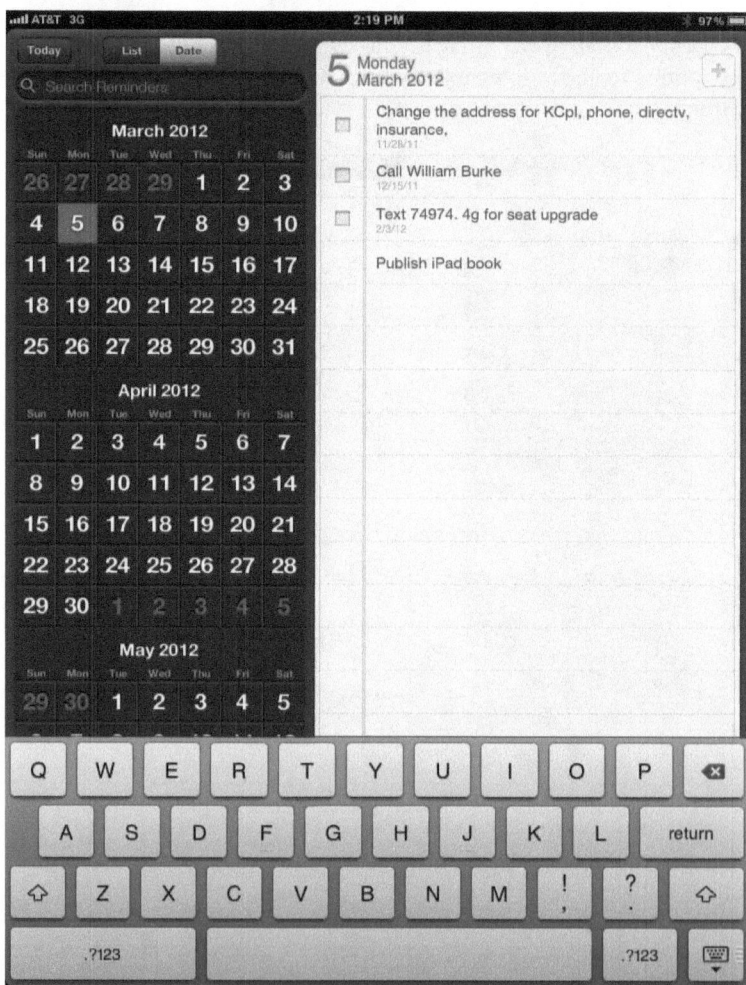

REMINDERS

Once an item is created, details about the reminder can be added. On this screen we are showing the short detail window. On this window, there is an option to "Remind Me" where you may select a date and time for the reminder. At that time, a reminder will flash on the screen. There is an option to show more detail about the reminder which will open the long version. To delete the reminder, select the delete button. The reminder can be cancelled by selecting the Cancel button or saved using the Done button.

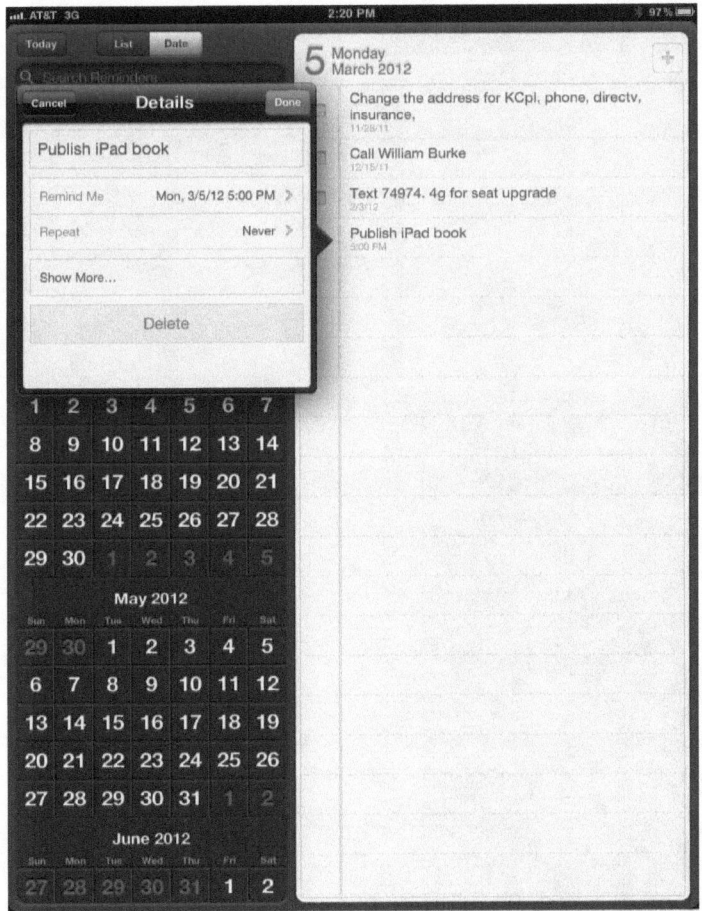

THE NEW USERS GUIDE TO THE IPAD

In the window below, we have selected to show more information about the reminder. On the long detail window, there are several additional options available. The Repeat option will allow for repeating appointments. The Priority option will allow you to create prioritized reminders. The Notes option will allow comments or notes to be added to a reminder.

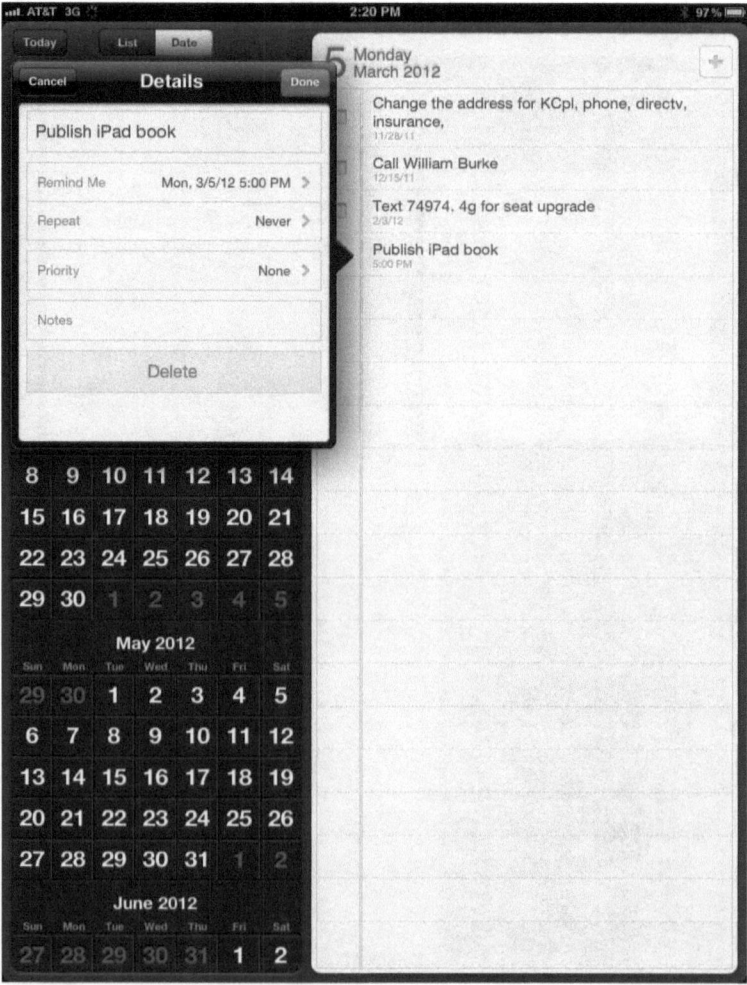

Page 262

REMINDERS

This is what the alert will look like on the iPad at the specified time when the reminder was set. When this alert goes off, the information about the reminder will be displayed on the main screen. If you use the MobileMe account from Apple, this reminder will also go off on all your Apple devices at the same time.

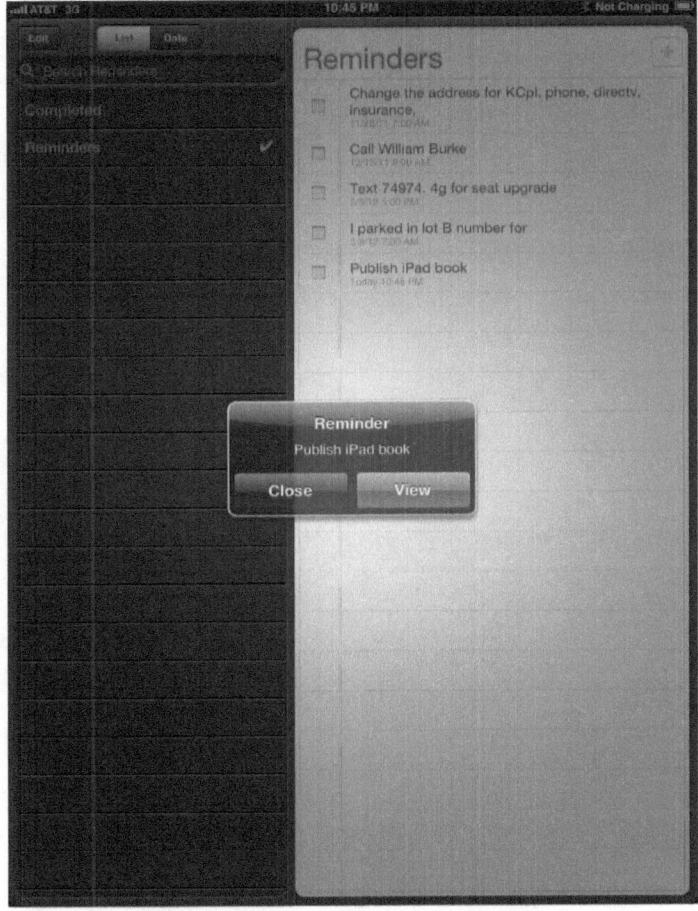

THE NEW USERS GUIDE TO THE IPAD

Photos

The Photos gallery on the iPad can be used to upload photos to websites or to do many other things.

PHOTOS

At the bottom of this photo, are a series of small thumbnails. Run your finger across these thumbnails to scrub through the photos in the library. In the upper left is a button to change libraries. On the upper right is a button to start a slide show of the photos.

THE NEW USERS GUIDE TO THE IPAD

On the screen below, we have selected one of the photos in our library.

PHOTOS

Move your finger left or right across the photo to move to the next photo in the library.

THE NEW USERS GUIDE TO THE IPAD

Use your finger and tap twice on a photo quickly, the photo will automatically zoom in. The other way to zoom on a photo would be to use two fingers placed on the photo, then move your fingers away from each other. Each time you perform this action, it will zoom in more. Place two fingers on the photo, and pinch the fingers together and the photo will zoom out. Double tapping on the photo will also cause the photo to zoom back to the original view.

PHOTOS

In the middle of the window, at the top, there are options to view the gallery of photos differently. The screen below shows the Photos view of the gallery.

THE NEW USERS GUIDE TO THE IPAD

The Photo Stream view will show the photos that are stored on the internet in the iCloud account. Photos from the main Photos folder will each be copied to the Photo Stream automatically. The last option at the top is the Album view. Albums are folders that can be created to organize photos into individual folders.

PHOTOS

At the top right is an actions button. The selected photo can be emailed to anyone from the email photo option. The selected photo can be sent with the messaging application to anyone that can receive messages using the message option. The assign to Contact option, will allow a user to assign a photo to a contact. Anytime you get information from this contact, the photo will be displayed. The Use as Wallpaper option will allow the photo to be used as the wallpaper screen or as the lock screen. The Tweet option will allow a Twitter user to tweet this photo. The Print option will use AirPrint to print copies of this photo to a printer that has AirPrint capability. The Copy Photo option will allow copies to be moved to other albums or locations while leaving the original in the existing location.

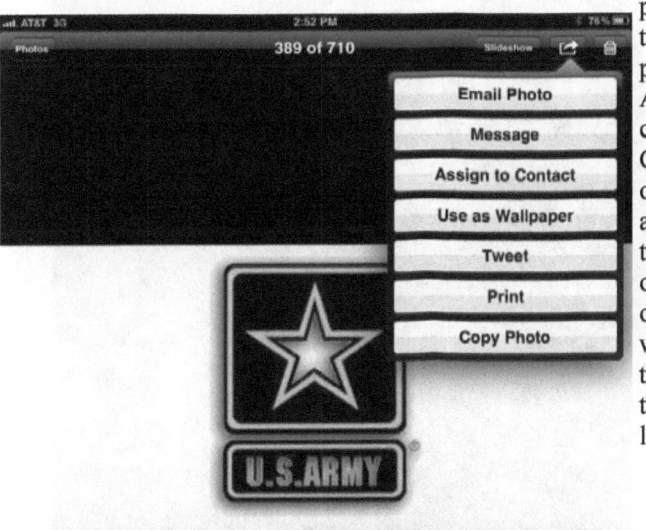

In the Albums gallery view of photos, the albums that we have created will be displayed on the main screen. There will be a preview of the photos in the album showing on the icon. In the upper right-hand corner is an edit button to edit the album.

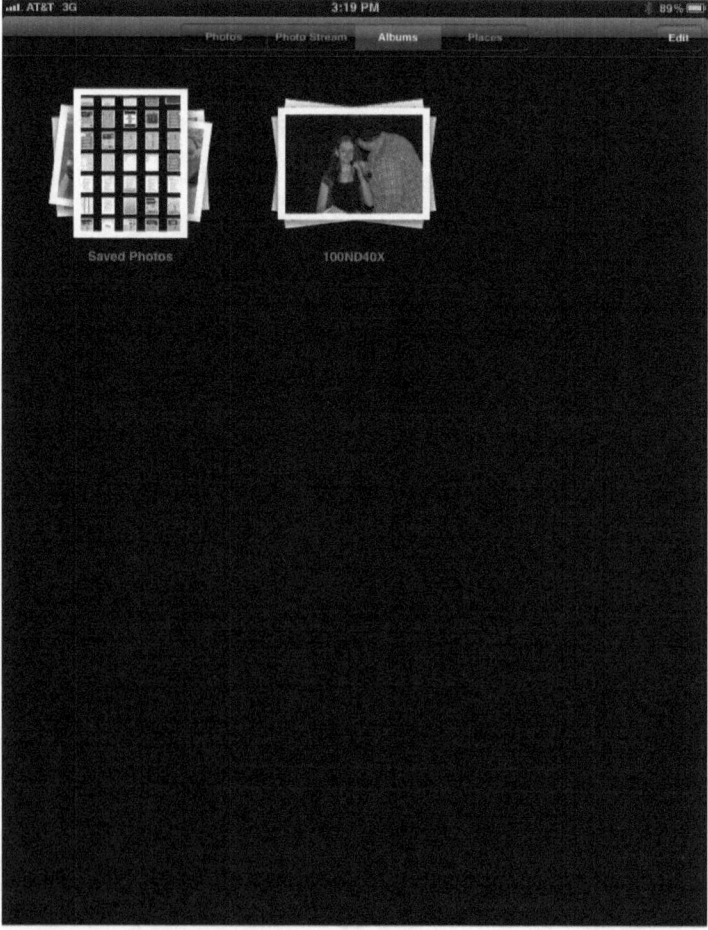

PHOTOS

In this photo, we are looking at an album where we have selected the Edit option on the previous screen. A new album can be created by selecting the New Album button in the upper left-hand corner. When a new album is created, a name is assigned to the album. After the album is created, a wizard will start asking what photos you would like to add to this newly created album. When the photos have been added, select the Done button to complete the new photo album. When the Edit option is selected, any album created by you will have an "X" in the corner to allow you to delete the entire album.

273

THE NEW USERS GUIDE TO THE IPAD

In this photo, we have added a new photo, so the wizard is asking for a name for the new photo library.

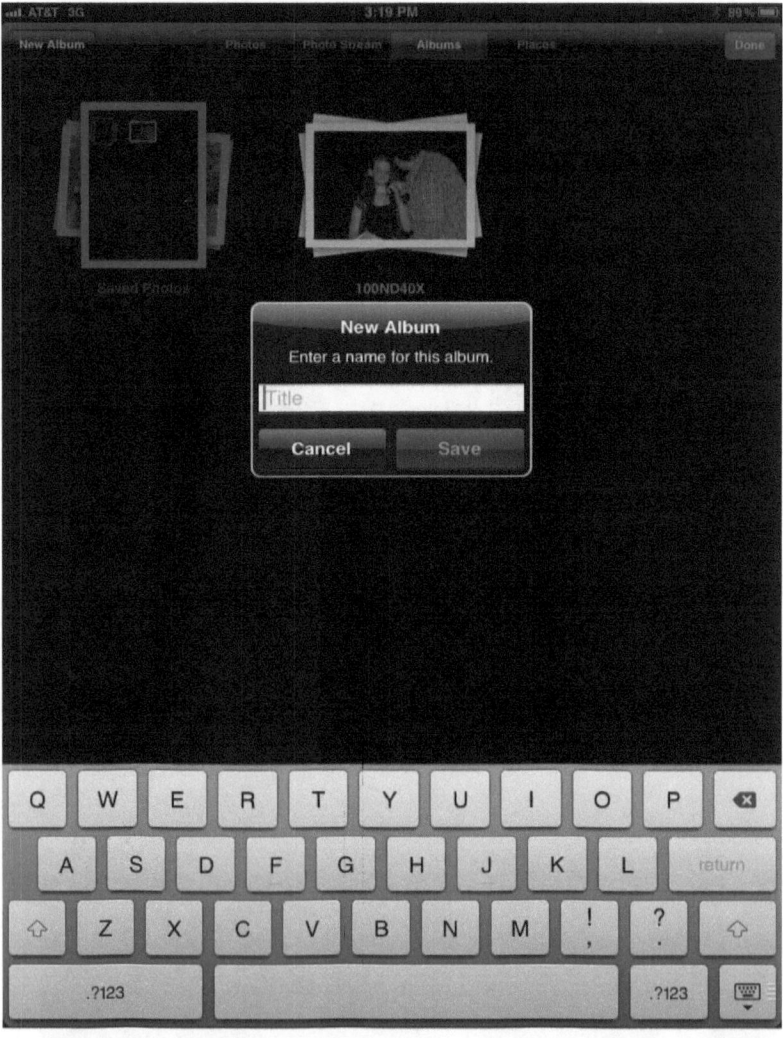

PHOTOS

Inside of an album, there are several options available. From the "Share" button, we can email the photo, Tweet the photo through Twitter, Print the photo, or send it through Message.

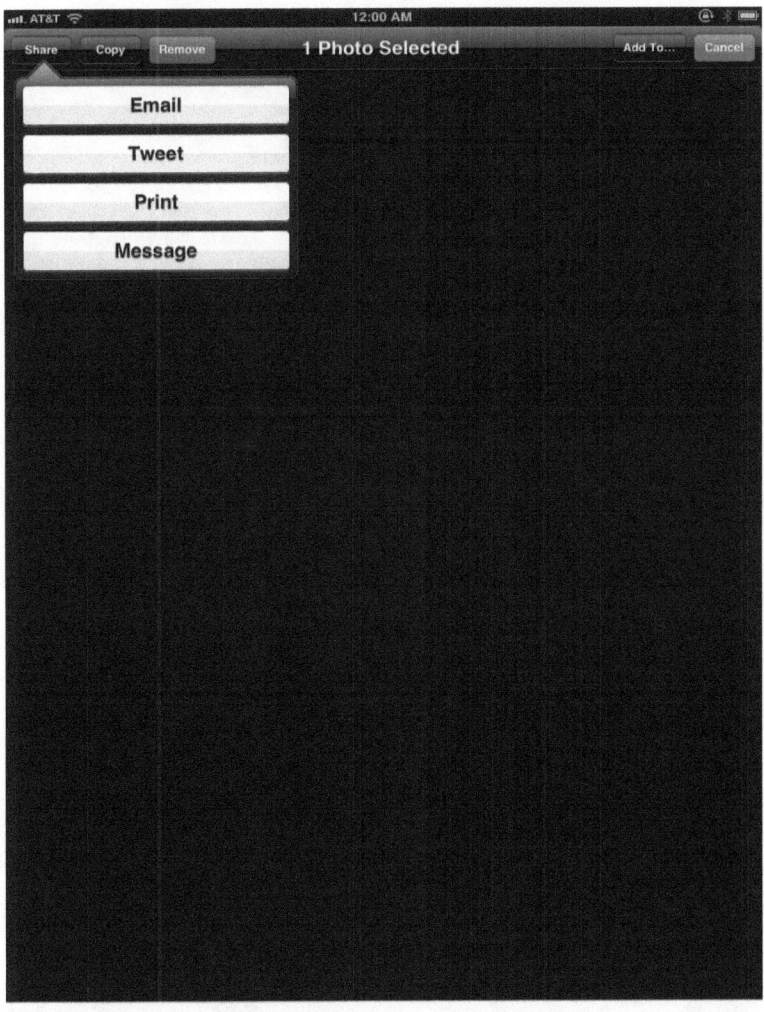

THE NEW USERS GUIDE TO THE IPAD

The "Add to…" button will allow us to take all the selections and add them to an existing album or add them to a new album.

PHOTOS

Select one photo or many photos. When the photos are selected, the selections can be copied to other areas or completely removed from the library.

The Slideshow button will display all the photos in the folder in a slideshow format. A song can be added to play while the slideshow is playing. The slideshow will only show each photo one time, and then quit. There are transitions that will decide how the photos will transition from one photo to the next. There are a few transitions to choose from.

PHOTOS

In this photo, we are in the process of pinching the photo to close it out. When the pinch is completed, the photo will be back in the gallery with all the other photos. For this option, just keep closing your fingers together until the photo closes out.

Place three or more fingers on a photo and the photo can be rotated on the screen of the iPad. Rotate it as far around as you would like.

PHOTOS

While using two fingers to shrink a photo, it can then be moved around on the screen by simply moving your fingers.

THE NEW USERS GUIDE TO THE IPAD

 iPad Music Player
(Note: On older IOS this is iPod)

The iPad music player was designed after the well-used Apple iPod. The controls along the top allow a user to control the music or other media that can be played.

 Software Volume Control

The controls below allow the ability to play, back up one song, go forward one song.

The area in the middle at the top will show us information about the song that is selected. The slider below the name is the scrubber to move through the music easier.

This button is the shuffle button, to shuffle the music rather than play them in their original order.

Along the bottom is a series of buttons to sort through the music. List all by songs, artists, albums, genres, or more. The icon that looks like an atom is the genius listing. The store button will take us directly to the iTunes store.

The additional options that can be sorted are listed in this photo.

Page 282

MUSIC PLAYER

The photo below shows our music listed by playlist. A playlist is a grouping of songs that were created by the user. A playlist can have only a few songs or a large list. The content in a playlist can be modified at any time. To modify a playlist, select the playlist to open it, then there will be an edit button on the upper right-hand corner to edit the play list. In the photo below there is a "New" button to create new and additional playlists.

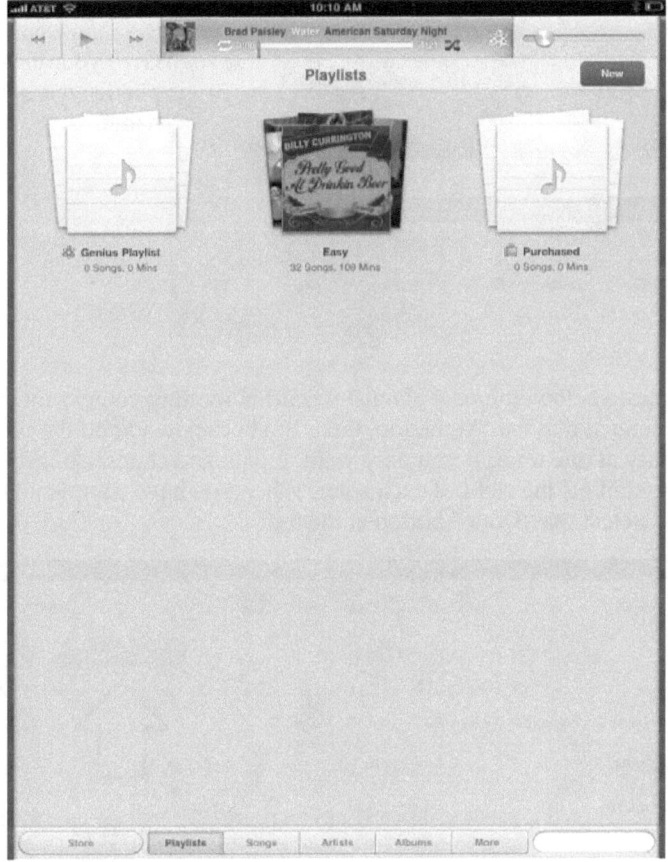

THE NEW USERS GUIDE TO THE IPAD

To create a new playlist, select the "New" button and let's get started.

Give your new playlist a unique name.

In the photo below, the new playlist wizard is wanting content for the newly created playlist. At the top, there is a button to add all the songs in the library at one time. If you only want to pick and choose songs, select the plus sign off the right of each song. When you have completed the playlist, select the "Done" button at the top.

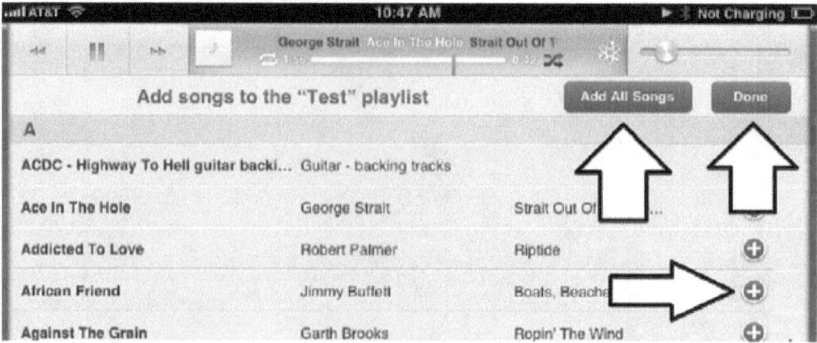

MUSIC PLAYER

To edit an existing playlist, select the playlist, then select the "Edit" button.

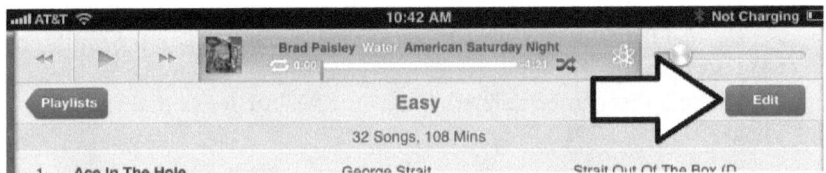

Once the "Edit" button is selected, the edit window will open. To remove a song from the playlist, select the minus sign to the left of the song. To add songs, select the "Add Songs" button and there will be an option to add individual songs. When the playlist is complete and you are done editing, select the "Done" button.

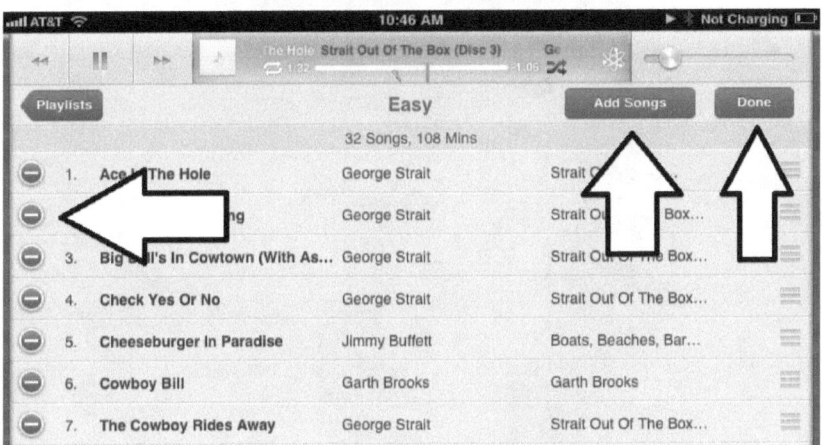

THE NEW USERS GUIDE TO THE IPAD

To delete a playlist, open the music library to show the playlists view.

Select the playlist to delete by holding one finger on that playlist until the "X" shows up in the corner, then release your finger. When the "X" is visible, the playlist can be deleted. Select the "X" to delete that specific playlist.

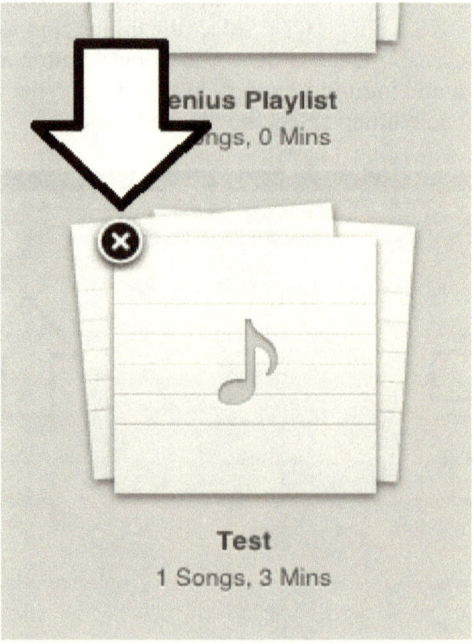

MUSIC PLAYER

Here is our music library listing by song. The song sorting is selected at the bottom of the page.

THE NEW USERS GUIDE TO THE IPAD

Artists view listing of music is shown on this page. If the cover art can be retrieved from the internet, you will see the cover art for the artist.

MUSIC PLAYER

Album view of music is shown on this page. If the cover art can be pulled from the internet, it will be displayed.

THE NEW USERS GUIDE TO THE IPAD

Additional sorting can be performed by selecting the "More" options at the bottom of the page and select sort criteria desired.

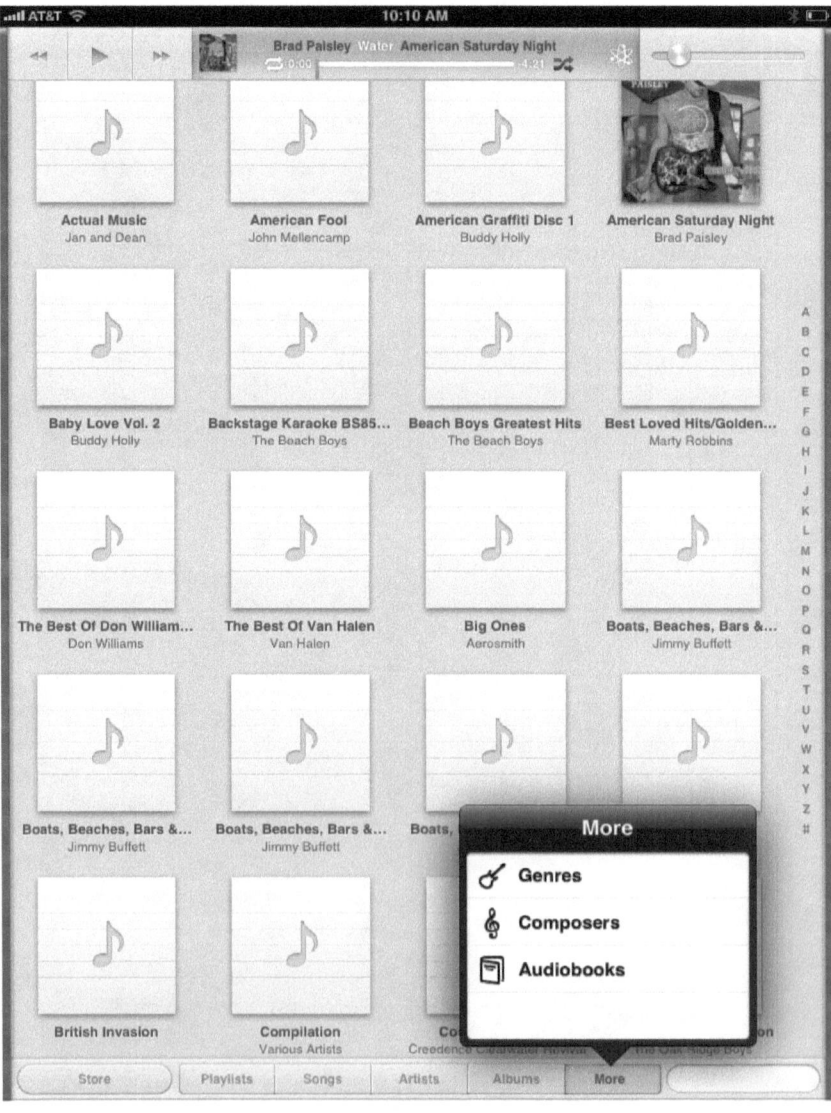

MUSIC PLAYER

THE NEW USERS GUIDE TO THE IPAD

 Messaging

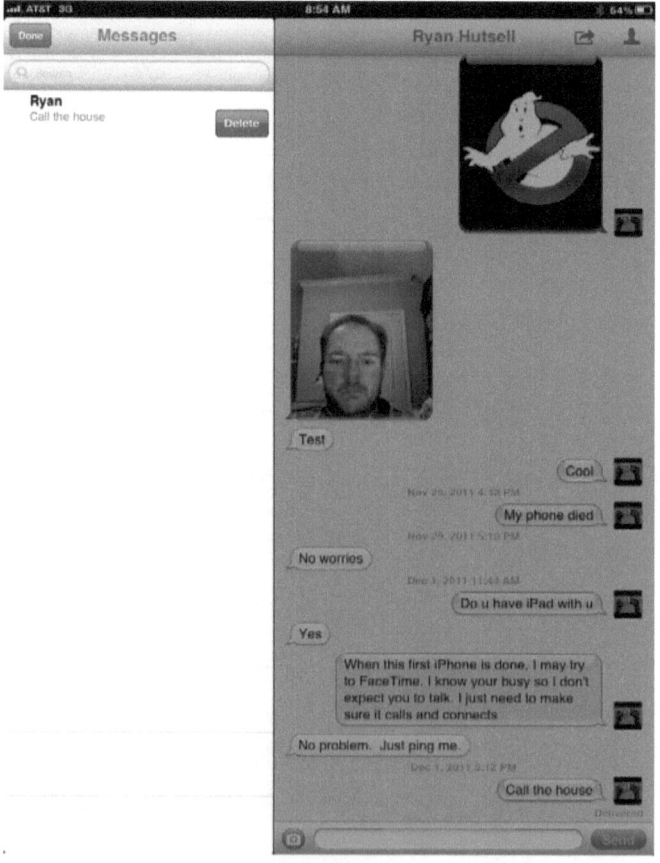

MESSAGING

Messaging is an IM (Instant Messaging) tool used on Apple devices. Messaging may be done with other Apple device users. In this photo, we have created a new message so that we can start a conversation.

We have to select which individual or individuals we would like to chat with. There is a plus sign to add users from our contacts list, or their information can be manually entered in the "To" box.

THE NEW USERS GUIDE TO THE IPAD

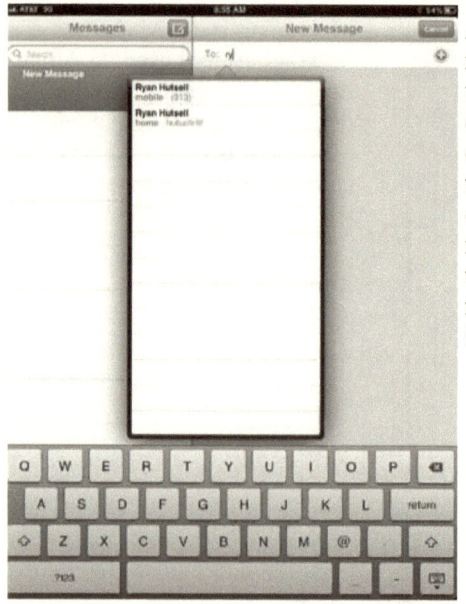
As we start to type the recipient's name, messaging will attempt to match the characters against known contacts in our contacts list. In this case, this contact has an email address and a phone number to choose from. Select the appropriate entry or manually type in the information for the recipient.

We have our recipient entered into the message. At this point, we can add additional recipients if desired. At the bottom of the screen is the box that will be used to type the contents of the message.

MESSAGING

 In this step, we have typed the initial words for our conversation to begin. When the information has been entered and is ready to send, select the send button to transfer the information to the conversation. Until the send button has been selected, the contents of the message can be changed. When the contents are sent, the information cannot be edited.

 In this step, the first words were sent to the conversation. If there is a photo associated with a contact, that photo will appear in the conversation.

THE NEW USERS GUIDE TO THE IPAD

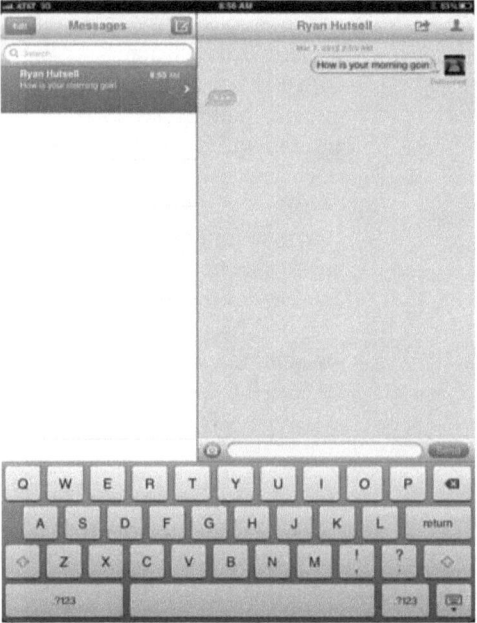

The three dots that are shown to the left, indicate that the other party is currently composing a message. The three dots will change to the actual words when the other person selects send.

To the left of our box for entering text is a small camera icon. This icon, when selected will allow us to send photos into the conversation. We can use a camera and take photos or select existing photos from our photo library.

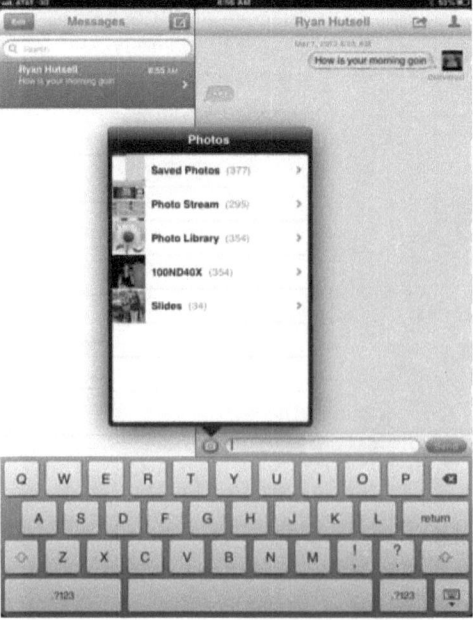

In this example, we have selected the camera icon. When the icon is selected, the user will be presented a list of the folders in the photo library where photos are currently saved.

MESSAGING

In this example, we have selected a photo from a hockey game. Once you have selected a photo, there is a "Use" button at the top to select. When the "Use" button is selected, the photo will be sent to all members of the conversation. Above this photo in the conversation, we can see that our three dots from earlier have now been changed into words.

When the "Use" button is selected, the photo is shown in the text entry box where additional words can be added to go with the photo into the conversation. All of the content, the photo and the words will go to the conversation when the "Send" button is selected.

THE NEW USERS GUIDE TO THE IPAD

 If there were additional conversations, they would be listed on the left side of the screen. In this example, the conversation we are showing is the only one available. The latest information in the conversation will be shown at the bottom of each conversation. This is an excellent way to view multiple conversations to see if you are current on its contents. The date and time of the last comment will also be shown there.

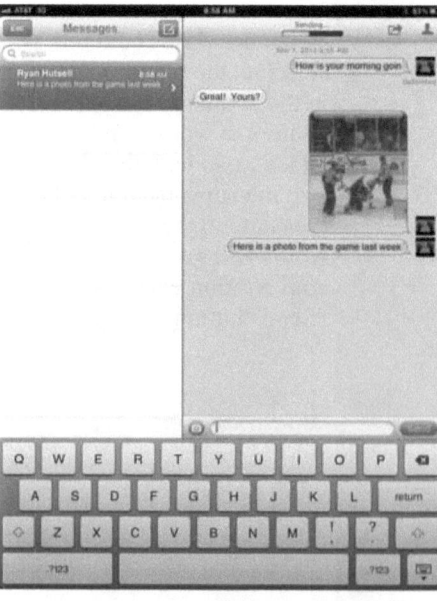 As you can see on the left of the photo, the words in the conversation are reflecting the last comments. At the top, you will notice that the information is being sent, due to the word Sending. Photos can be large and as such may take a few seconds or minutes to be delivered. If for some reason a photo cannot be sent, there will be an exclamation mark next to the photo to let you know it did not go.

MESSAGING

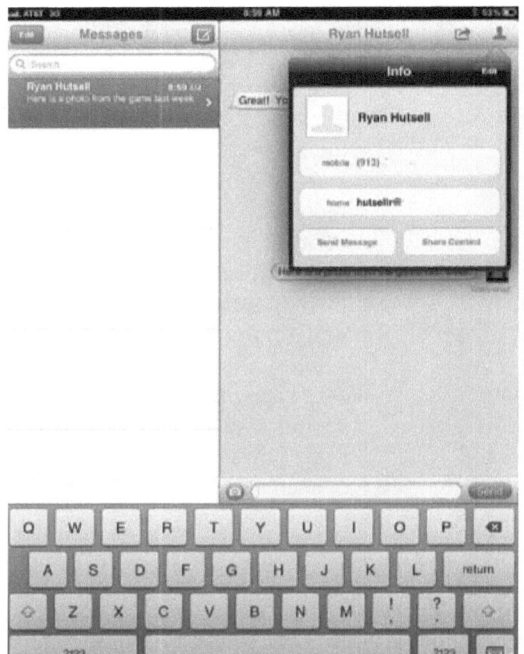

The icon that looks like a person will list all information about that user. From this window, the contact information can be shared with other contacts. The "Send Message" button will take you to the latest conversation or start a new conversation as necessary.

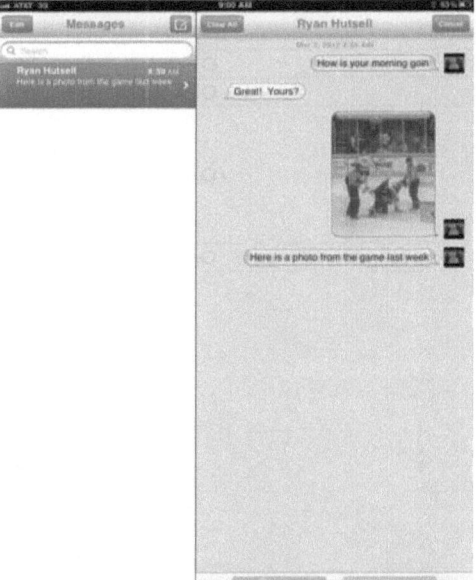

In this photo, next to the icon of a person, is an action button. Select the action button to clear the conversation, move the conversation or to forward the conversation to anyone else.

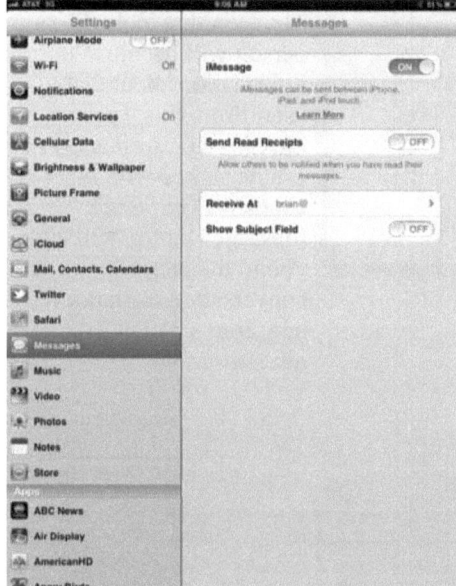

Messaging has a few options that can be turned off or on. Go to the settings and look for the Messages option. On this window, we can turn on or off the messaging application. This window reminds us that all messages will be visible on iPads, iPhones, or iPod Touches that are configured to use messaging on this account.

There is an option for Read Receipts if desired. These will let you know when a message has been read.

A subject field can be turned on or off.

The email address of the account that is configured to use messaging on this device, is shown on this screen.

MESSAGING

THE NEW USERS GUIDE TO THE IPAD

 Notifications

Notifications are simply messages from an app about a given event. If there is a weather app configured for your area, a notification will pop up in the event of poor weather conditions. Many of the News apps are designed to pop notifications on breaking news items. Each app has to have notification enabled in order to show them. When an app is installed, there will be a question asked about notifications. These are what the app is asking about. If you have changed your mind about an app, this setting can easily be changed. In the photo on the left, we see the Settings option with Notifications selected. The user can specify how they are sorted. Select a specific app to see its settings. Select the app from the apps list on the left to add notifications.

Page 302

NOTIFICATIONS

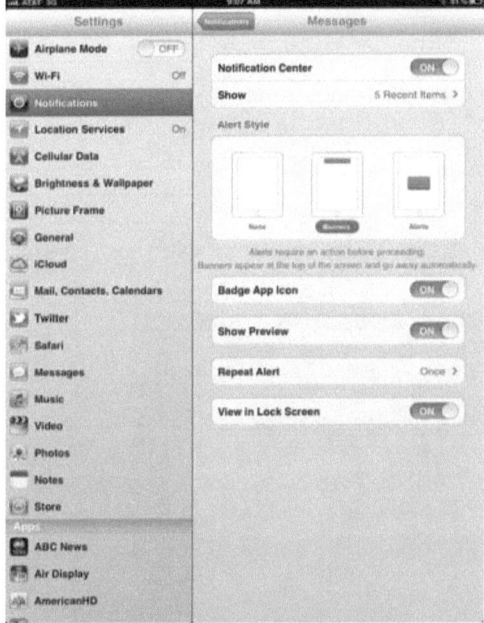

In this photo we see the Notifications option for the messaging app. On this app, we can turn it off completely. How many notifications to show is an option here. The alert style can be specified here. The other options are listed here too. If the "View in Lock Screen" is turned on, notifications will appear whether you are working on the iPad or not. The Badge app is the logo for the app that can show up on the notification. An example of a Badge app would be the eBay logo or CNN logo.

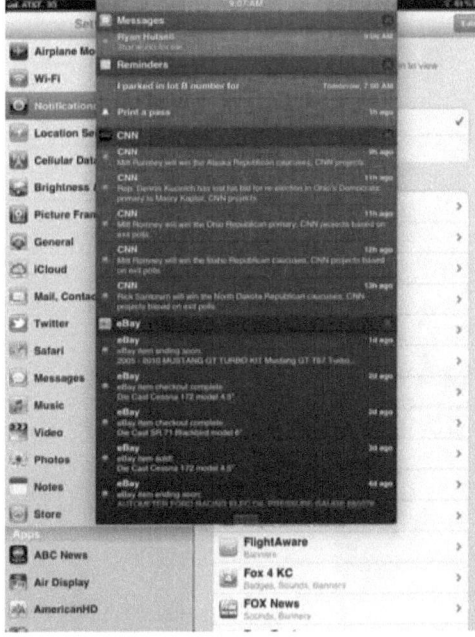

We can view all notifications at one time by placing one finger at the top middle of the iPad and dragging down. This motion will open the Notifications window where all the latest notifications are listed along with the time it was sent. There is an "X" to the right of each different app in the Notifications window. This "X" will clear all notifications in that group.

 IBooks

IBooks is the electronic book store built into the iPad.

Books that are purchased through the iTunes bookstore will show up in the iBooks app.

IBOOKS

Books can be grouped into collections. By default, there are collections already created. One collection for standard books and one collection for PDF files. Additional collections can be created and edited from this screen.

On this screen, we are viewing our PDFs collection. The collection name will be listed in the center of the bookcase at the top.

IBOOKS

The "Store" button will open the iTunes book selection where books may be purchased through your iTunes account. The cost of each book is listed next to the item. There are free books in the IBookstore as well.

Along the bottom is a menu to help locate books. At the top, results can be shown by featured items or listed according to release dates.

THE NEW USERS GUIDE TO THE IPAD

One option in the bookstore is the option to view the New York Times Bestseller list. These books are available in the iBookstore as well. At the bottom of the page are different views of books that are available.

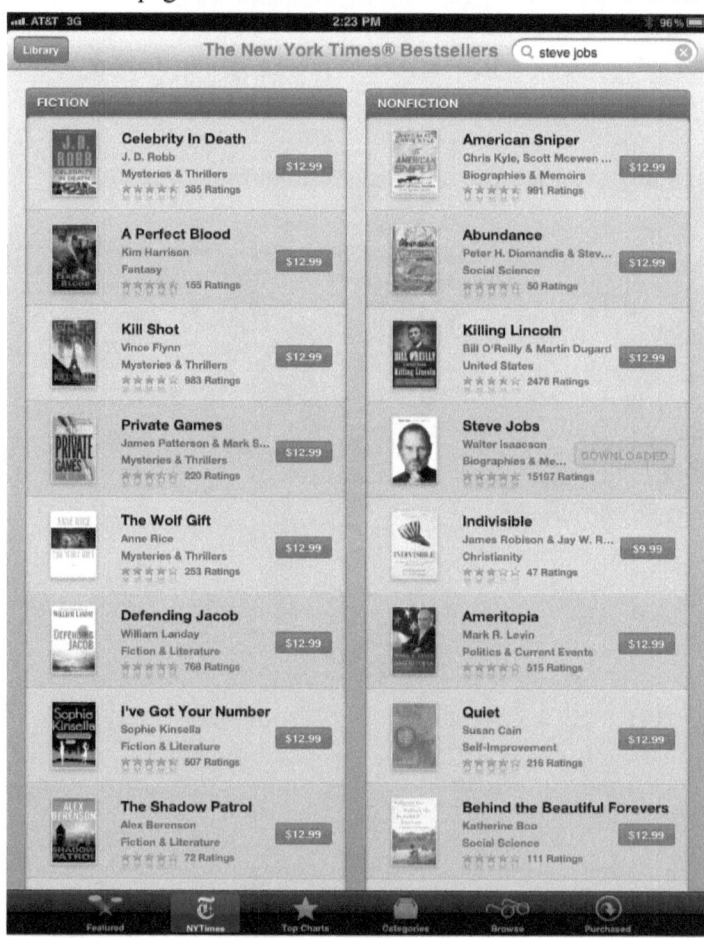

IBOOKS

Books can be viewed by category. Below we see a Top Charts list of the Top Paid books and the Top Free books. There is also a search box to look for specifics about a book.

THE NEW USERS GUIDE TO THE IPAD

Select the category to view books that have been classified in that category. The library button will take us back to our bookcase at any time.

IBOOKS

Here is the Browse option to look for books. Authors are listed alphabetically. There is an option to view free or paid books.

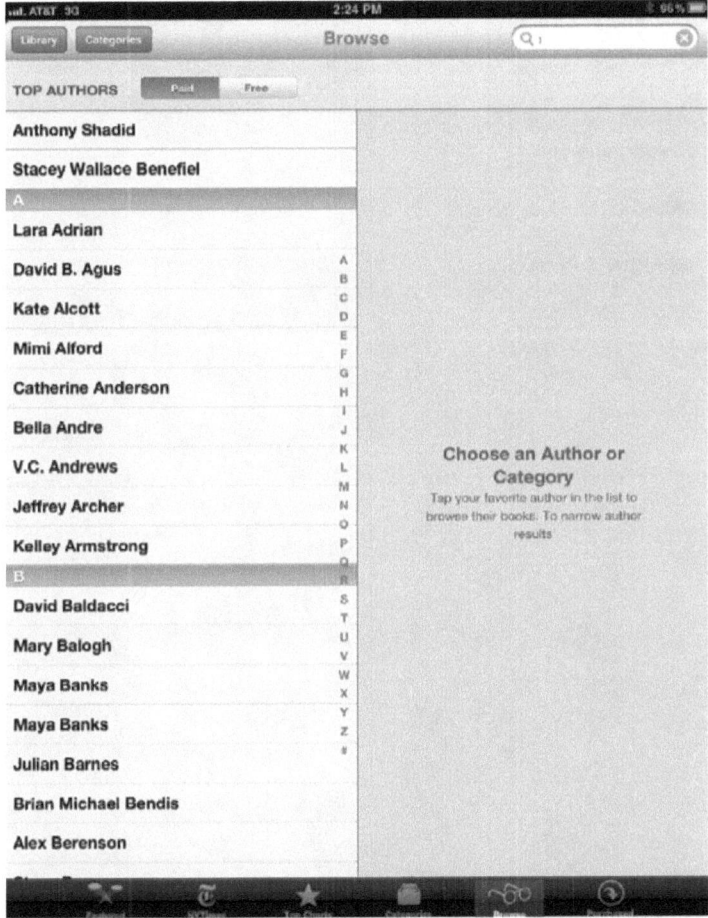

THE NEW USERS GUIDE TO THE IPAD

The diagram below shows a list view of the PDF files in our PDFs collection.

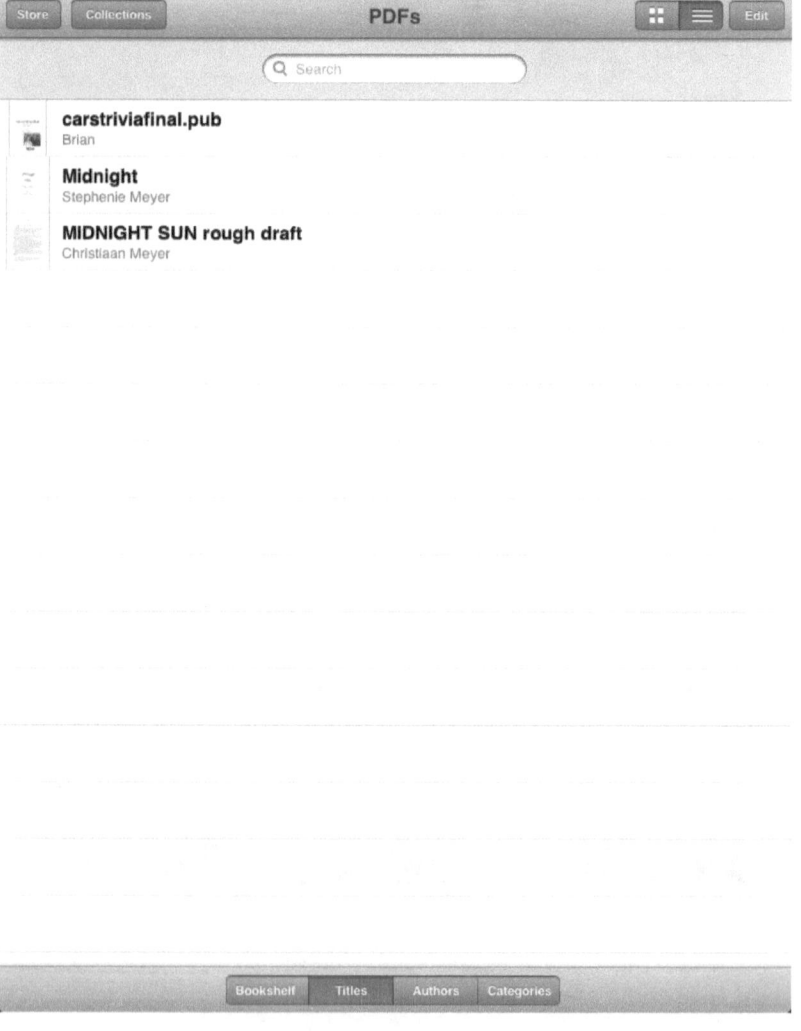

IBOOKS

By clicking the "Edit" button in the collection view, we see that we can move or delete individual titles or all titles in one location. Select the circle next to the title, then select to move or delete the selections.

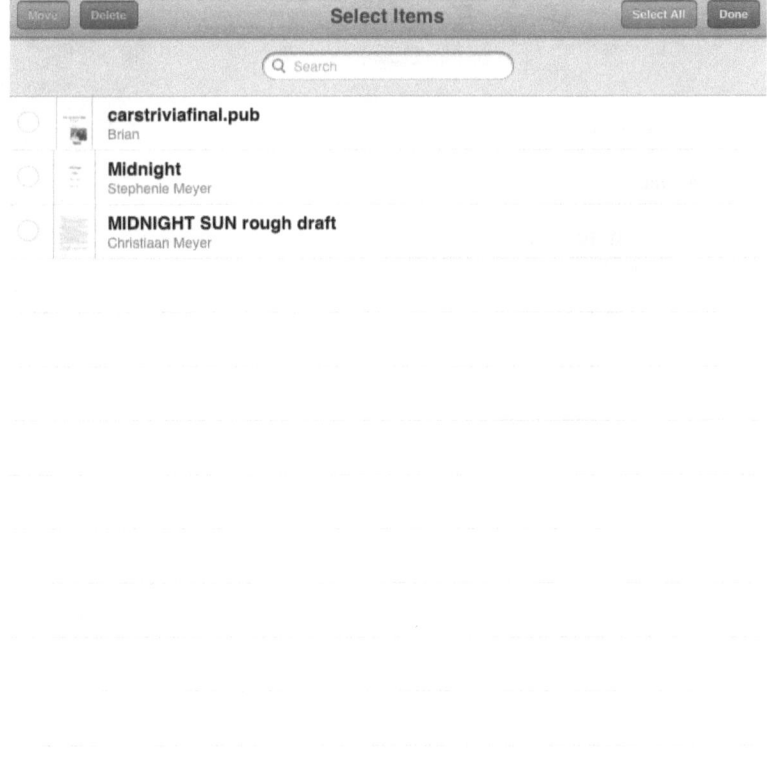

THE NEW USERS GUIDE TO THE IPAD

In the diagram below, we have selected one title to perform an action on.

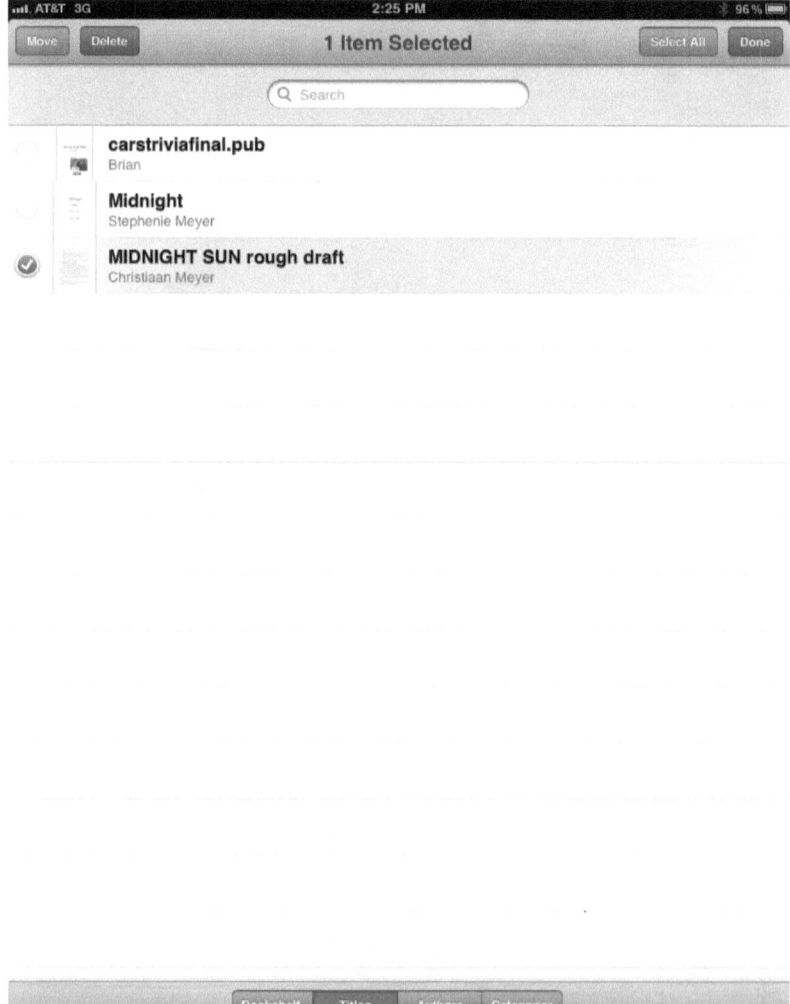

IBOOKS

In this diagram, we have opened one of our PDF books. This view allows us to see the options along the top.

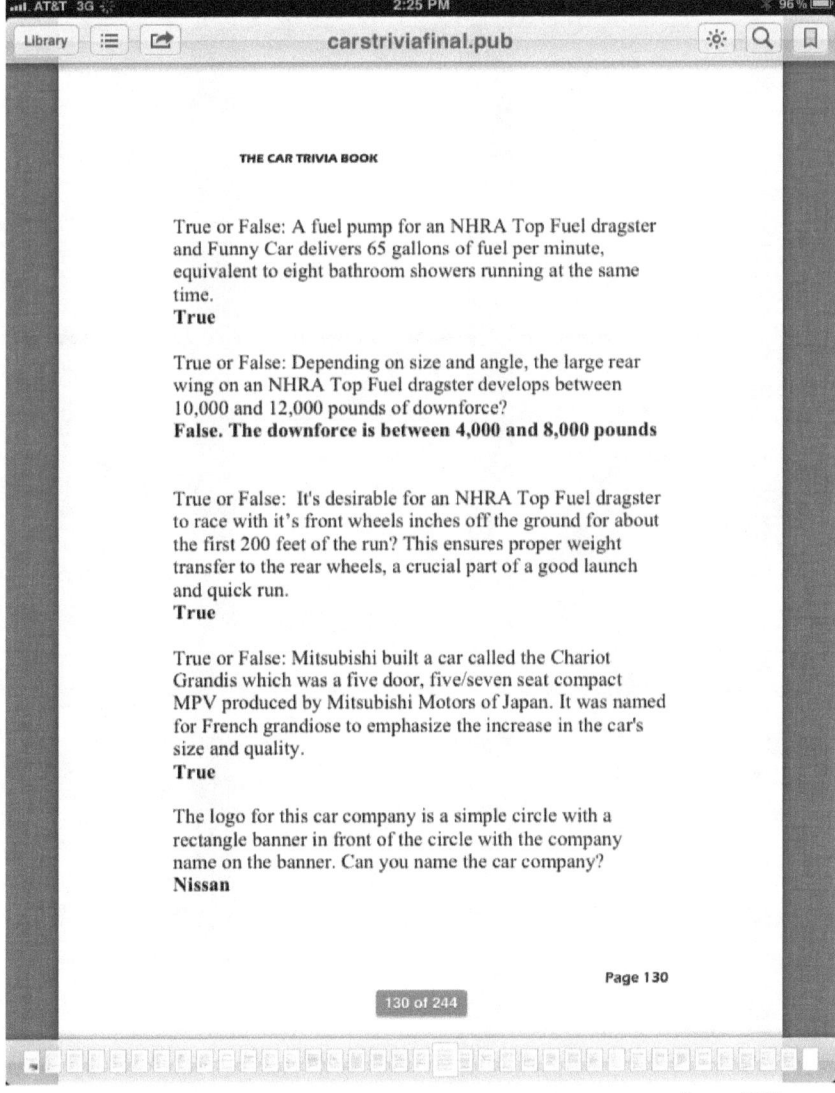

THE NEW USERS GUIDE TO THE IPAD

Here is a multipage view of our book.

Page 316

IBOOKS

The action button on this book will allow us to email the book or print the book.

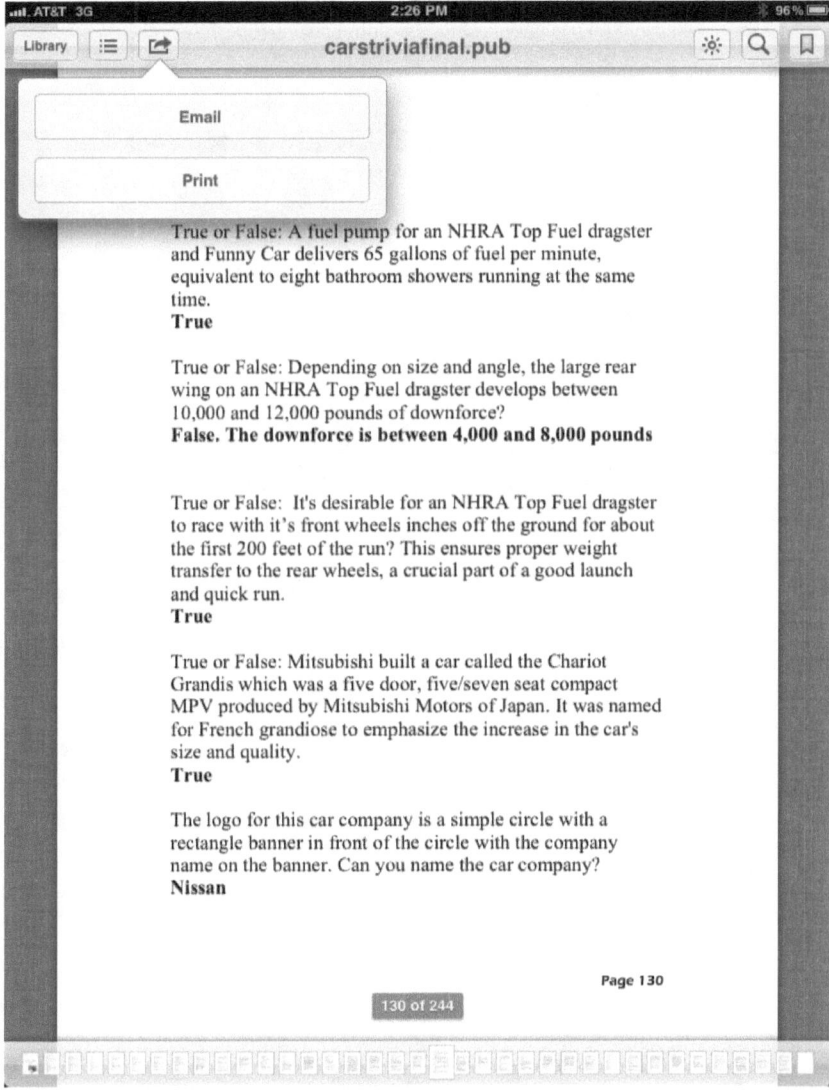

THE NEW USERS GUIDE TO THE IPAD

Some books do not allow the ability to be emailed. If the option is available to be emailed, when the action is selected, the file will be added to a blank email ready to send out.

IBOOKS

The brightness button allows the document to be lightened or darkened for better reading.

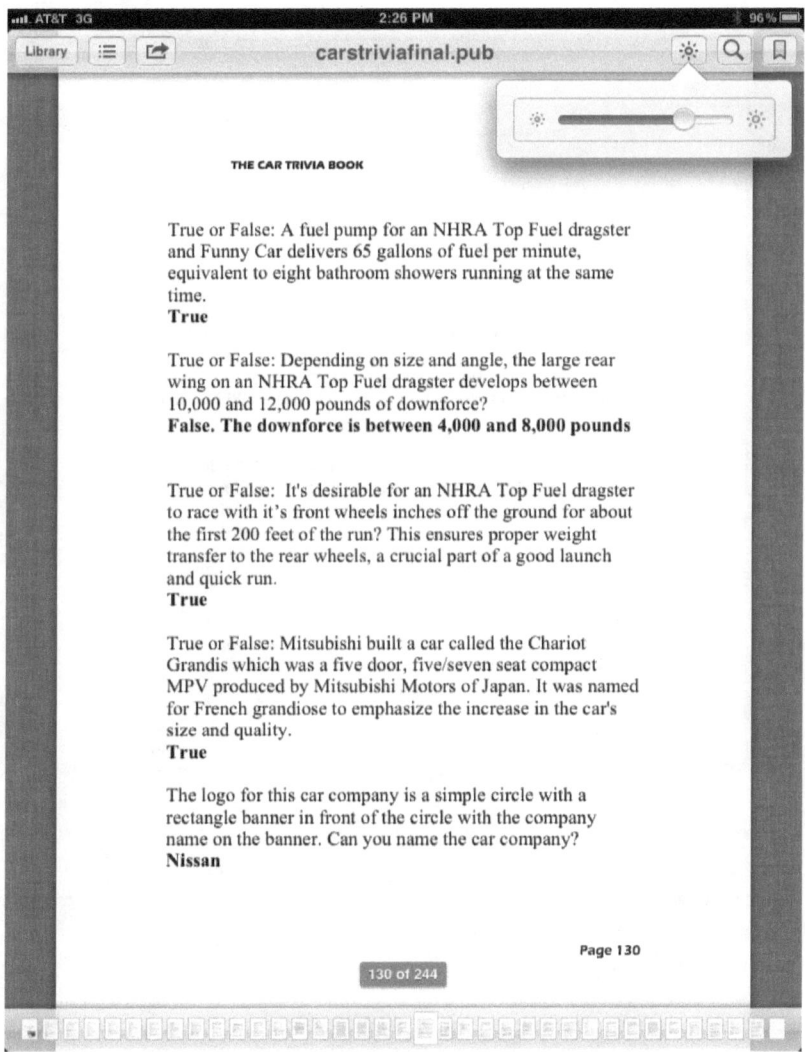

THE NEW USERS GUIDE TO THE IPAD

The magnifying glass will allow searching inside the book.

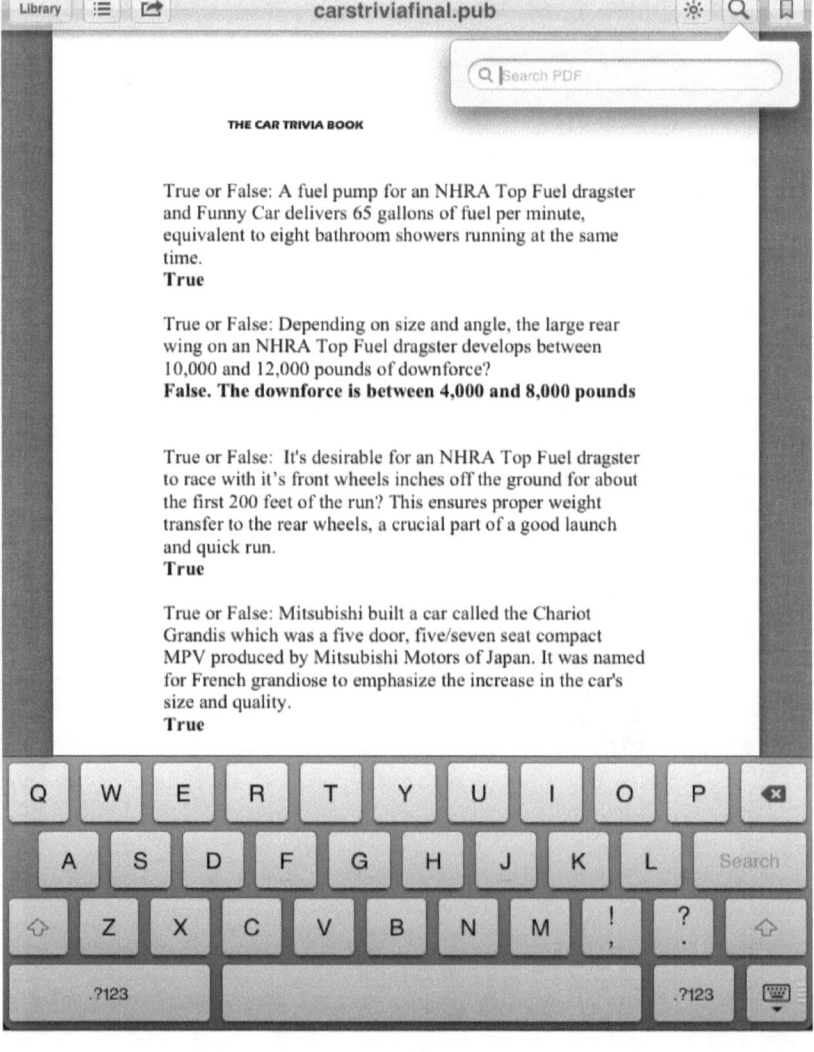

IBOOKS

The bookmark allows an electronic bookmark to be placed on a page.

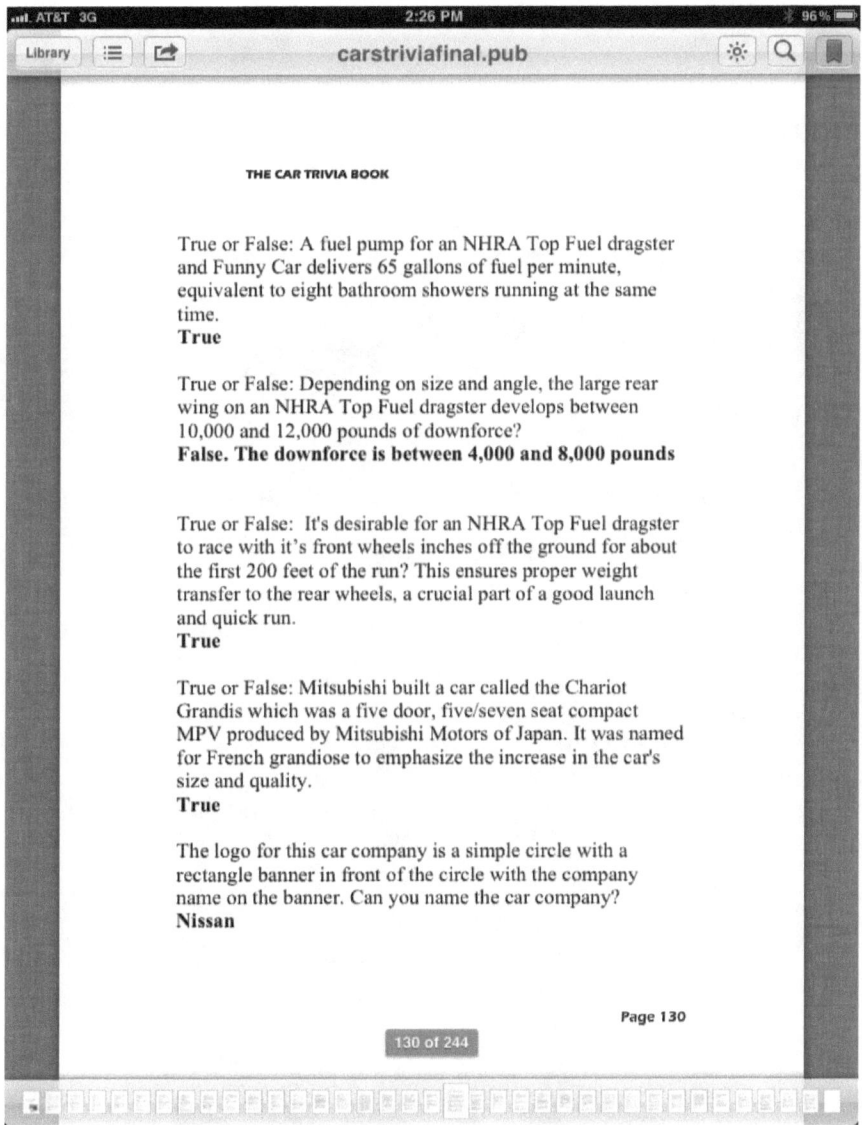

THE NEW USERS GUIDE TO THE IPAD

 Newsstand

The Newsstand app is similar to the iBooks app but Newsstand is designed for magazine, newspapers and catalogs. When you subscribe to something through Newsstand, the app will go out and get the latest editions.

NEWSSTAND

If we view the MotorTrend magazine in Newsstand, there are options to buy single-copy editions or subscribe to the magazine on a yearly basis.

Most of the magazines in Newsstand have a free preview of an edition.

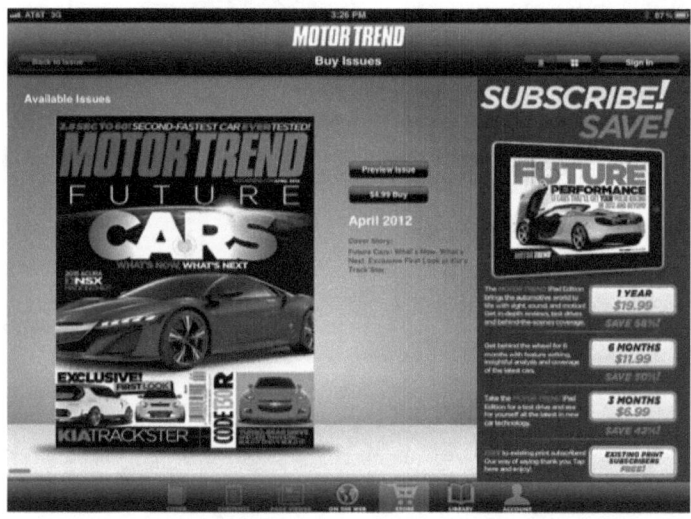

NEWSSTAND

Newsstand subscriptions can easily be transferred from one iPad to another.

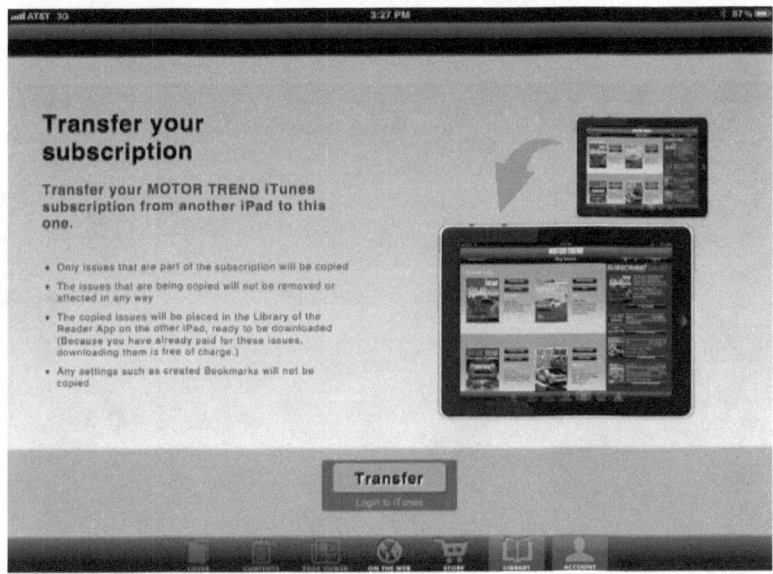

The magazine named "AppsMagazine" has the ability to use notifications. These notifications may let you know when a new edition is available.

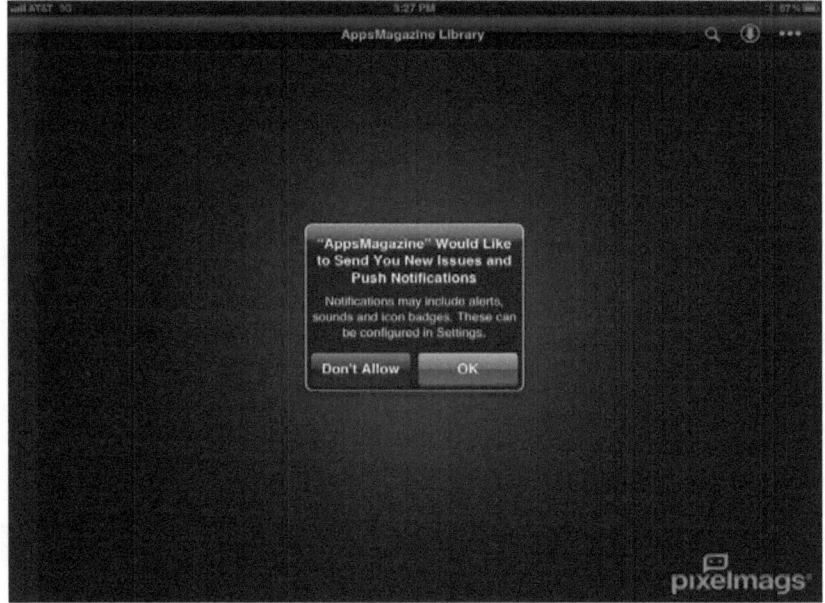

NEWSSTAND

Here we see that the "AppsMagazine" has a subscribe button at the top left. At the bottom, we see that there are regular issues and special editions available for purchase.

Three dots mean more information. On this More information screen about "AppsMagazine", there are settings, support and subscription information available.

NEWSSTAND

The download icon will tell us how many active downloads are happening right now. We can view how many downloads have completed successfully.

THE NEW USERS GUIDE TO THE IPAD

The search option will allow us to search through all of our downloaded versions of the magazine for specific words. The search will only work on items that have completely downloaded to the iPad.

NEWSSTAND

In this photo, we see the special edition of the magazine that is available for purchase.

THE NEW USERS GUIDE TO THE IPAD

 AirPlay

AirPlay is a function that will allow an iPad to stream media to a television or other external device.

Using an iPad, AirPlay will take video files, music, or photos and stream them to an Apple TV device for playing on a big screen television. In order for AirPlay to work, the Apple TV and the iPad have to be attached to the same wireless network. The iPad and the Apple TV have to be configured for Home Sharing with the same Apple ID account. When the configuration is complete, the option for AirPlay will be available.

Here we have a photo open on a network with an Apple TV. Select the AirPlay option and then select the output device.

The photo below shows the iPad in front of a 55" LCD TV.

AIRPLAY

Music output can be sent to the Apple TV for listening through the television or surround-sound systems. Select AirPlay then select the Apple TV for output.

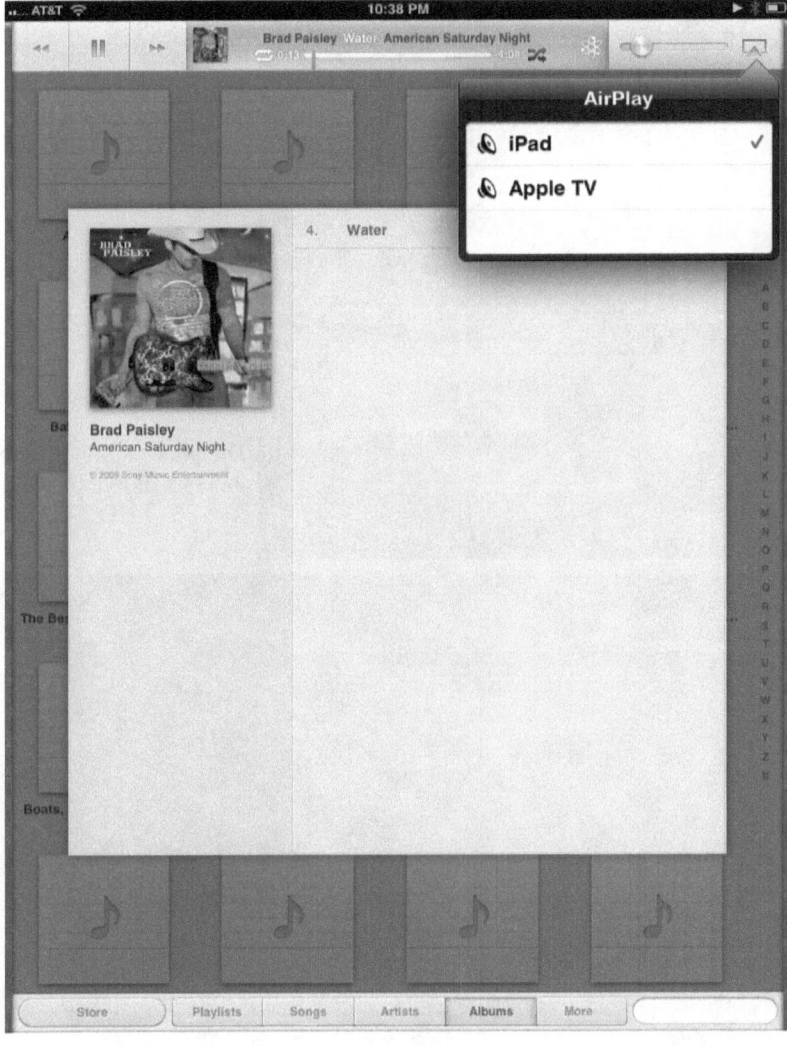

THE NEW USERS GUIDE TO THE IPAD

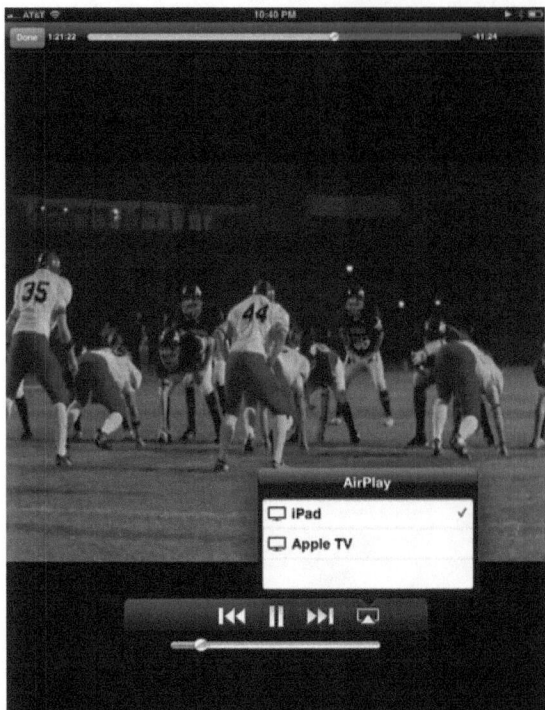

While a movie is playing, select the AirPlay option and the movie output will go to the Apple TV only. Movies are shown on one screen only unlike photos which show up on both at the same time.

The photo at the bottom shows a movie playing on a 55" LCD TV.

Page 334

AIRPLAY

During movie playback, the screen on the iPad will look like the photo below. Control for the movie is handled by the iPad. The play and scrubber controls will control the movie wirelessly on the Apple TV. To return to viewing on the iPad, select AirPlay, then select the iPad for the output.

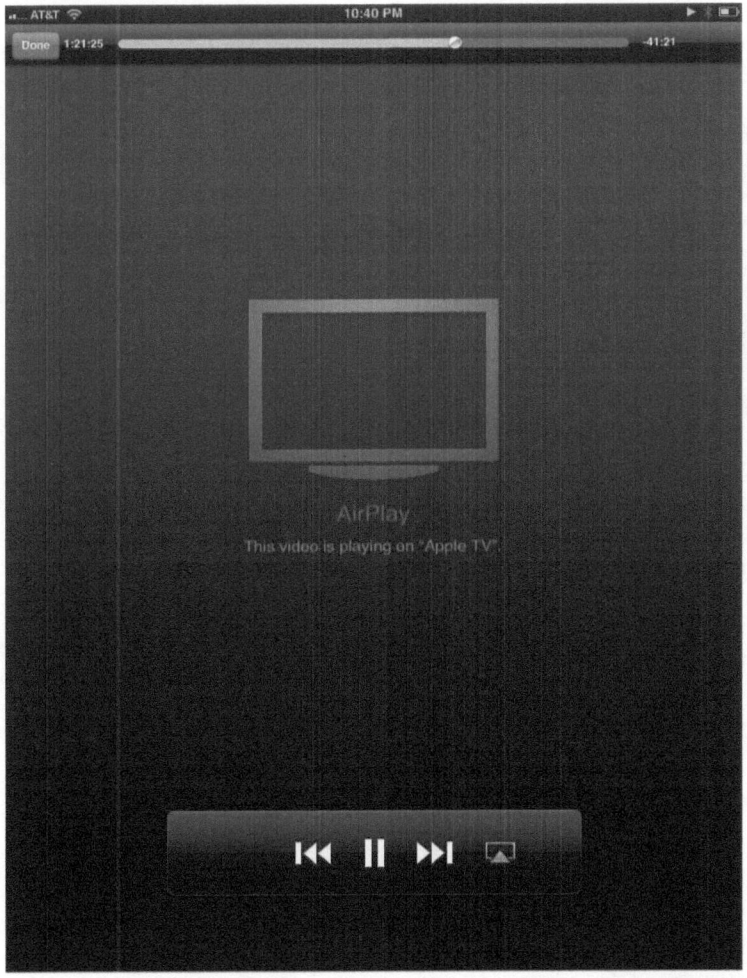

THE NEW USERS GUIDE TO THE IPAD

 AirPrint

Apple iOS 4.2 included a feature called AirPrint, which enables instant wireless printing from your iPad, iPhone and iPod touch apps. Users can automatically find printers that support AirPrint on their network and immediately print to them without needing to install drivers or download software.

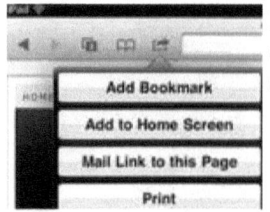 From the App, select the option icon with the arrow. If AirPrint will work with the app, the option will be there.

The printer must be connected to the same network subnet as your iPad or other iOS device.

AirPrint works *only* with wireless printers. It will not work with shared printers or printers connected directly to your PC. Some printers have Wireless 802.11 print capability, however the printer will not work unless the AirPrint option is also available on the printer.

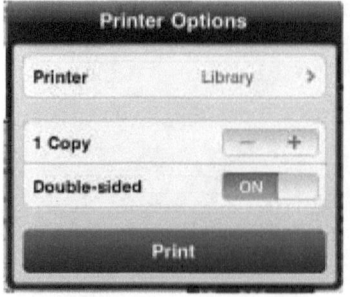 The print options windows will show what capability is available with that specific AirPrint printer.

AIRPRINT

Turn on – AirPrint is on by default, and nothing needs to be adjusted in your Settings app.

– To use AirPrint you just open an app that supports it – such as the built-in Safari, Mail, or Photos apps, and more 3rd party apps as they add support for the new feature.

– Once you're in an app that supports AirPrint, you just tap the Share icon (generally the one that looks like an envelope with a rightward pointing arrow in it).

– That will bring up a popup with a short list of actions you can take on the photo / email / web page you are on. Print will be one of those actions. Tap on that.

– Now you'll see the Printer Options popover. The first field in is Printer, with a prompt to Select Printer. Tap that and AirPrint will search for supported wireless printers on your network. If you have one, it should find and show your printer – just tap to select it.

– Once you have selected your printer, the only setting under Printer Options is number of copies to print. It defaults to one copy, but you can tap to adjust it. If you need to alter other print settings, you're going to need to do that on the printer itself or via your PC.

That's all there is to it. As you can see the hardest part is just having the right equipment.

On the Apple webpage is a complete list of printers that support the AirPrint option.

When purchasing a new printer, ensure that the AirPrint option is listed.

THE NEW USERS GUIDE TO THE IPAD

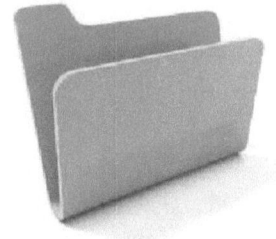 Folders and Desktop

The default Dock at the bottom of the iPad holds four icons initially.

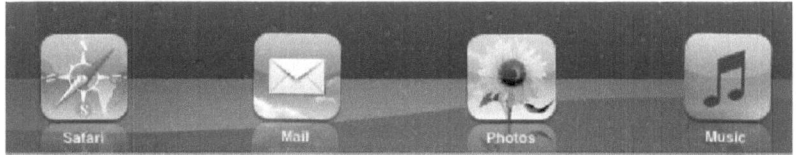

The total number of icons that can reside at the bottom row is six. Hold an icon until they start wiggling, then drag additional icons to the row and let go.

The dots above the dock indicate the number of screens that are configured with icons on the iPad. The iPad is limited to six screens and the spotlight search window. To remove a screen, move the icons to a different screen. A screen with no icons will simply drop off. If there are less than six screens, drag a new icon past the last screen on the right to increase the number of pages for icons.

FOLDERS AND DESKTOP

Hold down on one icon until they start to wiggle. When the icons are wiggling, they can be deleted by touching the "X" or moved by dragging them around the screen. Click on a folder to open the folder. The icons in the folder can be dragged out or deleted inside the folder. Folders can be moved around but not deleted. To delete a folder, move or delete all of its contents and the folder will disappear.

On this page, you will see that some icons are capable of being deleted and some are not. The original icons on the iPad cannot be deleted. The original icons can be moved or dropped into folders but they cannot be deleted.

THE NEW USERS GUIDE TO THE IPAD

To create a new folder for icons, drag one icon on top of another icon. The iPad will automatically start the create folder wizard. Once the folder is created, there is a name that is assigned to the folder; however, it can be changed at this time.

Once a folder has been created, it can hold up to twenty icons. Once the folder reaches twenty icons, no more icons can be dropped into the folder. If you attempt to drag the twenty first icon into a folder, the folder will simply move away and not let the icon be dropped into it.

FOLDERS AND DESKTOP

If a purchased program is deleted, and then you decide you would like to use that program again, go to the app store and repurchase the app. If you have paid for the app before, the subsequent times you will not be charged for the app.

If you push the Home button twice quick while the iPad is not locked, the iPad will open the controls as seen below. This screen will also show all the apps that are currently running. Close out the apps that are running to help increase battery performance as well as overall iPad performance.

THE NEW USERS GUIDE TO THE IPAD

Keyboard Shortcuts

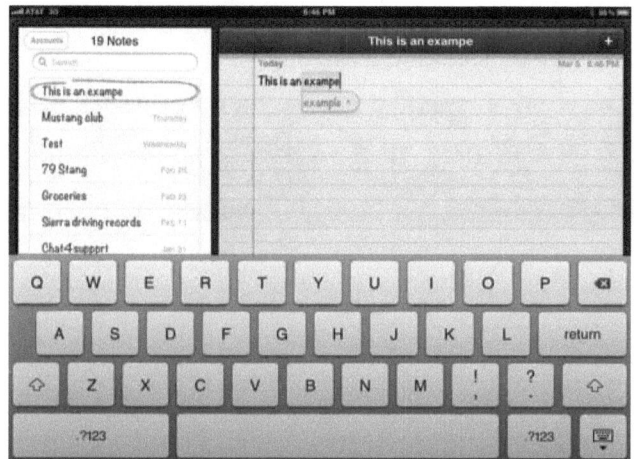

If the iPad finds a misspelled word, it will make a suggestion on the word. Click the word to change it or hit the space bar to change the word.

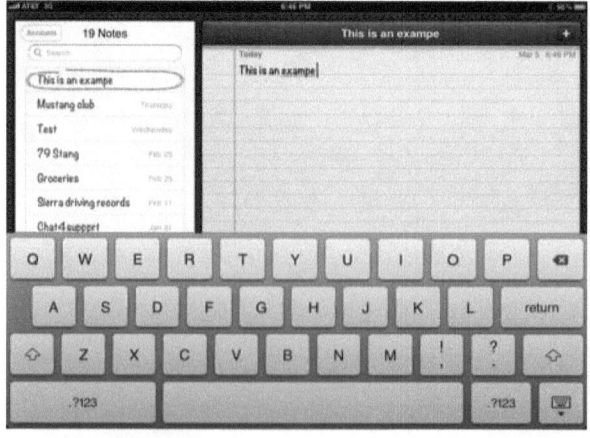

If you get past the suggested spelling, the iPad will indicate that the word is still incorrect. If you select the word, the iPad will make suggestions on correct spelling. The underline indicates a problem with the word.

KEYBOARD

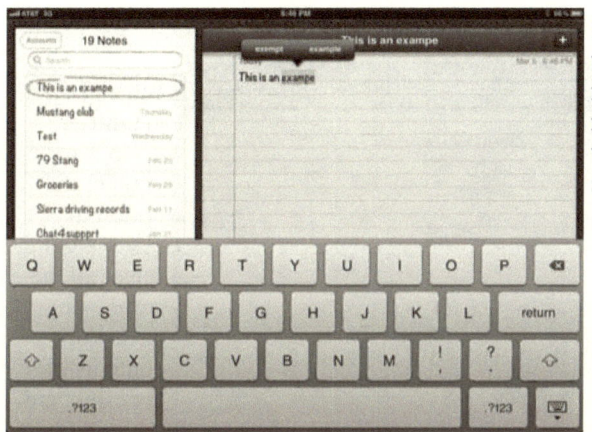

Select a word and the iPad will try to make suggestions regarding how the word should be spelled.

The magnifying glass is a way to select a location for correcting words.

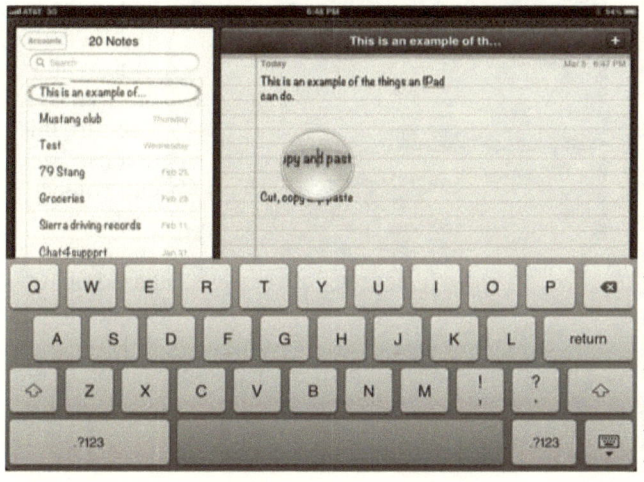

Hold your finger on a spot in the word until the magnifying glass shows up. When the magnifier appears, roll your finger slowly to the left or right until the cursor is exactly where you want it.

THE NEW USERS GUIDE TO THE IPAD

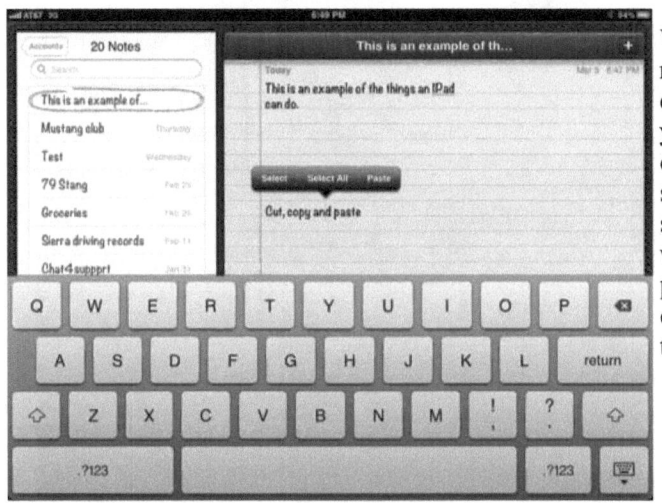

When the magnifier disappears, you get the option to select a word, select all the words, or paste the contents of the clipboard.

When an area is highlighted, there are points where the area can be expanded to add more text to the highlighted area. While the area is selected, this text can be cut, copied, pasted, changed based on suggestions.

KEYBOARD

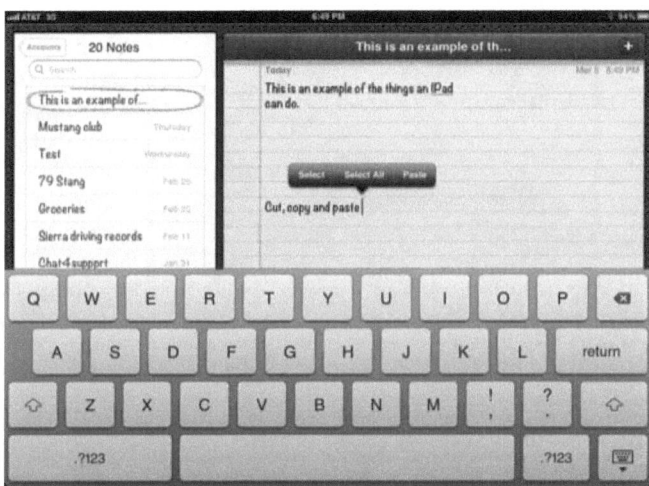

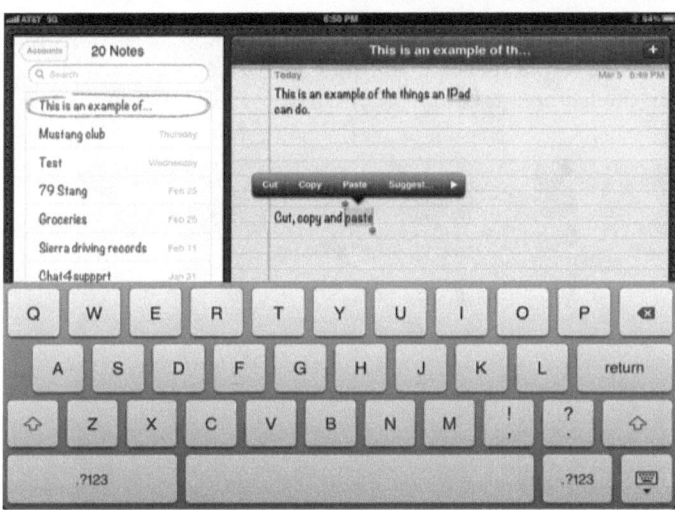

THE NEW USERS GUIDE TO THE IPAD

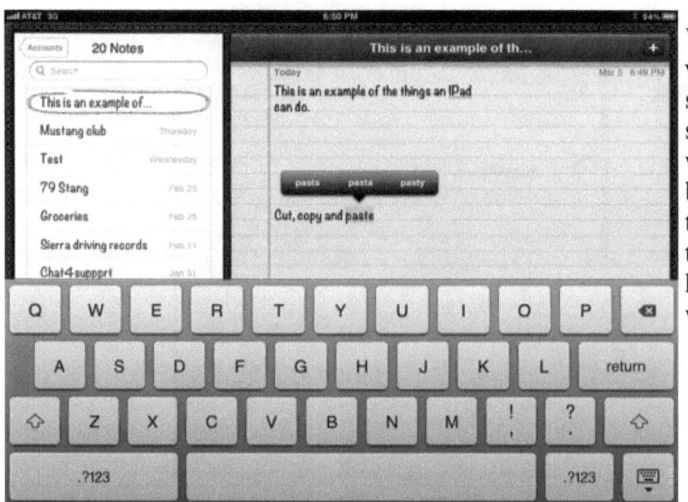

When a word is selected, suggested words will be shown to replace the highlighted word.

Splitting the keyboard will allow more of the document to be seen. Hold a finger on each side of the spacebar and slide your fingers apart. This action will split the keyboard. Bring fingers back together to join the keyboard

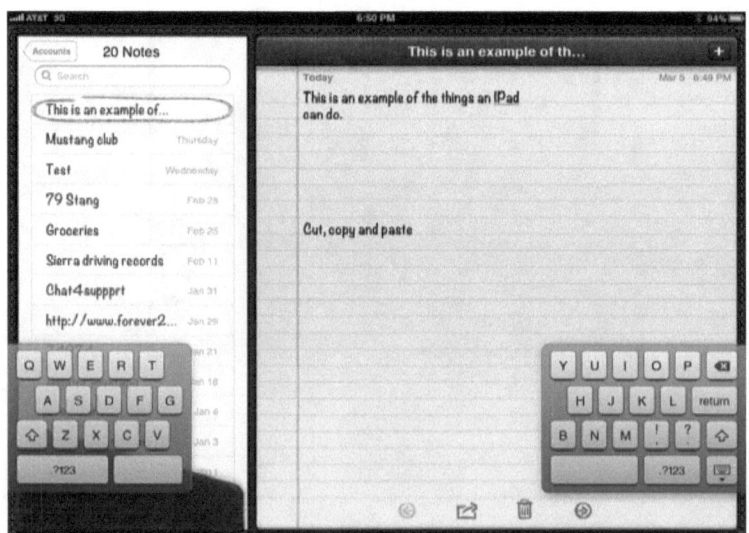

KEYBOARD

Select the shift key once to get the next character to show as a capital letter.

Press the shift key twice to keep the caps lock function turned on for all letters that are typed. To turn off the caps lock, press the shift key once.

Hold the key indicated below to get the alternate key to show up.

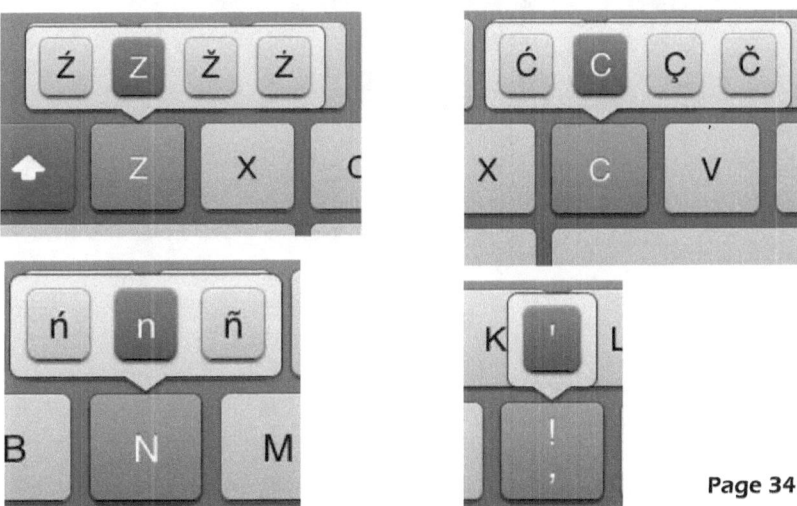

THE NEW USERS GUIDE TO THE IPAD

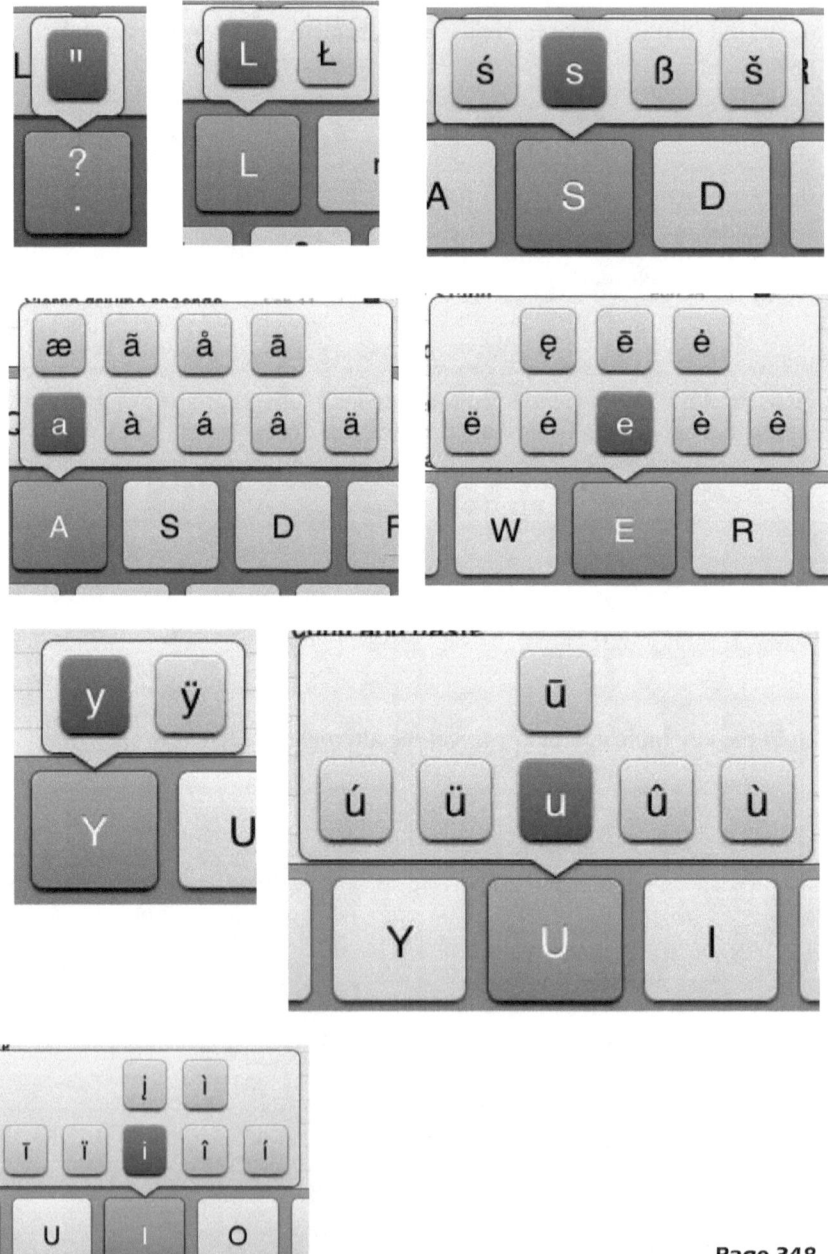

KEYBOARD

Page 349

THE NEW USERS GUIDE TO THE IPAD

When typing a web address, the www and the .com are not needed.

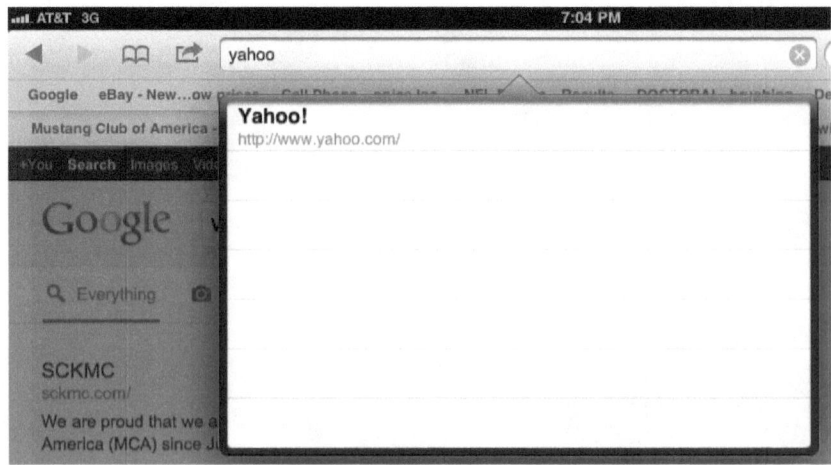

KEYBOARD

When typing the address of a website, hold down the .com key to get other domain extensions to display.

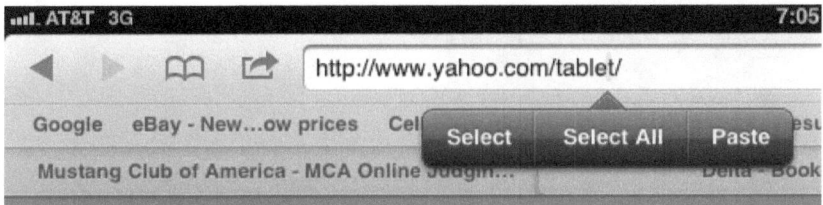

THE NEW USERS GUIDE TO THE IPAD

The new iPad has a new key next to the space bar. The key will allow for voice recognition. This button will work for dictating content in documents, notes, anywhere that you can enter text.

The keyboard button is usually used to hide the keyboard on the iPad but if you hold the key down for a few seconds, other options are available. We can split the keyboard with two fingers on the space bar, sliding our fingers apart. If we hold down the keyboard button, we can see there is also an option to split the keyboard there as well. Holding the keyboard key down will allow us to undock the keyboard. Undocking the keyboard will allow us to move the keyboard up further on the page.

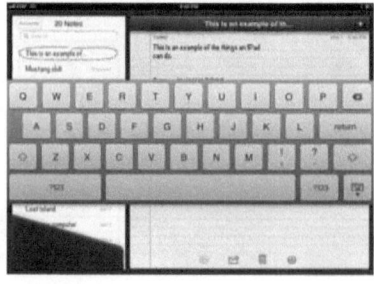

Here we can see the keyboard undocked and in the middle of the page. We can hold down the keyboard key again to dock it back.

KEYBOARD

When the keyboard is undocked, the keyboard key can be pressed again to show us the option to redock or to split the keyboard while it is undocked.

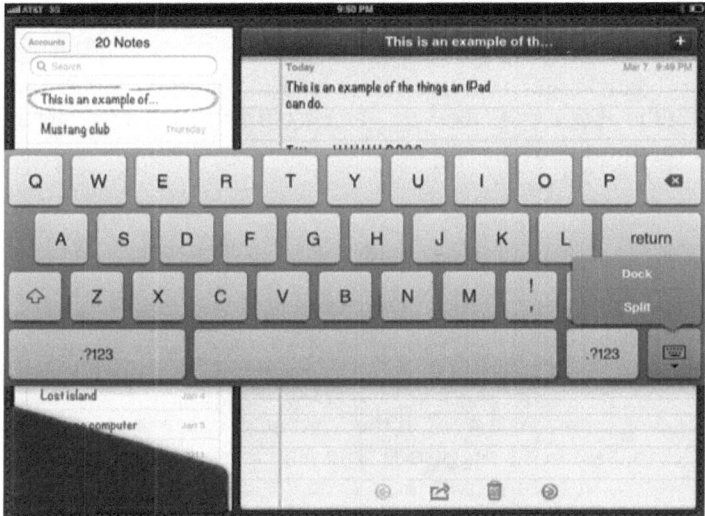

Here we see the undocked and split keyboard. Hold the keyboard button again to dock and merge it back into one keyboard.

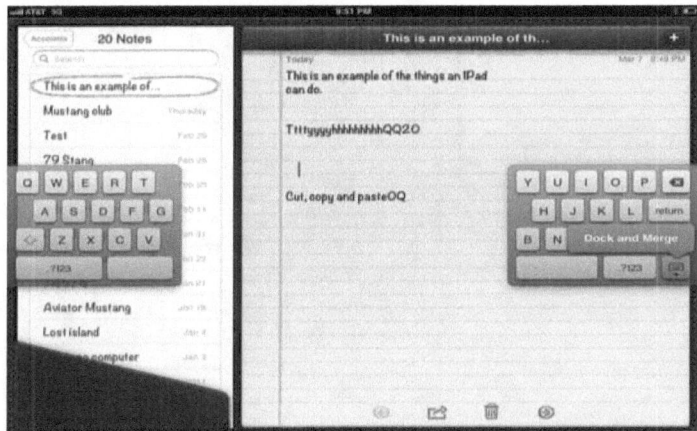

Page 353

THE NEW USERS GUIDE TO THE IPAD

When typing on the iPad, instead of trying to find the period for the end of the sentence, just hit the spacebar twice. Two taps on the space bar will automatically place a period and then a space to speed up typing. To enter two spaces, hit the spacebar once then wait a few seconds and hit the spacebar again.

When the keyboard is split, there are hidden keys that are available to be used. Type in the open area to the right of the letter "t" and you will get a "y". The other hidden keys are shown below.

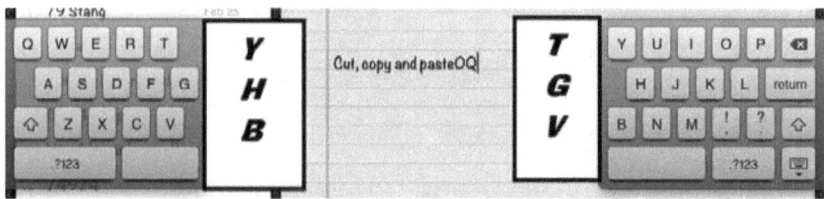

When the iPad recommends a word, if the word on the page is correct, select the "X" to dismiss the suggestion. The iPad is intuitive enough to learn about words. After a user hits the "X" on the same word multiple times, the iPad will realize that the word is a recognized word and stop making suggestions for that particular word.

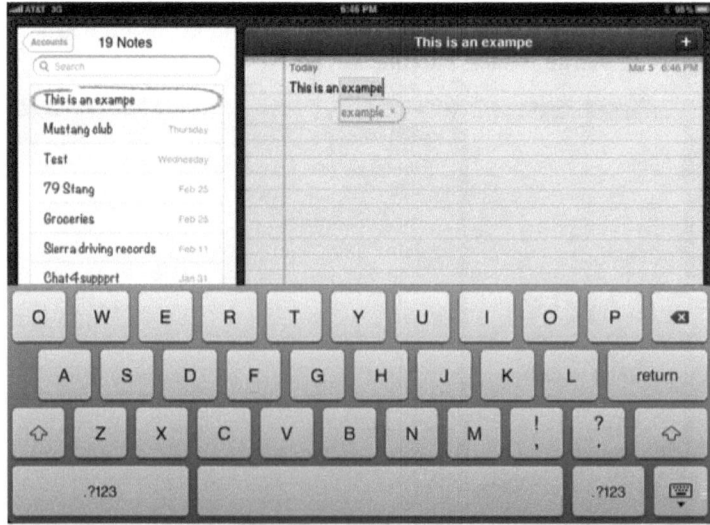

Page 354

KEYBOARD

The custom dictionary within the iPad will learn as you use the iPad. When the iPad suggests a replacement word for a specific word multiple times unsuccessfully, the iPad will eventually accept the word as a valid word. Through this process, the dictionary will grow to accept uncommon words that are valid.

If the dictionary has words that should not be kept or if the dictionary needs to be reset. Go to Settings, then General, look for reset.

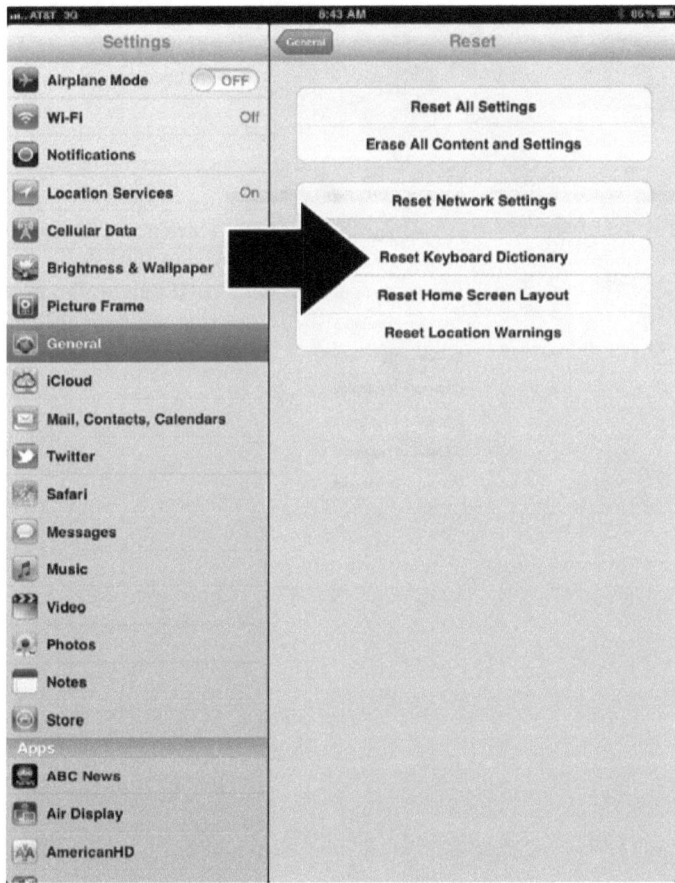

THE NEW USERS GUIDE TO THE IPAD

Change to different keyboards.

Go to the Settings option. Look for the Keyboard option. There is a button to "Add a New Keyboard". Click the button and the additional keyboard options will be displayed.

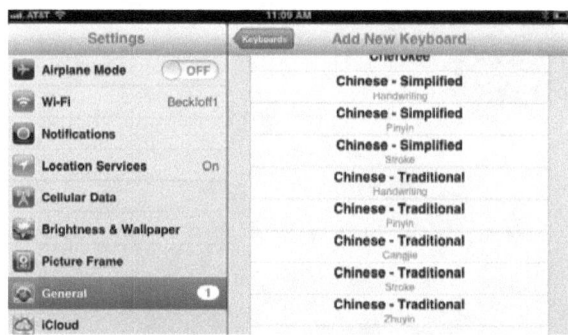

Here are a few examples of the different keyboards that are available.

KEYBOARD

 Alternate keyboard layouts may be selected.

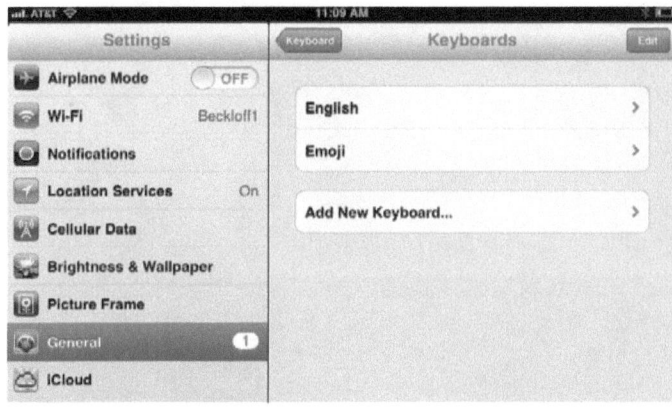 In this example we have selected the Emoji keyboard, which displays Emoticons.

Page 357

THE NEW USERS GUIDE TO THE IPAD

Once an alternate keyboard has been selected there will be a Globe key on the keyboard to select the alternate keyboard.

KEYBOARD

Below are the keys that are available from the alternate keyboard that we selected. This keyboard is full of Emoticons and icons to use.

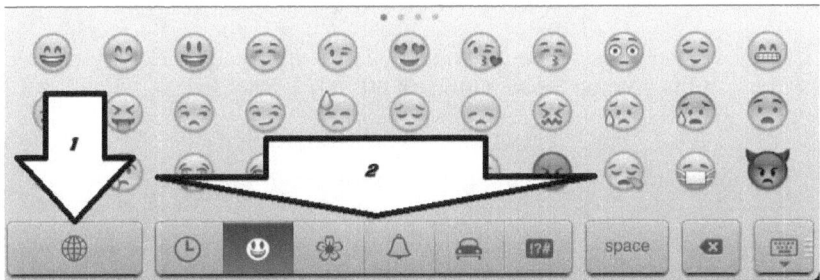

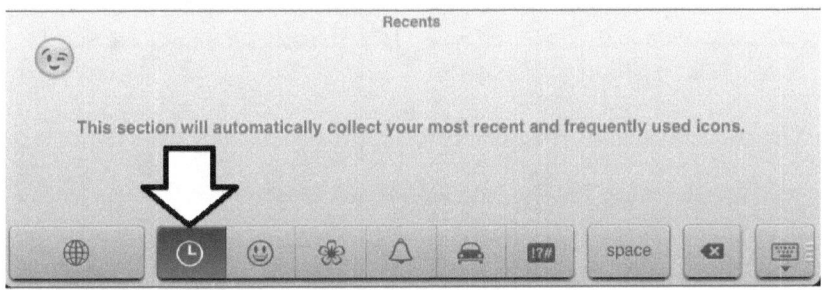

THE NEW USERS GUIDE TO THE IPAD

TIPS AND TRICKS FOR ALL IPADS

There are several ways to mute an iPad. The simple and quick way is to hold down the volume down button on the side of the iPad and the iPad will go mute.

If you are looking for something quick, swipe your finger across the screen until you get to the Spotlight Search. The spotlight search will look through the main portions of information on the iPad to find the information that you have selected in the search Criteria.

When the keyboard is split, there are hidden keys that are available to be used. Type in the open area to the right of the letter "t" and you will get a "y". The other hidden keys are shown below.

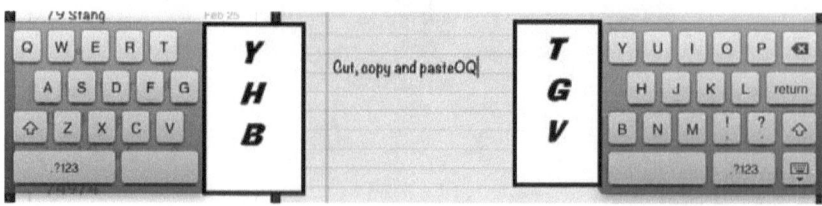

TIPS, TRICKS AND SECRETS

Keyboard

The keyboard can be split by holding a finger on each side of the space bar and sliding your finger apart. Reverse the process to rejoin the keyboard. Holding down the Keyboard button will also allow a split as well as the ability to undock the keyboard from the bottom of the screen.

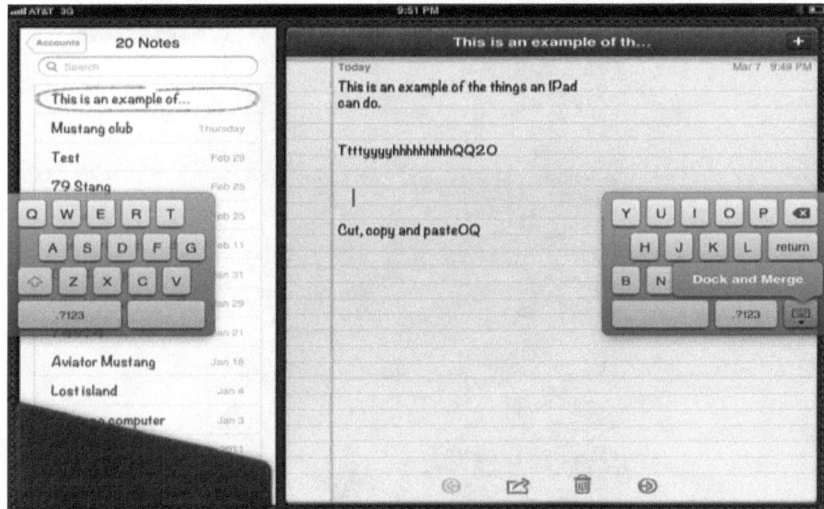

When the keyboard is split, there are hidden keys that are available to be used. Type in the open area to the right of the letter "t" and you will get a "y". The other hidden keys are shown below.

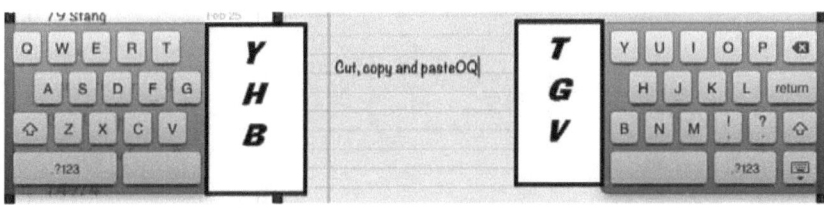

THE NEW USERS GUIDE TO THE IPAD

On the main screen of the iPad, touch in the middle at the very top of the screen. While holding your finger against the iPad, drag your finger down the screen. The Notifications for all apps that are configured to use Notifications will be displayed in one location.

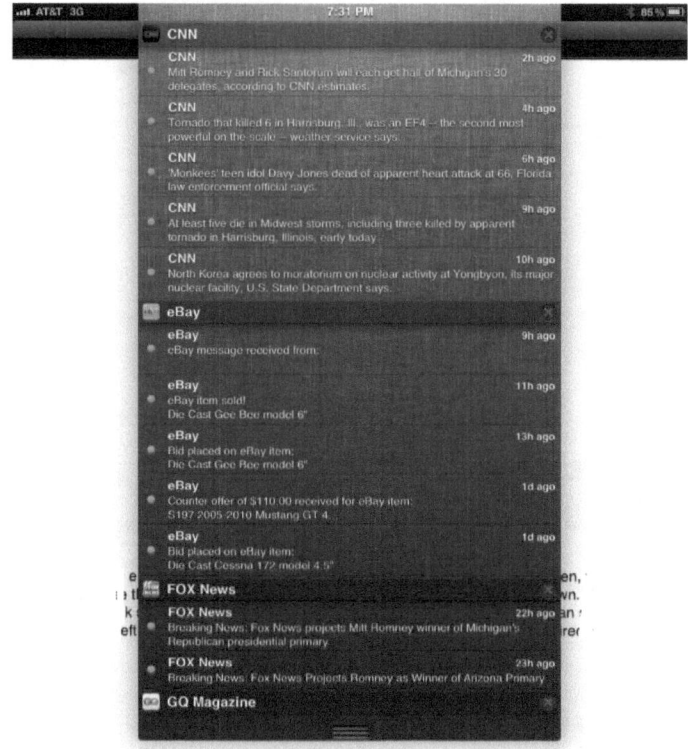

TIPS, TRICKS AND SECRETS

Passcode

This photo shows what a lock screen will look like. If you press the button on the top of the iPad, it will lock the screen. Even though the screen is locked there are some things that you can still do. There is a button on the lower right to start a slideshow while in lock mode.

THE NEW USERS GUIDE TO THE IPAD

If a song is playing using the music controls, the information about the song will be displayed on the lock screen.

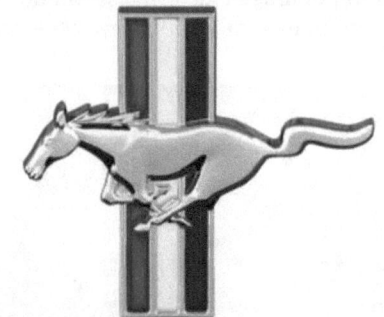

To change between the song name and the song controls, tap the Home button twice.

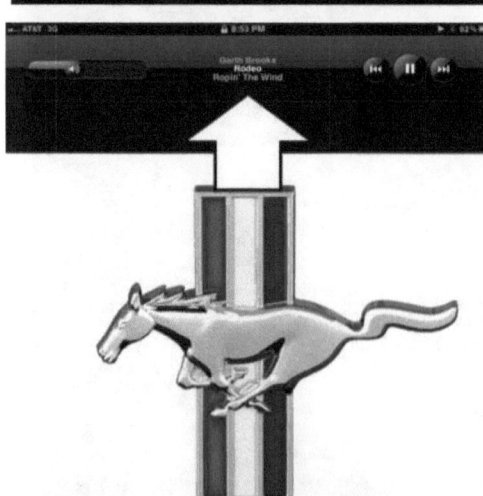

When the screen is locked while music is playing, the music controls will show up on the lock screen. Even though the iPad is locked, the music may be controlled from these controls.

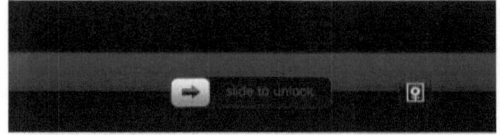

TIPS, TRICKS AND SECRETS

When the screen is locked, if you slide the slider, you will be presented with the password box. The standard password type would be a four digit numeric number. This password can be set to be more complex in the settings option area.

To make the password more complex, go to the settings app. Select the passcode lock option and then enter your existing password. Once you are past the password, turn the option off for simple password. Enter your old password then enter a new and more complex password.

Signals at a Glance.

 The symbol shown here indicates that the iPad is attached to a Wi-Fi network. The bars on the left indicate the signal strength of the Wi-Fi signal.

 The symbol to the left indicates that we are on a 3G cellular network and not Wi-Fi. The bars on the left indicate the signal strength of our cellular signal.

TIPS, TRICKS AND SECRETS

On a long website, when scrolling down through the site, to return to the top of the site quickly, tap twice where the arrow is pointing below. This will cause the browser to return to the top of the page.

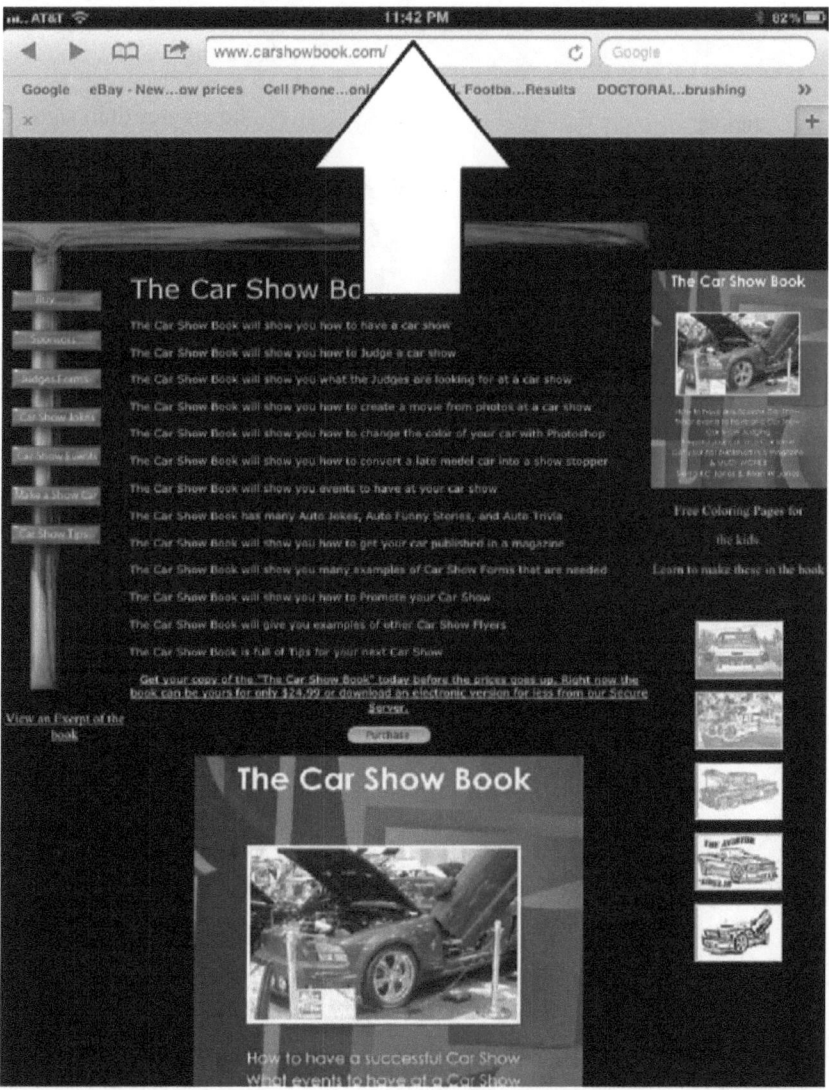

THE NEW USERS GUIDE TO THE IPAD

Wireless Problem

If you find you are attached to a Wi-Fi network but you are unable to get to any websites, this is the first thing to try. The button with the greater than sign, will give you more information about that network. The photo at the bottom will show you the detail page for a network. A check mark will show up next to the network you are connected to.

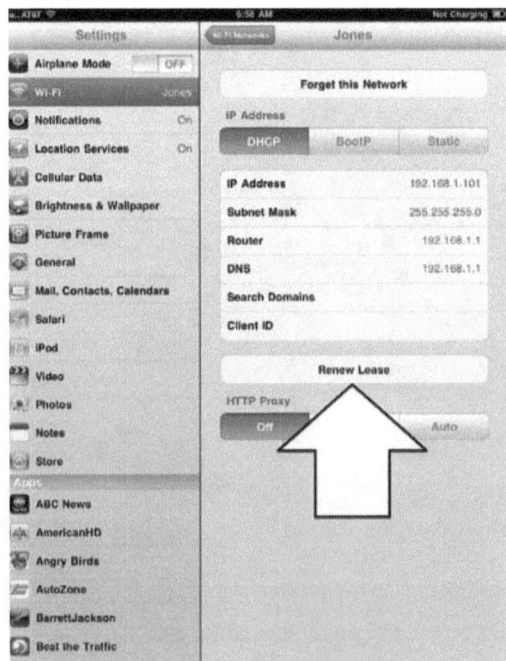

An IP address is a unique number given to you to access the internet. DHCP (Dynamic Host Control Protocol) means that there is a device giving you numbers. The Renew Lease button will get a new IP address. This process would be just like disconnecting and reconnecting to the same Wi-Fi network. This can solve many problems.

TIPS, TRICKS AND SECRETS

Scrubbing

When a series of icons are stretched along the bottom, drag a finger across the list to select one quickly. Dragging along this line is called scrubbing.

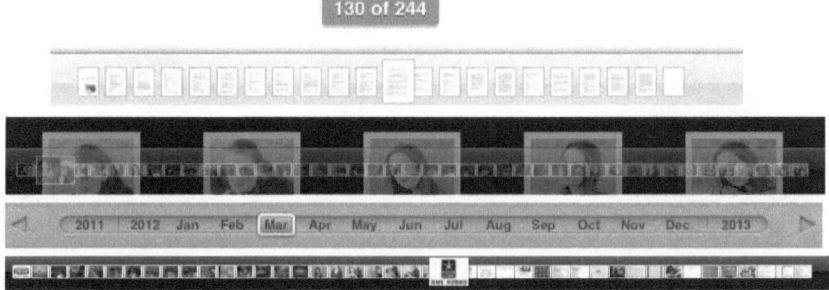

Scrubbing speed can be adjusted. Put your finger on the line then slide your finger down and away from the scrubber control. The further away from the control the more control and finer the adjustments are.

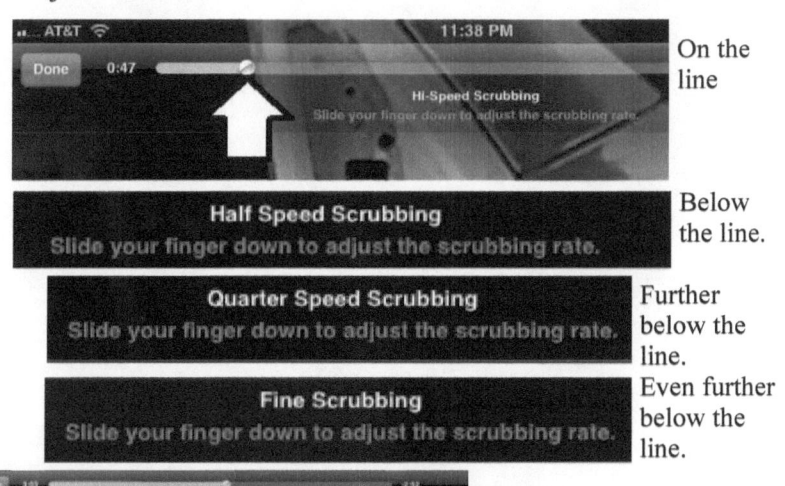

On the line

Below the line.

Further below the line.

Even further below the line.

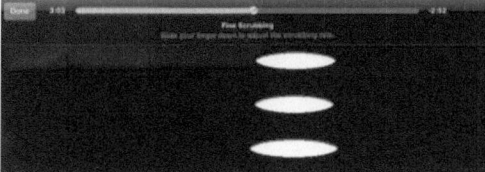

Each circle on the left indicates a different scrubbing speed.

How to clean an iPad screen

- Use only a soft, lint-free cloth. Abrasive cloths, towels, paper towels, and similar items may cause damage to the item.
- Disconnect your iPad from any external power sources.
- Disconnect any external devices and other cabling from the iPad.
- Keep liquids away from the product.
- Don't get moisture into any openings, and don't use aerosol sprays, solvents, or abrasives.
- Do not spray cleaners directly onto the iPad.

Screen protectors may be purchased to keep the screen on the iPad free of everything. The screen protectors are large clear adhesive plastic screens that attach directly to the screen on the iPad. After many hours of use, the screen protector can be removed and replaced with a shiny new one.

TIPS, TRICKS AND SECRETS

iPad Operating Temperatures

The iPad does not like temperatures less than 32 degrees or greater than 92 degrees F. Exposure to temperatures outside of these ranges can cause problems with the operation of the iPad.

If the device is left in a hot car for a period of time, you get the message in the photo below. If you get the message below, the iPad will need to be allowed to cool down before it will operate again.

- .

THE NEW USERS GUIDE TO THE IPAD

Battery percentage

In the upper right-hand corner of the iPad is a battery icon that will show the current battery charge state in graphic format. It would be nice to see a percentage there as well. Let's turn it on.

 Here is the default icon with the battery icon.

 If the iPad is plugged into a computer through the USB cable, it will not charge while the iPad is on, here is the icon.

Open the settings from the main page. Select the General setting and then select the usage option. The battery percentage can be turned on or off.

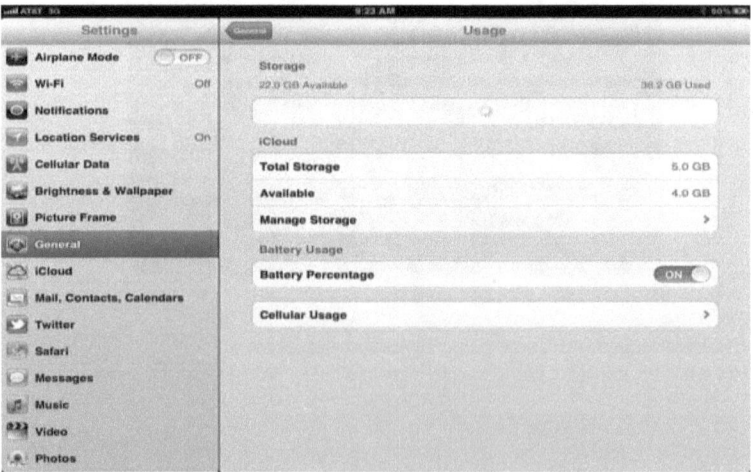

 Slide the switch to on, to view the battery percentage.

Here is the icon showing that the iPad is charging.

Page 372

TIPS, TRICKS AND SECRETS

How to reset an iPad

Similar to computers and smartphones, iPads utilize internal memory to run necessary programs and applications. Over time, this memory can become "full" and cause the device to "lag" A quick solution is to periodically reset your iPad with the following steps:

1) Hold the power button down for 3 seconds. It is the flat black button on the top right side of the device when viewing in portrait mode.
2) Once the slider button appears on the screen, slide it with your finger and the iPad will turn off.
3) Wait approximately 15 seconds after shutting down before restarting in order to allow for the device to completely power off.
4) To turn the iPad back on, hold the power button again for approximately 3 seconds.
Performing the above steps will allow you to clear any leaks or other occupied memory from the device and speed it up in the process

For problems with the iPad try a simple reset (reboot) of the iPad first. Hold both the Home and Sleep buttons for several seconds until the Apple logo appears. Ignore the "Slide to power off" arrow. The iPad will restart after a couple of minutes. Resetting this way will not hurt anything, and sometimes clears up mysterious problems.

As a last resort, you can do the factory reset. It will not require re-installing iOS 5. Go to Settings-General-Reset-Erase All Content and Settings. Then connect to iTunes and Restore the iPad from its last backup. You will lose any changes since the last Sync.

THE NEW USERS GUIDE TO THE IPAD

Battery Charging

To fully charge an iPad can take four to five hours. The best practice is to use the iPad until the battery is almost dead and then charge it to full capacity. Repeat these steps as often as possible. Repeatedly charging a battery that is not completely dead is not good for the battery and can lead to a shorter lifespan for the battery. Leaving the iPad plugged in to power is also a bad idea.

A charger is not a charger is not a charger. The charger that ships with the iPad is different than the charger that ships with the iPhone. While the two have the same connectors and will work to charge the device, the one that is shipped with the iPad is better for the iPad based on charging ability.

The battery on the iPad will not charge attached to a computer if the iPad is on. There will be an indicator at the top of the screen that shows a "not charging" status. Turn the iPad off while plugged into a computer and the iPad will charge; however, it is a much slower charge rate than being directly plugged into power.

Where is my Battery picture?

On the iPhone, there is a way to see the battery indicator on the main screen, this is not an option on the iPad.

TIPS, TRICKS AND SECRETS

Slideshow or Digital Photo Frame

While the iPad is charging in the evening, press the flower on the lock screen and the iPad will become a digital photo frame.

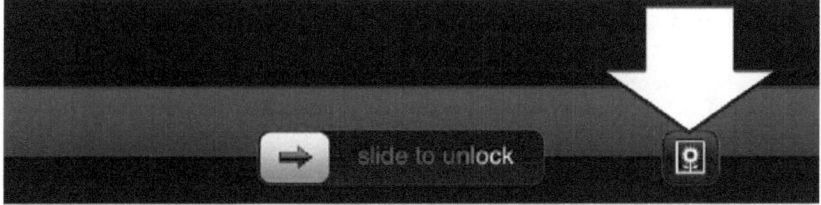

Be aware that while locked, the photo display will not show on an external device such as a computer monitor or television (using the appropriate connectors).

OPEN IN option

If more than one app have the ability to open a specific file type, when a document is selected, a menu will be presented allowing the user to select which program to open the file in.

THE NEW USERS GUIDE TO THE IPAD

Tap to Top

On a long scrolling website, rather than scroll all the way back to the top, you can tap the spot shown below and the website will automatically go right to the top of the page.

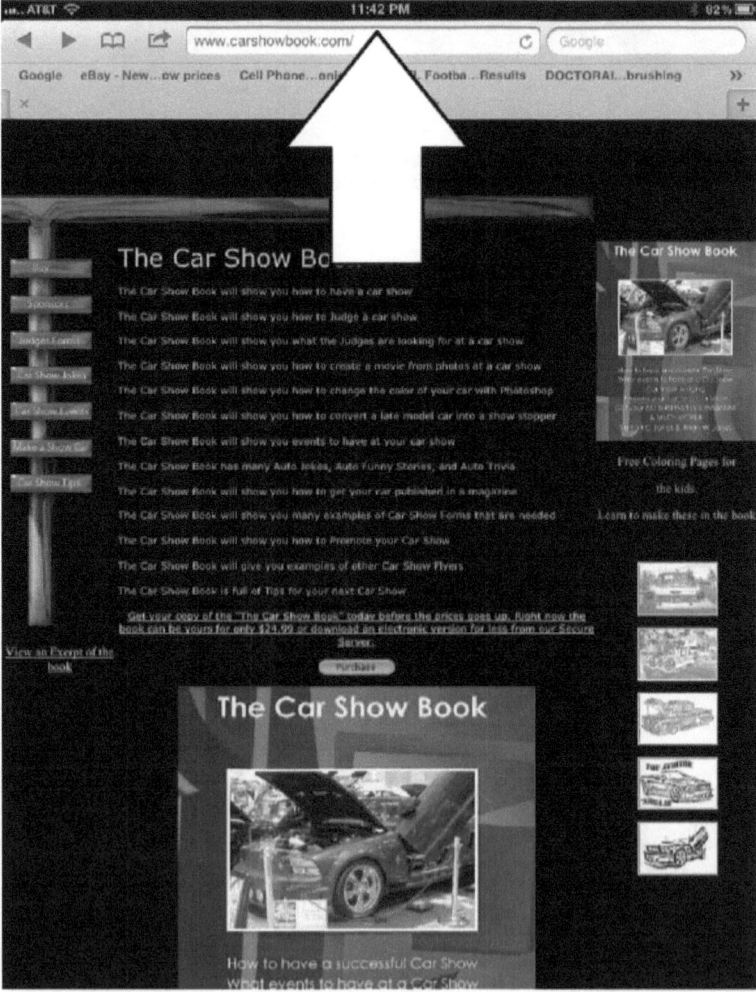

TIPS, TRICKS AND SECRETS

Wi-Fi Problems

Having difficulty connecting with a Wi-Fi hotspot or staying connected to a Wi-Fi hotspot, try the following.

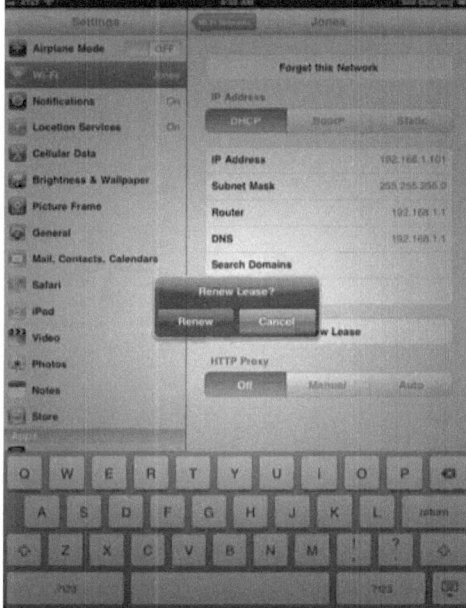

Go to settings, look for Wi-Fi and click the "Renew Lease" button. This will get a new address from the router.

Try plugging the iPad into power.

Reset the iPad by holding the power button at the top left, until you see a message that says "Slide to turn off." When the iPad is black, power it back on.

Try dimming the display.

Reset the network adapter by going to Settings, look for General, then look for Reset and "Reset Network Settings."

Try placing the iPad into Airplane mode. Go to Settings, look for Airplane mode, and slide the switch to on for a few seconds, then slide it back to the off position.

The final thing to try if problems persist with Wi-Fi connectivity, look for software updates in Settings, then General, and finally Software Updates.

Fast Switching of Photos

A complete swipe across the screen will allow a user to get to the other photos. Swipe left or right to advance through the photos. You can also swipe through the photos using small swipes on either side of the screen. Using one finger in a short motion where the arrows are located swipe in motions less than one inch. Small swipes can be made in left or right direction.

TIPS, TRICKS AND SECRETS

Shake the iPad

While typing, the iPad can be physically shaken. When shaken while typing, there are options that will pop up. Shaking the option will allow users to redo typing or undo typing. Undo and redo work for cut, copy and paste as well.

THE NEW USERS GUIDE TO THE IPAD

View Running Programs

Push the home button (round physical button at the bottom of the screen, on the front of the iPad) twice to open the multitasking window. All open programs will appear in the window at the bottom. Running programs take away performance, so if there are a lot of things running, the iPad may slow down. Scroll to the right to see the additional programs that are running.

TIPS, TRICKS AND SECRETS

Close Running Programs

Double click the home button so that all running programs show. Hold a finger on any of the apps that are running. The apps should start wiggling and also have a minus sign in the corner of each one.

Select the minus sign on the apps that you would like to close.

THE NEW USERS GUIDE TO THE IPAD

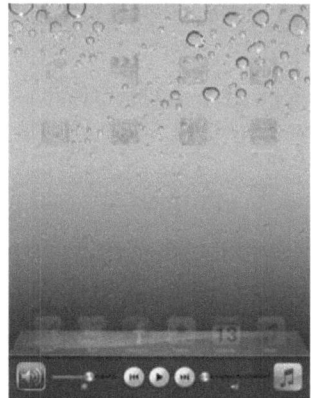 Double click the home button to access the multitasking window. Scroll all the way to the left and the music controls will be found.

Arrow one—In this example, this button is a mute button. This button can also be configured to be a screen rotation lock button.

Arrow two—Brightness control. Use to dim or brighten the display.

Arrow three–Music controls. Play, Pause, Back, or Next.

Arrow four—Volume control.

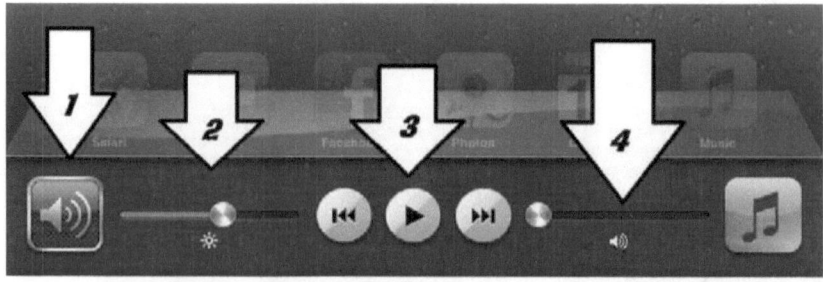

TIPS, TRICKS AND SECRETS

Change Slide Control

On the side of the iPad is a physical slide button. The functionality of this button can be changed between a mute button and a lock screen rotation button. To change the behavior of the button, go to Settings, select General and then look for the section titled "Use Slide Switch for."

Place a check next to the desired function.

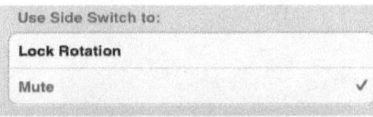

Mute function selected. The Multitasking view of the button will change based on this setting.

Multitasking button is showing the screen is locked from rotating.

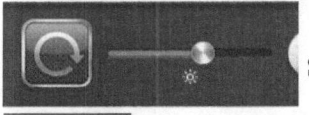

Screen will rotate.

Mute Button

Page 383

THE NEW USERS GUIDE TO THE IPAD

Take a Screenshot

If you would like to capture a snapshot of your iPad, there is a function that will allow that to happen.

Press and hold the physical power button at the top left of the iPad. While holding down on the power button, press the home button at the bottom front of the iPad, then release both buttons. The iPad will capture your screen and store that capture as a photo in the photo library.

TIPS, TRICKS AND SECRETS

Fast Web Content

Google has a site set up to view webpages with no photos or graphics. This special page will load web pages lightning fast to read textual content.
Go to www.google.com/gwt/n   type in the URL address and go.

www.cnn.com

Zoom in Apps

In some apps such as Maps and web videos, there are ways to zoom fast. Tap the screen twice and the screen will zoom right in. Tap the screen again twice and it will zoom back out.

At any time, the finger zoom functions also work. Hold two fingers on the screen and slide them apart for one zoom function and slide them together in a pinching style to zoom the other way.

Ways to Scroll

On a long website, using a finger you can easily scroll down through the website no problem; however, if there is a frame on the web page that also allows scrolling, try using two fingers inside of the scrollable frame to scroll only inside the frame.

TIPS, TRICKS AND SECRETS

Navigate between Screens

The iPad can have up to seven different screens to hold icons, apps and folders.

To navigate between screens, swipe across the screen with a finger.

To navigate between screens, swipe in small motions at the sides of the iPad.

To navigate between screens, tap the sides of the iPad just above the dock area.

The dots indicate the number of pages and the current location in the pages.

THE NEW USERS GUIDE TO THE IPAD

Wipe an iPad

You have decided to give your old iPad to someone so that you can get one of the brand new models but how do we remove all of our personal settings and information? Erase them!

Go to settings, General, Reset, look for Erase All Content and Settings.

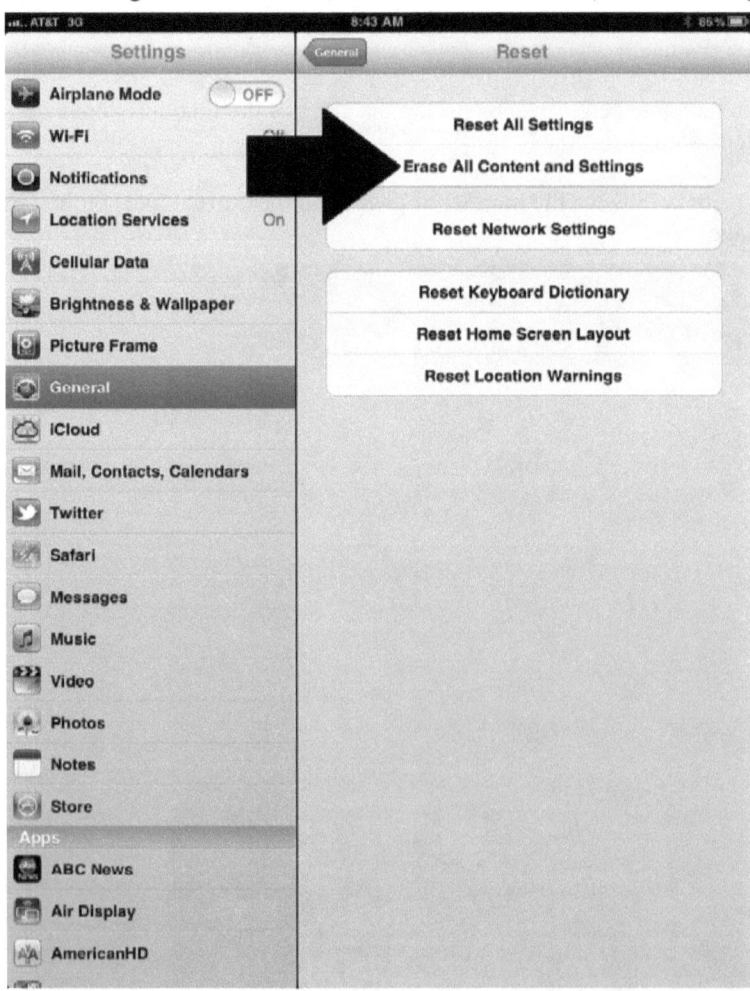

TIPS, TRICKS AND SECRETS

Reset Home Page

You have been using your iPad for a while, you have installed and deleted several different apps. You do not like the way the Home page is laid out with all the changes and settings. How do we reset our home page?

Go to

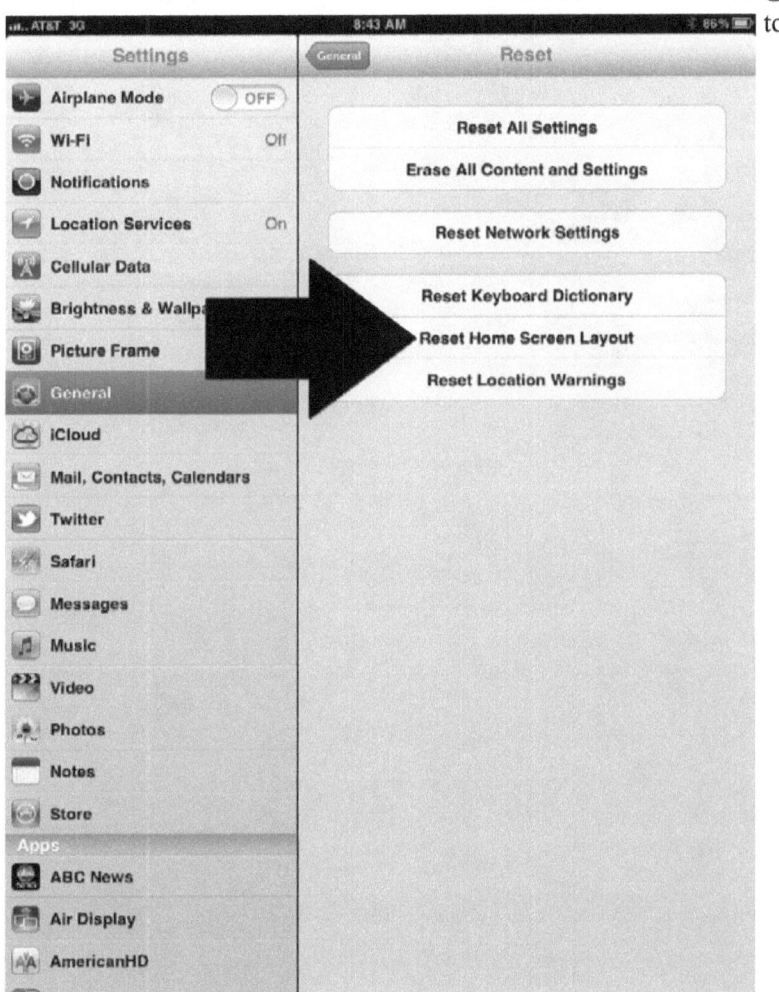

Turn off Auto Correction and Spell Check

The auto correction function and spell check is very nice but if a user decides they longer want to use these functions, this can be turned off.

Go to Settings, General, and then look for Keyboard. On the keyboard page, there is a toggle to shut off auto correct and spelling check.

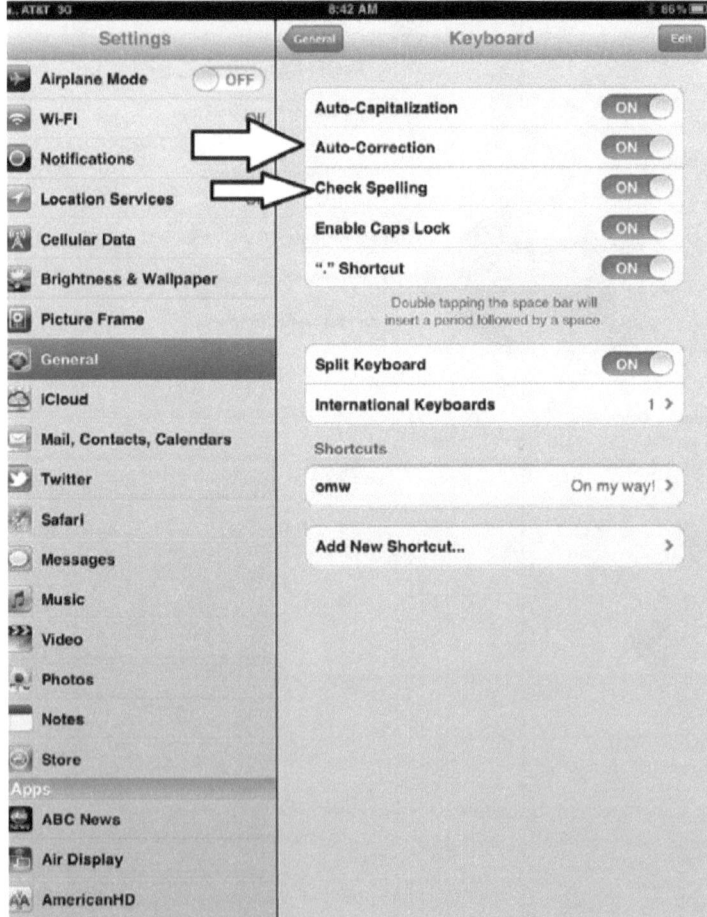

TIPS, TRICKS AND SECRETS

iPad Ambient Light Sensor

Whenever you unlock your iPad, it should be in the "dark room mode" first and will brighten if it detects you're in a well-lit room. It should get brighter if you start in a dark room and move to a bright room.

An option would be to fool the iPad by covering the sensor with your hands to cause it to start in dim mode. An option would be to wake up the iPad while it is being held next to a bright light, to cause it to open in bright mode.

Add Holidays to the Calendar

 1. Tap the Settings icon
 2. Tap Mail, Contacts, Calendars
 3. Scroll down and tap Add Account...
 4. Tap Other
 5. Tap Add Subscribed Calendar
 6. In the server field, input: ical.mac.com/ical/US32Holidays.ics - then tap Next
 7. On the next screen, change the name of the calendar under "Description" if you choose - then tap Save

There are many other calendars that can be added in the same manner.

THE NEW USERS GUIDE TO THE IPAD

A question that many people ask, "Is there a way to password protect specific apps on the iPad?"

The answer is no, not easily. There are many articles on the Internet regarding this topic; however, there is no capacity for this natively on the iPad. In searching the App store, there seems to be very few apps that deal with this. Several apps in the App store claim the ability to password protect folders with photos and videos, but none seem to have the ability to protect apps. This is one area where it would be great to see a change in a future IOS version.

The iPad does have the ability to restrict types of apps based on ratings or other criteria; however, there are no criteria for individual app support. An app developer does have the potential to add this option to their app when developed, but the settings would need to be set in the app's own settings.

Restrictions work great on several functions such as email accounts, notes, app purchases, app deletions, friend requests and more.

TIPS, TRICKS AND SECRETS

Lost iTunes/Apple ID Passcode

One way to reset the iTunes passcode is to use the website at: https://iforgot.apple.com/

There is a link on most Apple ID log in screens to email a link to a webpage where the passcode can be reset.

Lost Apple ID or iTunes ID

Go to the following website and follow the prompts https://iforgot.apple.com/

Lost Restriction Passcode

Restore the iPad to factory, not from your backup unless the backup was prior to adding the restriction passcode. When the iPad is restored to factory defaults, then sync data from iTunes.

Lost iPad Lock Passcode.

Restore the iPad to factory defaults through iTunes. Once restored, sync data from iTunes. Apple's official instructions to restore an iPad are:
1. Connect iPad to your computer.
2. Select iPad in the iTunes sidebar, then click the Summary tab.
3. Click "Check for Update." iTunes tells you if there's a newer version of the iPad software available.
4. Click Restore. Follow the onscreen instructions to complete the restore process. When restoring, it is recommended that you back up iPad when prompted. When the iPad software has been restored, you can choose to set up iPad as a new iPad.

If the device is locked and asking for iTunes to unlock it, try this.
1. Turn the iPad off.
2. Hold home, then connect to iTunes while holding home until a different "Connect to iTunes" screen appears.
3. Restore with iTunes.

THE NEW USERS GUIDE TO THE IPAD

Swipe right to delete. There are many apps that allow items to be deleted by swiping your finger to the right across an item.

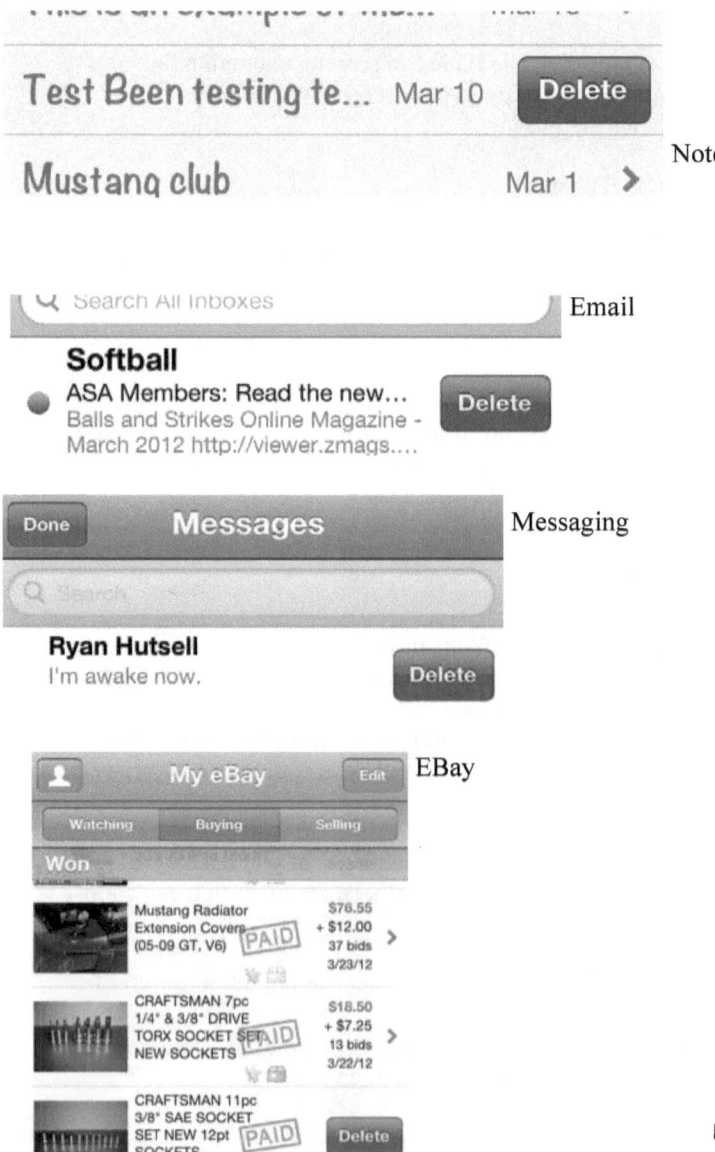

TIPS, TRICKS AND SECRETS

Speedy Keyboard Changes

When it is necessary to switch between the alpha keyboard and the numeric keyboard, there is a quicker way to enter numbers from the alpha keyboard. Press the number button on the keyboard and keep your finger in contact with the button, do not take your finger off the button.

While your finger is in contact with the button, the keyboard will change to the numeric version. Keep your finger on the screen and slide your finger to the number or character on that keyboard. While your finger is on that key, release your finger. When a finger is released off the key, the item will be used and the keyboard will return to the alpha keyboard.

THE NEW USERS GUIDE TO THE IPAD

Stop a program that is running.

Select the Home button twice quickly.

A list of all running programs will be displayed.

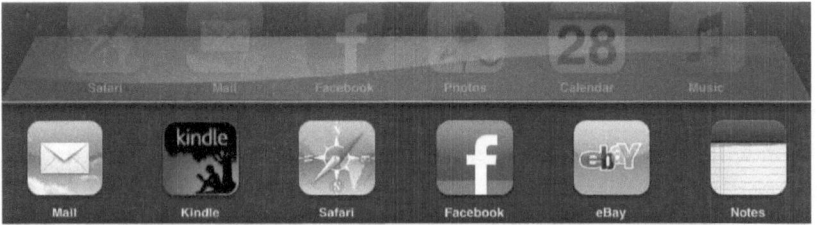

Hold a finger on any one of the apps until they start to wiggle and a minus sign appears. Select the minus sign to close out an app.

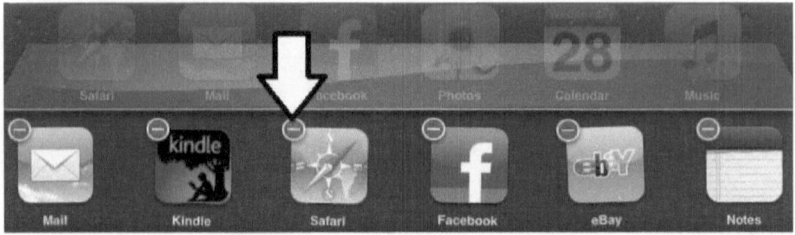

TIPS, TRICKS AND SECRETS

Reader

When a reader button appears in the address box, this will allow the web site to be presented with no graphics and in textual format only.

Web page in reader format is shown below.

THE NEW USERS GUIDE TO THE IPAD

Digital Photo Frame

The iPad can make a great electronic photo frame for your photos. While the iPad is charging at night, start the slide show of your photos and the slide show of photos run. Lock the iPad and then click the flower icon to start the slide show.

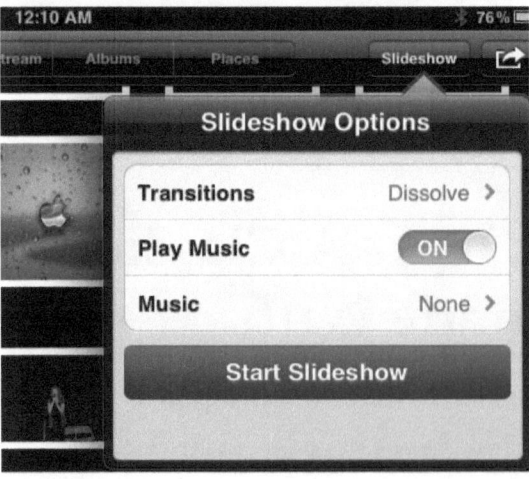
The other way to watch a slide show, would be to start it from the Photo Album. The slideshow from the Photo Album can also play music during the display of photos. This slide show will only show each photo one time and you can only select one song for the slideshow.

Note: If you plug your iPad into the accessory external display connector to show the slideshow on a VGA Monitor or a television, be advised, the external connector will NOT display the photos while the iPad is locked. The iPad WILL display the photos using the external connector while the slideshow is playing from the photo album.

TIPS, TRICKS AND SECRETS

iPad SIM security option.

If you enable the SIM PIN, entering the SIM passcode will be required when powering the iPad on in order to connect to the internet via the cellular data or internet network. The same is true when turning data or internet access on via the cellular network after turning it off. It is additional protection along with the Passcode Lock feature to prevent unauthorized internet access via the cellular network with your iPad in the event your iPad is lost or stolen.

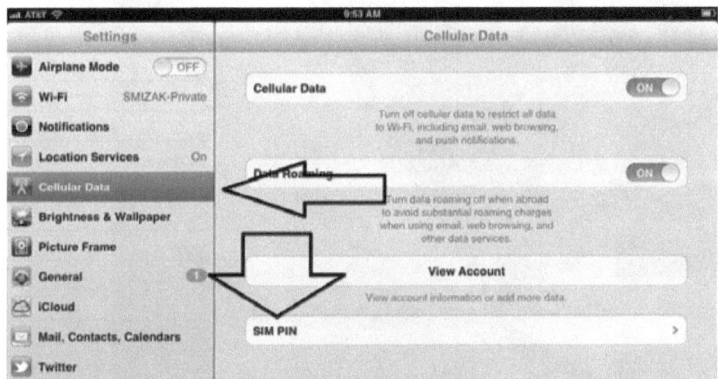

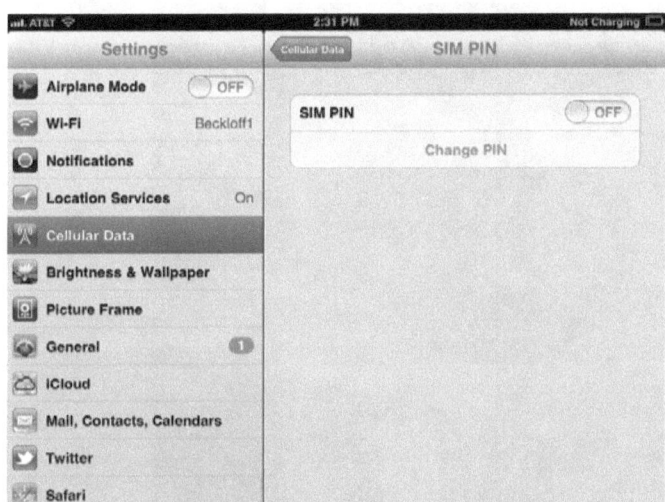

THE NEW USERS GUIDE TO THE IPAD

Remove a SIM Card from an iPad

On the side of an iPad is a small door with a small hole. Apple makes a tool to open this door; however, a small paper clip works as well. Insert the clip into the hole to eject the drawer and remove the SIM Card.

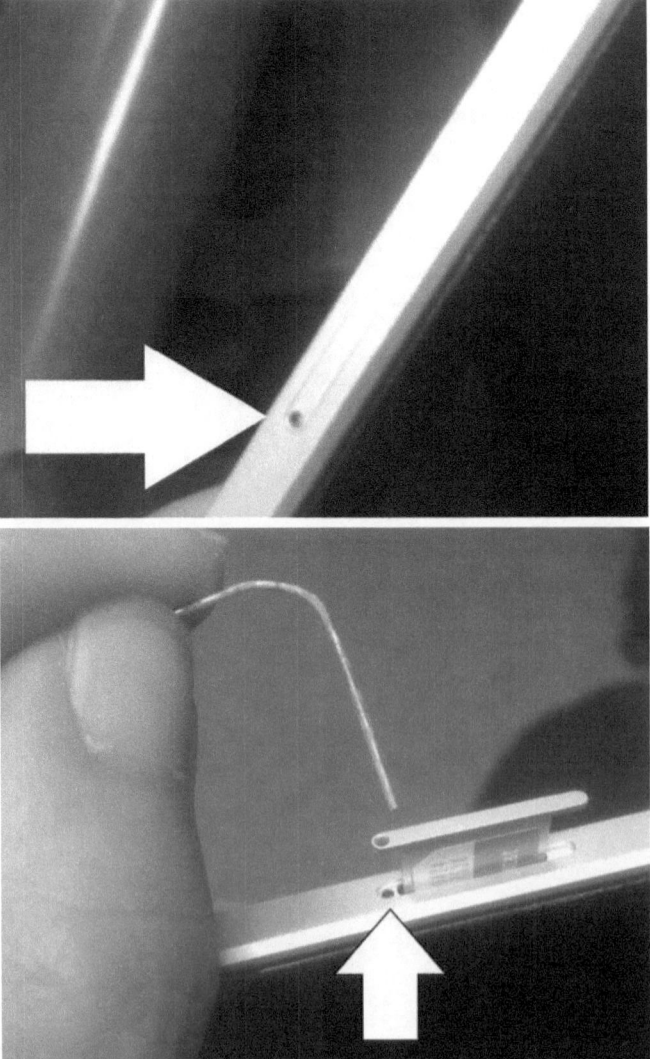

TIPS, TRICKS AND SECRETS

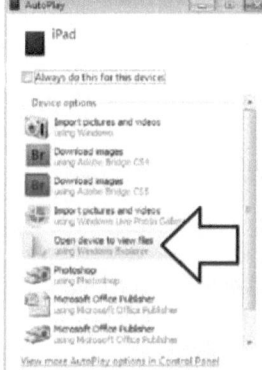

Copy Photos without iTunes Sync

Plug the iPad into the sync cable and the other end will connect to a USB port on computer.

When the Autoplay options open, select the open folder to view the files.

We can also open My Computer and look for the Apple device.

Select the internal storage folder. There may be additional folders with letters and numbers in the folder name. Keep opening folders until you find the DCIM folder.

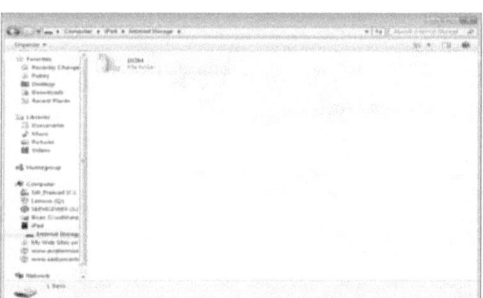

Open the DCIM folder on the iPad. The files inside the DCIM folder can be either copied and pasted out or drag and dropped out.

Any photos that are dropped into this folder will be available on the iPad.

Give an App as a Gift

If you would like to gift an app, here's a quick explanation.

If you're on a Mac or PC using iTunes, you'll first need to look up the app of your choice in the App Store. Once you find it, look for the down arrow to the right of the price button. Click the arrow and a small window appears with "Gift This App" as the first choice. Select "Gift This App" and the "Give a Gift" screen appears requesting information. Simply select the delivery method, fill in the blanks with the appropriate information and click "Continue." You'll then be prompted for your iTunes password. Enter your password and an iTunes "bill" appears. If your information is correct and you want to proceed with the purchase, click "Buy Gift." You know you're finished when the "Thank You!" screen appears and you can select either "Done" or "Gift Again."

If you want to gift an app directly from your iPad, look up the app in the App Store and click on the app to get more details. In the upper right-hand corner of the app details screen, you'll see "Gift This App." Click on the link and follow the on-screen directions to gift your app.

TIPS, TRICKS AND SECRETS

Twitter on the iPad

There is now a setting on the iPad to configure your Twitter account and use it on the iPad. Go to Settings and look for Twitter, on that page, you will need to enter your Twitter ID and password.

Here's a quick, useful iPad tip that will help you out if you've ever accidentally deleted an app you had installed on your iPad. Or perhaps had a child who accidentally deleted an app you still want on your iPad. Luckily, regardless of how an app was deleted, it's very easy to get it back on your iPad. There are a few ways to get a deleted app back. Here is the list, with the easiest method first – here are the steps to get back deleted apps on your iPad:

Use the Purchased Tab in the iPad App Store:
– Open the App Store app on your iPad.
– Tap on the Purchased button in the bottom nav bar.
– Tap on the 'Not On This iPad' tab at the top of the screen. That will give you a complete listing of all apps that have been purchased (including free apps) that are not currently installed on the iPad.
– Tap on the download symbol next to the app you want to restore – it's the symbol next to the app name, a cloud with a downward arrow inside it.

Search for and Reinstall the App in the iPad App Store:
– Open the App Store app on your iPad.
– Use the Search box at top right to search for the app you want to reinstall. The App Store will recognize that you have previously purchased the app and instead of a Price listing / Buy button next to the app name you'll see a button that says Install.
– Tap the Install button.

Sync with iTunes:
An iTunes sync will also reinstall any missing apps if you have selected to sync all apps or have the missing app chosen among selected apps to sync. In iOS 5 you can sync via Wi-Fi as well as when connected to a PC and iTunes on the desktop.

The only time that this will likely be the quickest method is if the deleted app you want to restore is a very large app. If so, sync when connected to your PC will likely be the fastest option. You can check the file size of an app on its detail page in the App Store. Just below the app's icon there is a listing that shows what category the app is in, when it was last updated, its version number, file size and more details.

TIPS, TRICKS AND SECRETS

Here's a neat little iPad alternative way to select multiple photos in the iPad photo library.

The way we have always known to select multiple photos in any album in the photo library is to tap the Share button at the top right of the screen and then tap on each photo you want to select. This of course comes in very handy when you want to copy or delete a number of photos at once.

The new method takes some getting used to, but is quite effective once you get the hang of it. Here's how it works:

– Go into any album in your iPad photo library, and tap on the Share button at the top right of the screen

– Tap with two fingers held close together (I find index and middle easiest) and hold just for the briefest moment and then drag the two fingers across all the photos you want to select.

It seems that this works best when the iPad is laid flat or otherwise held in a very stable position; and when the tap and drag is as close to one continuous motion as possible – as in, tap and drag in one smooth motion across a row of photos. You can also drag up and down – but it seems more difficult to do more than about three rows at a time. That's 21 photos though, so that's not bad – especially when you want to do a quick clear out in an album.

It takes a few tries to get this method working well.

 Find my iPhone

The "Find my iPhone" app is designed to keep track of all your Apple devices. The devices have to have internet access either through Wi-Fi or cellular and be online to be located. This app is great if your device is stolen, lost, misplaced or other problems.

Start the app and then login with your Apple ID and password.

FIND MY IPHONE OR IPAD

The Apple device will show up on a map showing the exact location of the device.

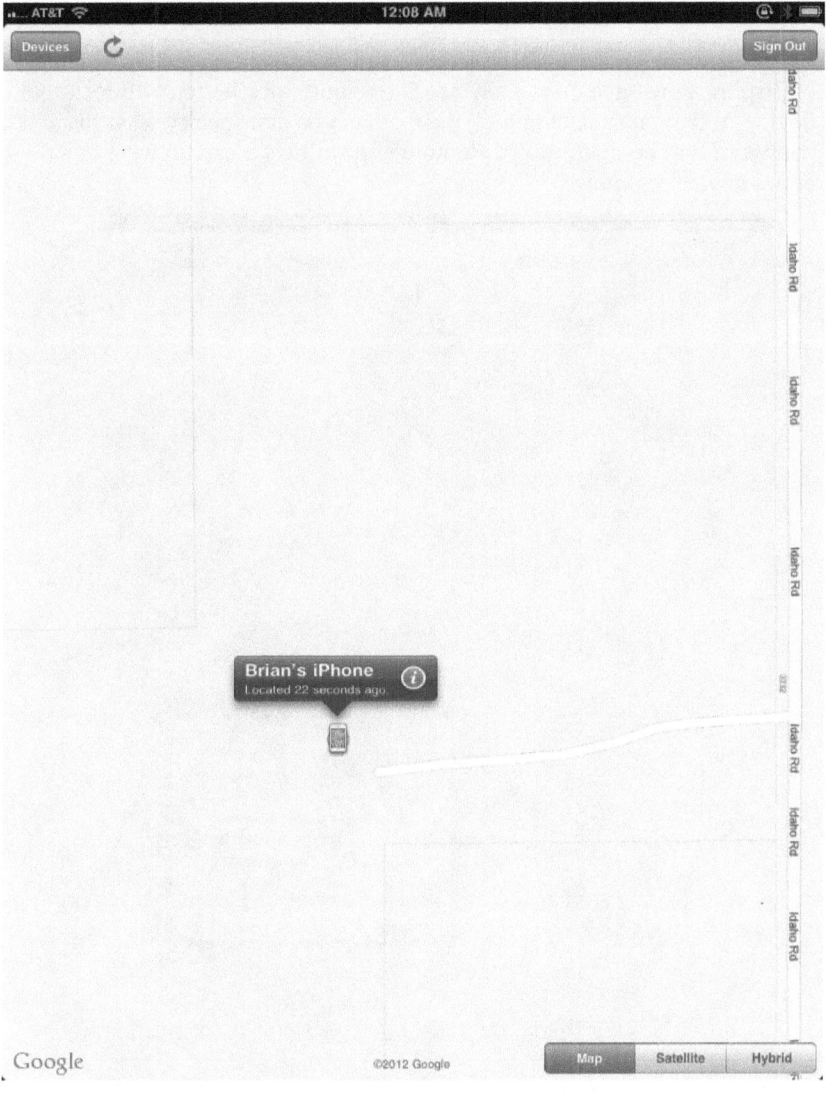

THE NEW USERS GUIDE TO THE IPAD

 Select the "i" to get more detailed information on the device.

From the more information screen, we can have the device play a sound or display a message on the device. The remote lock button will lock the device. When you select to lock the device, you can specify what the password will be to unlock it. Remote wipe allows a user to wipe the entire device remotely.

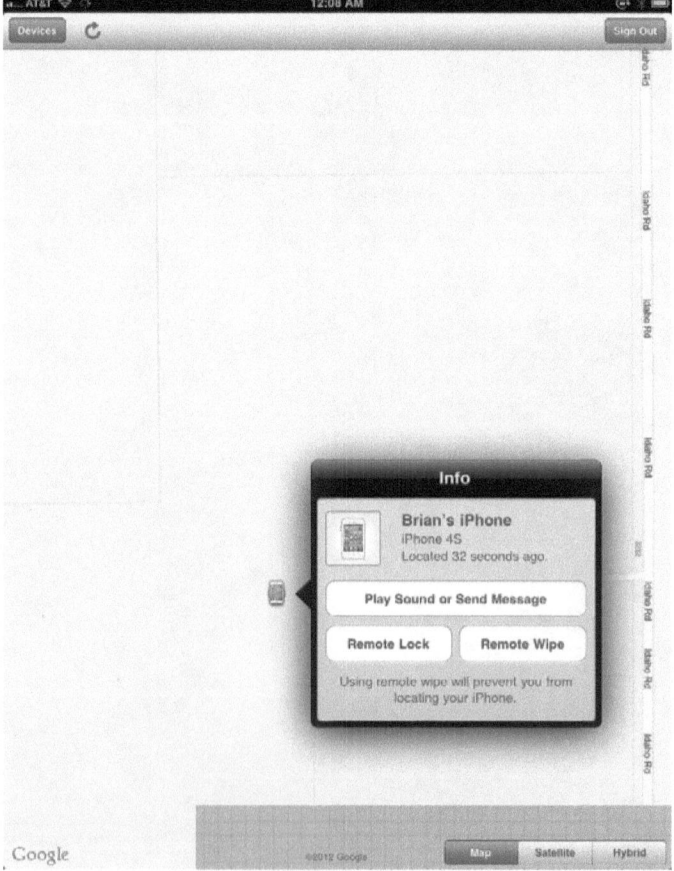

FIND MY IPHONE OR IPAD

The Devices button will allow you to see all of your Apple devices that are attached to the internet, and see their location. All of devices have the capability to have a message displayed, a sound played, a remote lock, or a remote wipe. Select the device to view its location. The button next to the devices button is a Refresh button to refresh their location.

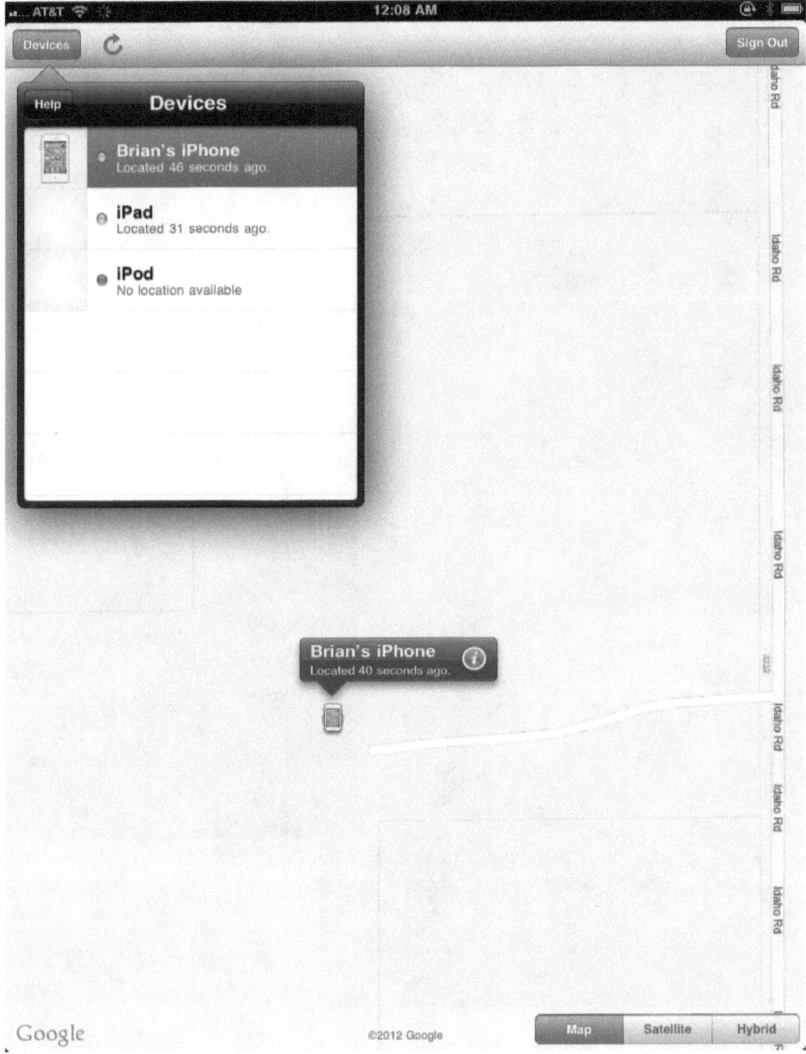

The apple device can be shown with a satellite image rather than a map image.

FIND MY IPHONE OR IPAD

A hybrid image of the location will show a satellite image with roads, streets, highways, cities, and more labeled and named on the map.

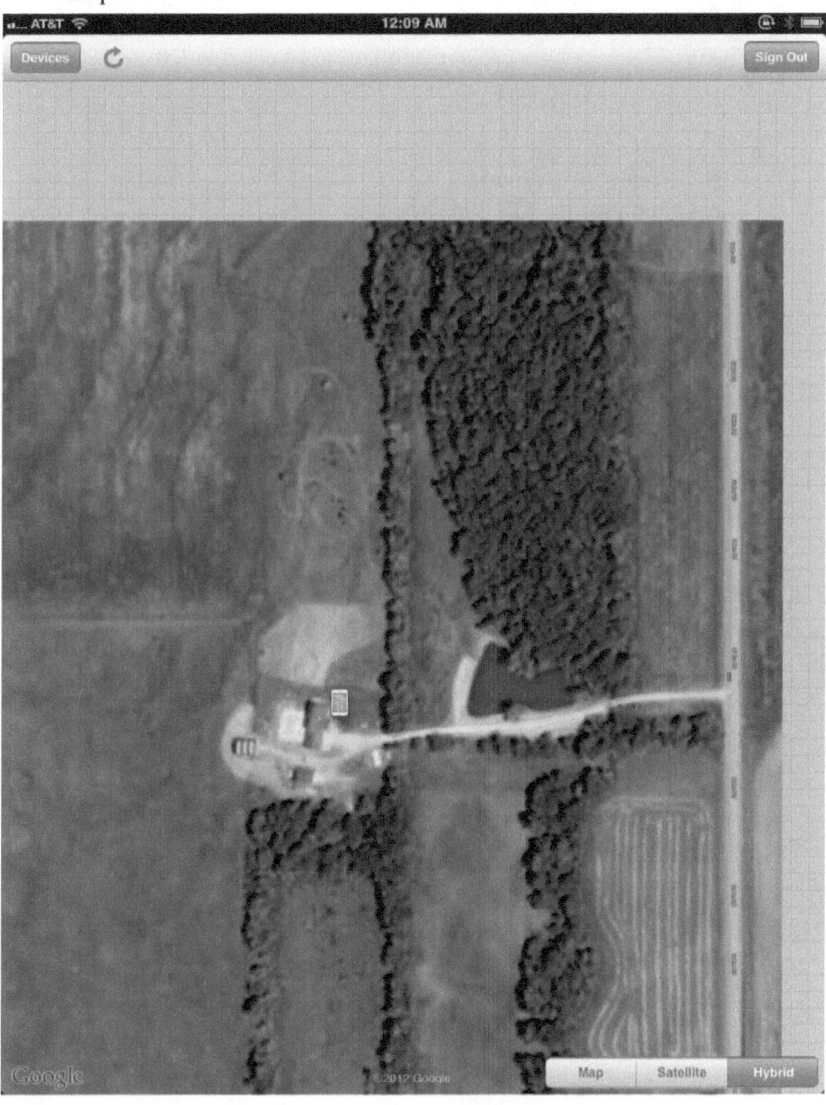

Facetime

Facetime is a video chat app that will allow Apple device users that have a camera in their device to connect to one another and have a video conversation.

Requirements for Facetime
 A device with a camera.
 A version of the IOS that supports Facetime.
 A Wi-Fi connection. (Facetime will not work on Cellular).
 A second party with a device that meets the requirements.

To start a face time conversation, go to the contact for the person that you would like to communicate with.

On the contact record, scroll down to the Facetime button to start the conversation.

FACETIME

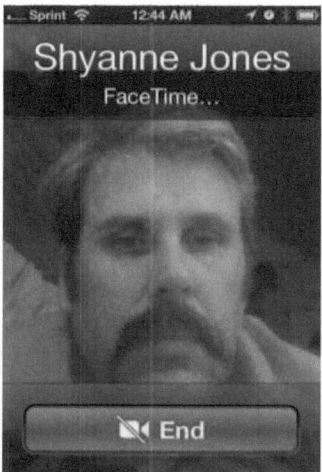 Here we are waiting for the other party to accept our call.

 On the iPad there is also a button to start the Facetime call.

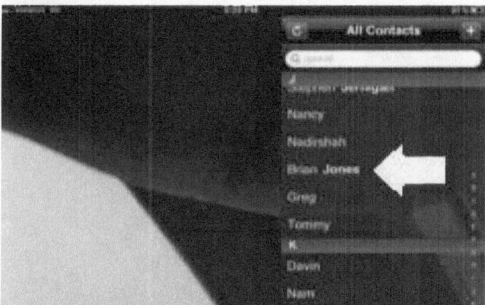 When Facetime opens, locate the contact to communicate with.

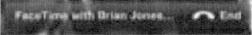

During the conversation, the video for the other party will show on the device. When the conversation is completed, click on the "End" button to close out of the conversation.

Note: If there are problems with communicating with Facetime, make sure that you are attached to a Wi-Fi network.

Make sure the IOS on the device is new enough to support the device on the other end. In this case, my four year old iPhone may have trouble communicating with a brand new iPad if the iPhone does not have the latest software updates and patches.

FACETIME

Home Sharing

Home Sharing in iTunes is designed to let you share and transfer content between multiple iTunes libraries on your home network and stream from those libraries to an iOS device or Apple TV (2nd generation).

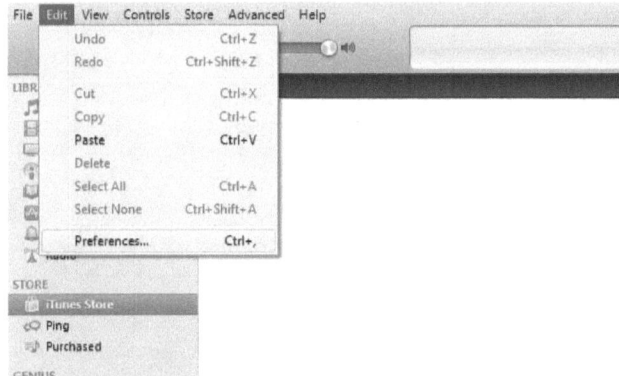

To set up home sharing, open iTunes on your computer. At the top, select the Edit menu and look for Preferences and select it.

On the Preferences window, look for the tab for Sharing. Click the Sharing tab. On the Sharing tab there are options to enable Home Sharing by placing a check in the box "Share my library on my local Network." On the Sharing options tab, you share the entire library or only select specific content to share. Home Sharing has an option to require a password. Once this is set up, we need to next configure the iPad and other devices for Home Sharing.

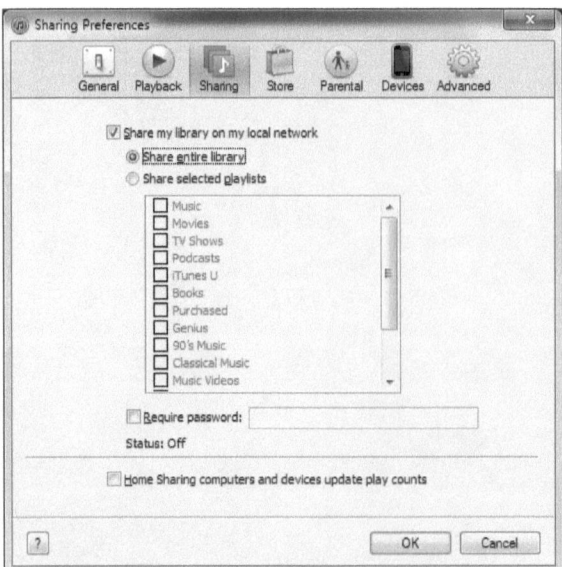

Page 416

HOME SHARING

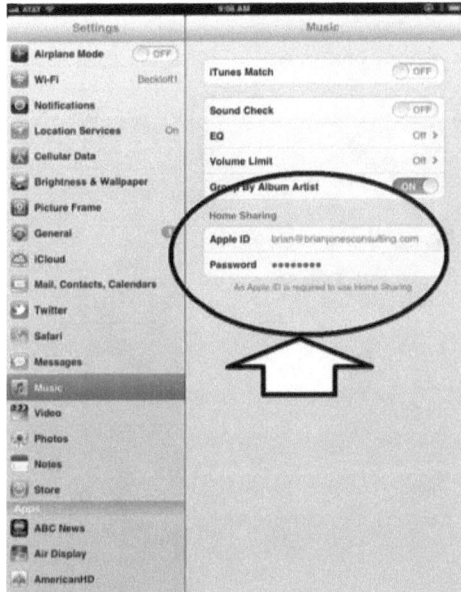

Home sharing has two locations on the iPad where it must be configured to work.

In the Settings, go to the Music settings. On the side is a section for Home Sharing. Enter your Apple ID and password into the Home Sharing information to use music with Home Sharing.

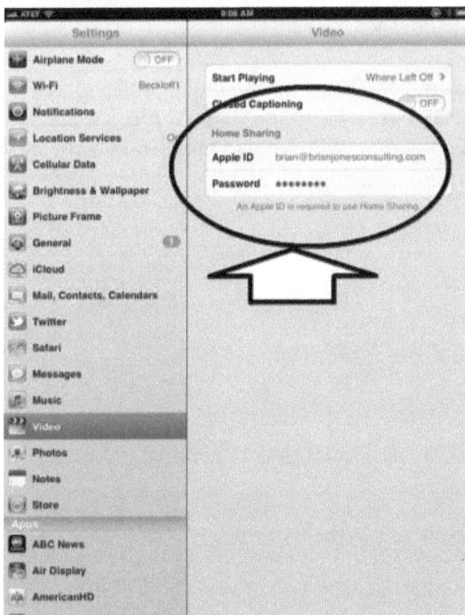

In Settings, go to Video, and then look for the Home Sharing section. Enter the Apple ID of the Home Sharing account that will be used throughout your network. This ID needs to be the same in all devices for the sharing to function correctly.

When these two settings are complete, Home Sharing is ready to use on your wireless network.

To use an Apple TV with the Home Sharing network, this will need to be set up on the device. On the menu, under computer, look for the option to turn on Home Sharing.

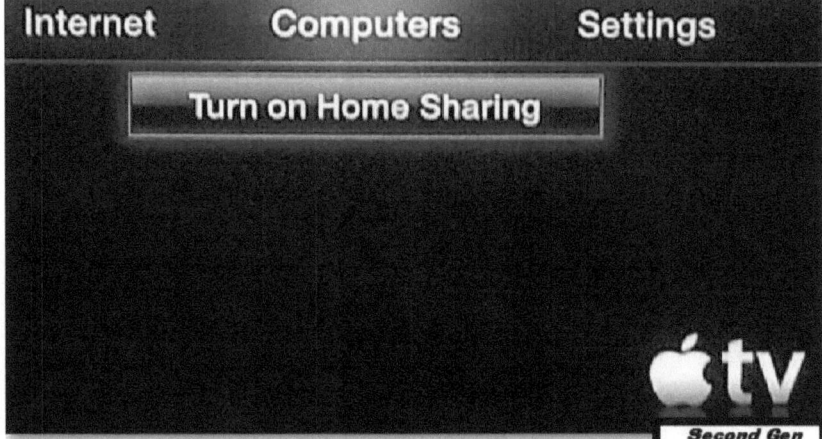

To set up Home Sharing, the Apple ID and password will need to be entered into the settings on the Apple TV.

With all devices configured for Home Sharing, all the music and video can be played on any Apple device in your network. The Apple TV can now accept input from your iPad as well as play music and video directly from the iTunes library on the computer using AirPlay.

APPLE TV

 Apple TV

An Apple TV is a device that is connected to a television in the home or business. The latest generation of Apple TV boxes use a standard HDMI video cable to connect the device to the television.

Once the Apple TV is connect to the television, the television is now capable of playing music, photos, videos, television shows, and more, that are stored in the iTunes library of the computer. Multiple computers within your wireless networks may be used to pull media and play them through the Apple TV.

The interface on the Apple TV has a very easy and intuitive navigation structure.

Attach an HDMI video cable to the HDMI port on the Apple TV. Attach the other end of the cable to any HDMI ports on the television. Change your television to the corresponding HDMI input, and you are done.

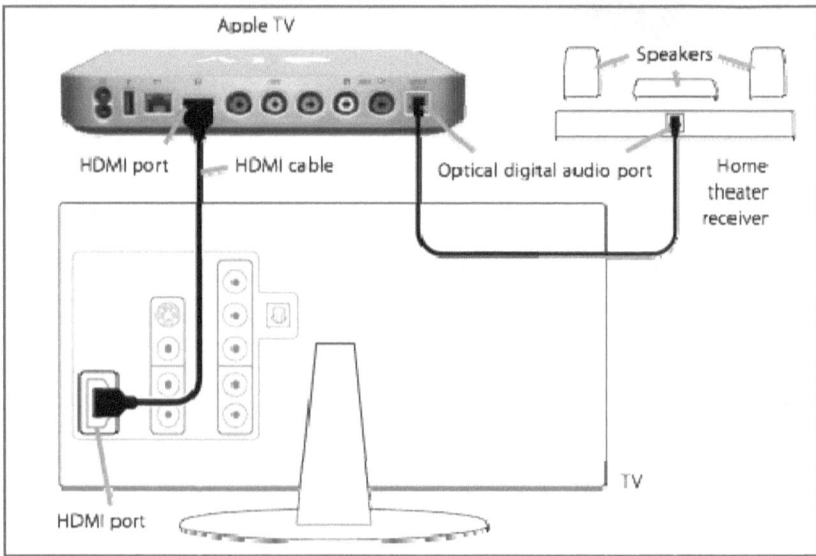

Using the AirPlay function of your iOS device, music that is played on the device can be sent to the Apple TV to play. In essence, the television becomes the speakers and monitor for your media files. While the media is played on the iOS device, the iOS device is now a remote control. The movie or music can be stopped and restarted on the iOS device.

If multiple Apple TV devices are installed in your home or business, the output can be sent to any of the devices, as long as they are all attached to the same wireless network.

APPLE TV

THE NEW USERS GUIDE TO THE IPAD

 iCloud

The iCloud is a location on a server hosted by Apple where the iOS devices can backup their data on a regular basis. An iCloud account can be created when the iOS device is initially installed. Follow the wizard during the set up of the iOS device to create the iCloud account.

From a computer, go to www.icloud.com

Click the button to log into the iCloud. This account information is typically the Apple ID.

ICLOUD

Once logged into the iCloud account, there will be several icons that are available.

The mail icon will allow a user to see the email that is configured on the iCloud account. This will allow the use of email to be sent and received without having to use the iPad. Any changes in the email will be reflected on the iPad in the mail app.

The contacts icon will allow access to the contacts that are stored on the iPad in the iCloud account. Phone numbers, addresses, and more can be pulled directly from the website rather than using the iPad.

The calendar icon will allow the use of the iCloud calendar. New meetings and schedules will be replicated to the iPad.

The find my iPhone icon will allow a user to locate the exact location of their iOS devices. For this function to work, the device must have access to the internet through Wi-Fi or cellular. If the iPad has 3G enabled or is attached to a wireless network, the location will be displayed on a map showing the exact location. Using this app, a user will have the ability to lock the device remotely, play a sound and a message, or completely wipe the device remotely. Would be thieves, beware of this function before stealing someone's iOS device.

The iWork icon will allow access to presentations, documents, spreadsheets and more that are stored on the iCloud. This function is great for those that tend to leave their iOS devices at home or at work but need access to these business tools. All changes will be reflected on all iOS devices configured to use this iCloud account.

THE NEW USERS GUIDE TO THE IPAD

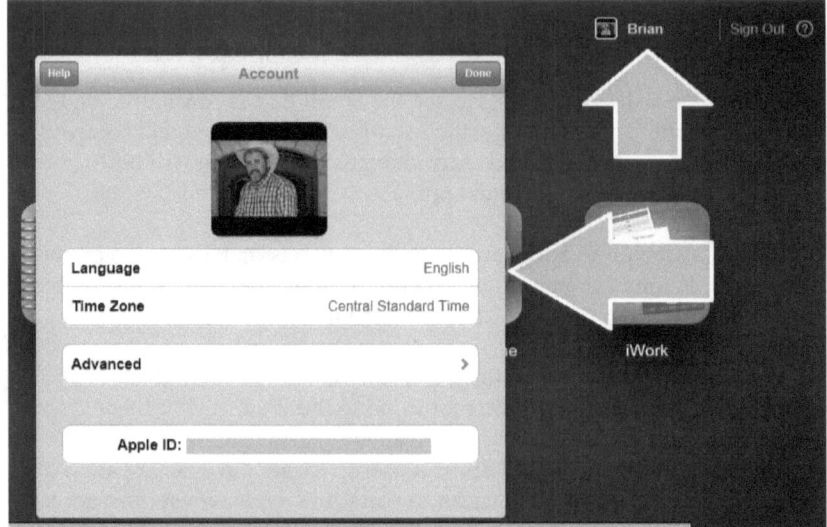

At the top of the iCloud page, there will be the username of the person logged into the iCloud account. To access information about the user, click on the name.

The default information that is configured for the user can be changed here.

The language and time zones can be adjusted.

At the bottom of the page will be the Apple ID for this user.

The advanced button will allow additional functions.

ICLOUD

The Advanced option will allow a user to reset the Photo Stream of photos from the different iOS devices that are configured to use the iCloud account.

The Photo Stream will be a grouping of photos from the different iOS devices. As photos are gathered or taken on an iOS device, a copy will be replicated or streamed to the iCloud account as a backup. Once photos are streamed to the iCloud account, they will be kept for a period of time on the iCloud servers. Eventually the photos will be deleted off the photo stream. This reset will NOT remove any photos from the iOS device, only from the iCloud.

The reset will remove all photos that are stored on the iCloud servers. Individual photos can be removed from the iCloud servers using the iOS device, if the iOS is version 5.1 or higher.

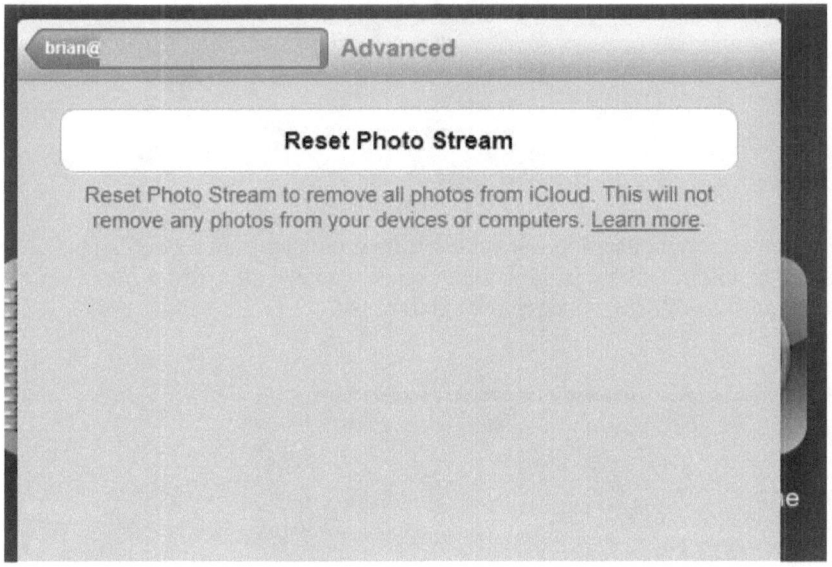

THE NEW USERS GUIDE TO THE IPAD

To access the iCloud settings on the iPad, open the Control Panel and look for the iCloud option on the left. At the top we see the account name. At the bottom we see the ability to delete this iCloud account.

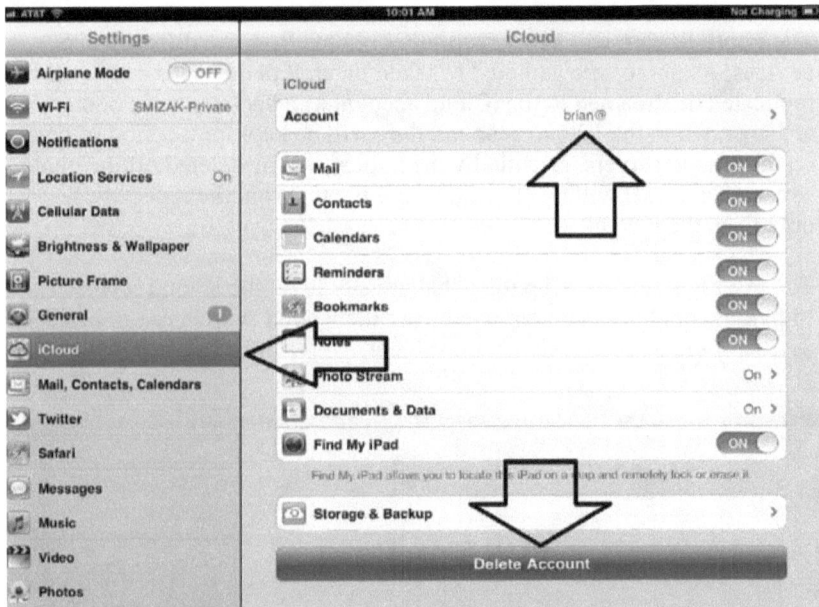

Tap the account name to open the information about the account. This screen will also show us how much space we have allotted for our iCloud account. Additional space may be purchased.

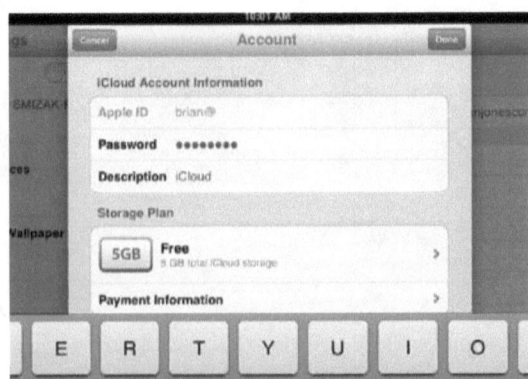

ICLOUD

This screen shows the bottom half of the account page. We can see on this screen the email that is configured for the iCloud account. If there is a greater than sign next to the option, it indicates that there is more information available for that option.

Tap the mail option.

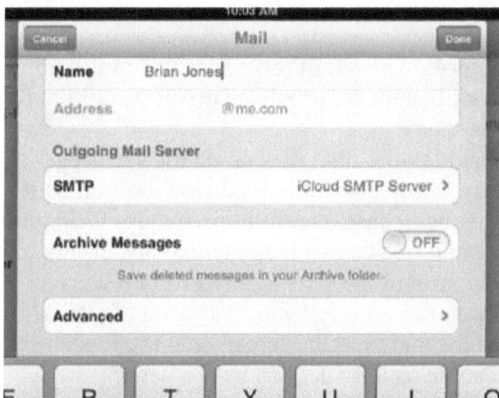

Here we see the information regarding the detail of our email account being used on the iCloud. There is an option on this screen to archive deleted emails for a period.

Tap the advanced option for more settings.

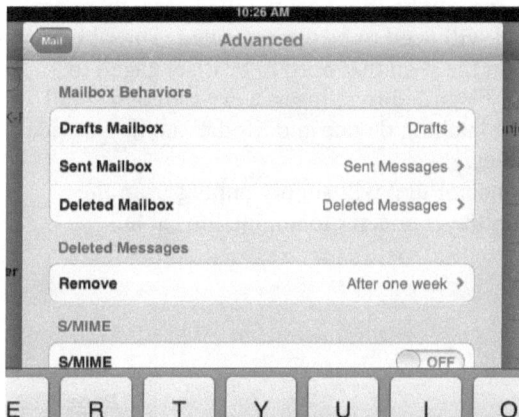

The advanced screen has additional mailbox behaviors.

Drafts, sent, and deleted folders can be mapped to other folder in the account if desired.

The time period to keep deleted emails is set here.

Page 427

Replace an iPad Cracked Screen or Digitizer

The biggest fear an iPad user has is the potential of dropping their device and seeing the screen shatter into pieces. Replacing a glass screen on an iPad is not extremely difficult however it does take a little time and patience. There are companies that will replace a glass screen on an iPad for a few hundred dollars which is the easiest solution for some users. For the DIY users, here are the steps needed to replace a glass screen.

There are two parts to the screen on an iPad. The LCD glass screen and a digitizer. If the damaged iPad still functions by touch and only the glass is damaged, then the glass replacement screen is all that is needed. If the functionality has been affected by the damage, you will probably need a digitizer as well.

1) Assemble the necessary tools. The list of tools is as follows: iPad case tool (metal ones work better), #4 torx head driver, small flat tip screwdriver, and electronic tape.
2) Find a nice flat surface and lay the iPad face up on the surface. We will take the screen off by starting with the iPad case tool. Insert it between the glass and the metal case, carefully prying up. Work your way around the case in small one or two inch increments, prying a bit as you work your way around the screen (a flat tip screwdriver is handy to keep the gap open as you work your way around). This process will release the tabs that hold the screen onto the iPad case. If these tabs break, and some usually do, just have a set of replacement tabs on hand.
3) When the glass is loose and can be lifted off the iPad case, there are several ribbon cables that will need to be disconnected. The ribbon cables have connectors on the iPad that need to be disengaged to allow the ribbon cable to be pulled free. Insert a pry tool or a small flat tip screwdriver in the latching device and lift the latching device up to free the ribbon cables.
4) There will be a plug connector that will simply unplug from the motherboard. Just pull on the connector to unplug the cable.

MISC

5) While lifting the screen up from the back case there will still be another connector that is attached and has to be removed. This final connector has a small hinge that you must pull up and then it stays with the ribbon when you pull the connector out. To remove the LCD you will need to lift up the ribbon cable that is held on with a piece of tape. This ribbon cable will come out with the LCD.
6) You will now have to remove 8 #4 torx head screws that are holding the LCD to the touch panel frame.
7) When you have removed the screws and before you separate the LCD from the touch panel assembly there is a piece of tape that needs to be lifted up slightly in order to remove the LCD from the touch panel assembly. This tape is usually located on the side of the screen that did not have any screws.
8) Gently pry up the LCD from the touch panel assembly. Using a small flat tip screwdriver at each of the screw locations can help pry it up. Be careful prying the LCD up as it is adhered around the edges.

Now the iPad LCD has been successfully removed from the iPad, to replace the screen, simply reverse the steps. Replacement parts can be found online through Amazon.com, EBay.com, or many other parts retailers. The tools and clips needed are also available online.

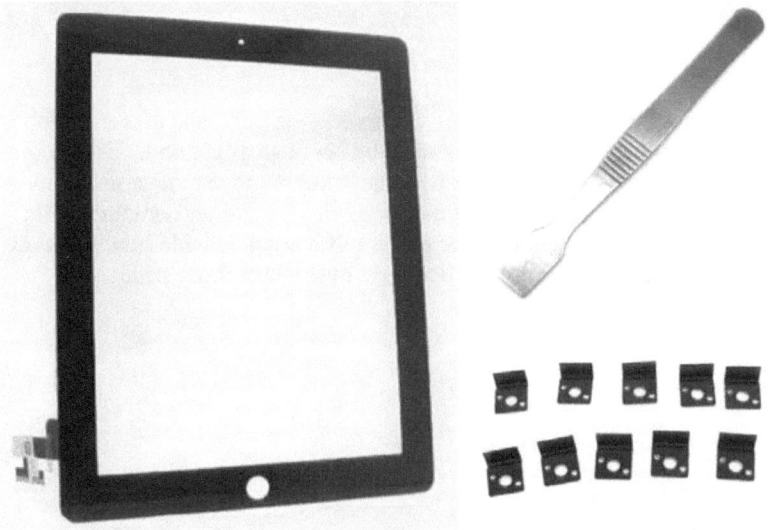

Accessories

Stylus-a pen-like device with a capacitive end, which can be used on an iPad screen. The use of a stylus can make life better for a user that needs more refined motions or needs more precision accuracy.

iPad VGA or RCA connector docks-used to attach an iPad to a standard computer monitor (VGA) or to standard video equipment such as a VCR, projector, or television. These devices allow the output of the iPad to be displayed on other devices.

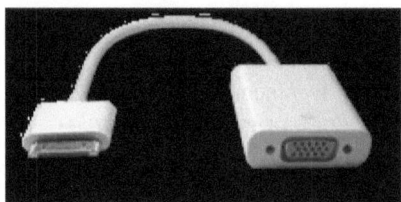 

Cases-there are a variety of cases which may be purchased for use with an iPad. Some cases allow the iPad to be set at an angle on a desk. Some cases allow the use of a built-in Bluetooth keyboard. Some cases allow the ability to be stored inside of a bound book or leather container. The cases that are available today are extremely varied. Decide how the iPad will be used and then decide which case best meets those needs.

MISC

iPad Stands-stands can be purchased that mount to a desk, set on a desk, fit into a vehicle cupholder, fit onto the headrest of a vehicle, mount to the windshield of a vehicle, mount to a knee, mount to a bike, mount to a boat, and much more.

iPad Chargers-Apple supplies a charger with each iOS device; however, it is very convenient to have additional chargers. Chargers can be purchased not only for a standard electrical outlet but also for vehicle 12 volt connectors. Some chargers, such as the iPhone chargers, are 1 amp (5 watt) while the chargers included with the iPad are 2 amp (10 watt) chargers. Either will charge an iPad but the lesser amp chargers will take longer to charge the device. There is no damage that can occur using a lesser amp charger.

Docks-iPad docks are stands that have built-in chargers. Many docks have attached speakers for listening to the iPad while it is charging. Some docks have a built-in alarm clock so that it fits well on a nightstand.

Bluetooth Accessories-there are many different types of Bluetooth devices available for the iPad. Bluetooth keyboards are great for typing and entering data through a traditional stand alone keyboards. Bluetooth headsets will allow a user to listen to music or other iPad sounds without the need for wires or a cable.

App enabled devices-there are many devices designed to work with specific apps. Blood pressure kits allow a user to take a blood pressure reading on the iPad. Baby monitor devices allow the use of viewing children from anywhere inside your wireless network, on the iPad. Universal remote control devices turn the iPad into a universal remote control for audio-video equipment. Meat thermometers allow the use of the iPad to ensure grilled meat is grilled at the proper temperature. Scales that can be read and used to track individual weight and calculate such things as body mass indicators. There is a company that builds a cabinet that looks like an arcade cabinet from the 80s where the iPad is the screen used to play games, such as Pac-Man or Space Invaders. Remote control helicopters and cars can be controlled by an iPad app. App enabled devices are all over the board on what is available and only the imagination of developers will limit the possibilities of these cool devices.

www.ingramcontent.com/pod-product-compliance
Lightning Source LLC
Chambersburg PA
CBHW031814170526
45157CB00001B/54